Index *to* Wills
of
Charleston County
South Carolina

- 1671-1886 -

**Compiled under the direction
of the
Charleston Free Library**

**Southern Historical Press, Inc.
Greenville, South Carolina**

This volume was reproduced from
A personal copy located in the
Publisher's private library

Please direct all correspondence and orders to:

www.southernhistoricalpress.com
or
SOUTHERN HISTORICAL PRESS, Inc.
PO BOX 1267
Greenville, SC   29601
southernhistoricalpress@gmail.com

Originally published: Charleston, SC.   1950
Copyright 1950 by: Charleston Free Library
ISBN #978-1-63914-029-9
All rights Reserved.
Printed in the United States of America

PREFACE

Among the plans of the Federal Works Progress Administration to preserve and make more easily available selected classes of historical records was one to prepare typescript copies of all wills filed prior to the year 1869 in the various counties of South Carolina. In due course this useful work was completed. In every county in which wills of this period were found, two copies, and in one case (Charleston County) three copies, were made. One set of these copies was then deposited in the county office controlling the originals, and another set was sent to the South Caroliniana Library of the University of South Carolina, which thereby became the custodian of a complete file. The extra set prepared in Charleston was deposited in the Charleston Free Library.

In 1946 Mrs. Martha Lou Houston published the *Indexes to the County Wills of South Carolina* containing indexes prepared by the South Caroliniana Library for each county except Charleston. The present volume, therefore, completes the series of indexes to the WPA transcripts of South Carolina wills.

The importance of Charleston as a center of probate records is well known. The only probate court (court of ordinary) in South Carolina was located there until 1782 when a beginning was made of carrying out a provision in the Constitution of 1778 requiring similar courts in other judicial districts. It may be said, then, that, with a few exceptions, all South Carolina recorded wills prior to 1782 are covered by the following index.

The preparation of the index to Charleston wills was under the direction of the reference department of the Charleston Free Library. The actual work of indexing was done by NYA students of the College of Charleston, and the typing, as it now appears in photolith form, was done by WPA workers assigned to the same institution.

J. H. EASTERBY

Historical Commission
of South Carolina

EXPLANATION OF METHOD

THE LONG S

The long s has been copied interchangeably as f and s by typists. A double lower case letter has been treated in the same way. No attempt has been made to correct spellings.

The information in the index appears in columns as follows:

| | *Name* | *Volume* | *Page* |

PAGING

The page number is that of the typed copy, rather than that of the original will book, the latter having been omitted from the transcripts. Unnumbered pages have been lettered a, b, c, etc., and are so referred to in the index.

DOCUMENTS
OTHER THAN
WILLS

Form of document has been indicated when other than a will as: memorandum, order, substitution of trustee, etc. These have not been noted when they appear in addition to a will under the same name. Duplicates of documents have been noted after page number.

SYMBOLS

*   Incomplete wills
**   Destroyed in original will book
[ ]   Alternate forms of name
( )   Additional forms of name

ABBREVIATIONS

ve — widow
fm — wife
SOB — son of Benjamin
P.C. — person of color

Name	Volume	Page

A

Abbott, Ann	47 (1851-56)	756
Abel, Nicholas	9 (1760-67)	170
Aberegg, Gottlieb	50 (1862-68)	292
Aberly, John	11 (1767-71)	37
Abrahams, Emanuel	28 (1800-07)	354
Ackerman, George	15 (1771-74)	607
Ackerman, Stephen	23 (1786-93)	706
Ackles, Margaret	7 (1752-56)	328
Adams, Barnard	29 (1800-07)	541
Adams, Catharine A. (Substitution of Trustee)	40 (1834-39)	277
Adams, Catharine Ann	31 (1807-18)	204
Adams, David	21 (1783-86)	798
Adams, Elizabeth M.	37 (1826-34)	203
Adams, Enoch	25 (1793-1800)	117
Adams, John	19 (1780-83)	103
Adams, John	23 (1786-93)	636
Adams, John S.	32 (1807-18)	632
Adams, Nathaniel	21 (1783-86)	751
Adams, Robert	1 (1692-93)	61
Adams, Samuel	25 (1793-1800)	222
Adams, William	1 (1687-1710)	37
Adams, William	2 (1729-31)	108
Adams, William	18 (1776-84)	305
Adams, William	29 (1800-07)	616
Adams, William	36 (1818-26)	1103
Adams, William (Woo.)	7 (1752-56)	489
Adcock, Elizabeth	42 (1839-45)	439
Adderly, John	4 (1736-40)	222
Addifson see Addison		
*Addison, Allen	18 (1776-84)	109
Addison, James	31 (1807-18)	297

2

Name	volume	Page
Addison, Joseph	33 (1807-18)	1292
Addison, Joseph S.	51 (1862-68)	493
Addison, Thomas (Addifson	18 (1776-84)	340
Adger, James	48 (1856-62)	338
Adger, William	46 (1851-56)	367
Adier, Andrew	16 (1774-79)	9
Aertsen, Guilliam (Guillaim)	30 (1800-07)	1038
Affleck, Thomas	8 (1757-60)	248
Afsalit, Jean Marie Honore Joseph	39 (1826-34)	976
Ahrens, Christopher	45 (1845-51)	505
Ahrens, John	49 (1856-62)	969
Ainger, Hannah	13 (1767-71)	935
Ainger, John	6 (1747-52)	618
Ainger, John	8 (1757-60)	181
Ainslie, John	16 (1774-79)	69
Air, Amaranthiea S.	49 (1856-62)	563
Air, Ann	10 (1760-67)	447
Air, Charles James	29 (1800-07)	431
Air, James H.	31 (1807-18)	242
Air, William	7 (1752-56)	241
Airs, George	34 (1818-26)	275
Aish, Marmaduke	6 (1747-52)	367
Akeen, Thomas	27 (1793-1800)	832
Akerman, Albert	11 (1767-71)	3
Akin, Ann	22 (1786-93)	186
Akin, Ann	39 (1826-34)	852
Akin, Eliza	42 (1839-45)	404
Akin, Elizabeth	11 (1767-71)	105
Akin, James	8 (1757-60)	226
Akin, James	19 (1780-83)	140
*Akin, James	20 (1783-86)	97
Akin, James	44 (1845-51)	87
Akin, Margaret	8 (1757-60)	5

Name	volume	Page
Akin, Thomas	7 (1752-56)	485
Akin, Thomas	19 (1780-83)	189
Akin, Thomas	42 (1839-45)	288
Akins, John	2 (G1729-31)	6
Albertson, Sarah	39 (1826-34)	1050
Albrecht, Nicolaus	48 (1856-62)	450
Albright, Susan	45 (1845-51)	544
Alder, George	6 (1747-52)	196
Aldert see Aldret		
Aldret, Sikke [Aldert]	51 (1862-68)	572
Aldrich, Robert	45 (1845-51)	835
Alexander, Alexander	29 (1800-07)	546
Alexander, Ann Sarah	40 (1834-39)	354
Alexander, Charles	25 (1793-1800)	210
Alexander, David	7 (1752-56)	117
Alexander, John	1 (1687-1710)	12
Alexander, Joseph [Alexander]	22 (1786-93)	2
Alexander, Martha	9 (1760-67)	269
Alexander, Mary	31 (1807-18)	112
Alexander, Mary	32 (1807-18)	625
Alexander, Peter	16 (1774-79)	89
Alexander see Alexander		
Alison, Hecter [Hector]	11 (1767-71)	238
Alison, Hugh	21 (1783-86)	484
Alison, Regina	33 (1807-18)	1219
Allan, Cecilia S.	45 (1845-51)	555
Allan, John Williams	32 (1807-18)	580
Allan, Robert M.	41 (1834-39)	932
Allan, William	37 (1826-34)	219
Allan, William	51 (1862-68)	494
Allan see also Allen		
Allen, Andrew	3 (1732-37)	221
Allen, Elizabeth Wigfall	1 (1722-24)	21

Name	volume	Page
Allen, James	9 (1760-67)	405
Allen, John	6 (1747-52)	83
Allen, John	24 (1786-93)	996
Allen, Josiah	26 (1793-1800)	502
Allen, Mary	6 (1747-52)	343
Allen, Samuel	28 (1800-07)	212
Allen, Sarah	6 (1747-52)	125
Allen, Sarah	10 (1760-67)	663
Allen, Sarah [Allan]	44 (1845-51)	50
Allen, Stephen	35 (1818-26)	687
Allen, Thomas	1 (1721-22)	44
Allen, Thomas	37 (1826-34)	260
Allen, William	5 (1740-47)	280
Allen, William	6 (1747-52)	296
Allers, Carsten	48 (1856-62)	438
Allifson, James	30 (1800-07)	1130
Allston, John	6 (1747-52)	358
*Allston, John	6 (1747-52)	568
Allston, Josias	17 (1774-79)	527
Allston, Mary Coachman	48 (1856-62)	479
Allston, Peter	6 (1747-52)	146
Allston, Robert Francis Withers	50 (1862-68)	231
Allston, Sarah	10 (1760-67)	469
Allston, William	5 (1740-47)	292
Alston, Thomas Pinckney	49 (1856-62)	835
Alston, William	41 (1834-39)	939
Alston, William Algernon	51 (1862-68)	762
Amacher, John	15 (1771-74)	593
Ames, William H.	39 (1826-34)	984
Amory, Jonathan	1 (1687-1710)	5
Amory, Martha	1 (1687-1710)	7
Amory, Sarah	13 (1767-71)	809
*Amos, James	18 (1776-84)	139
Ampau, Etienne Pascal	31 (1807-18)	445

Name	volume	Page
Amyand, Isaac	4 (1736-40)	199
Ancel, Peter	29 (1800-07)	499
Ancrum, William	31 (1807-18)	83
Anderson, Abraham	10 (1760-67)	593
Anderson, Alexander	10 (1760-67)	704
Anderson, Ann	31 (1807-18)	88
Anderson, Archibald	28 (1800-07)	188
Anderson, David	3 (1732-37)	185
Anderson, George	48 (1856-62)	395
Anderson, Hannah	32 (1807-18)	833
Anderson, Hugh	9 (1760-67)	365
Anderson, James	9 (1760-67)	271
Anderson, James	13 (1767-71)	969
Anderson, James	19 (1780-83)	288
Anderson, James	33 (1807-18)	1341
Anderson, James	42 (1839-45)	418
Anderson, John	16 (1771-74)	346
Anderson, John Southgate	31 (1807-18)	291
Anderson, Joseph	10 (1760-67)	571
Anderson, Kennedy Y.	42 (1839-45)	194
Anderson, Mary	24 (1786-93)	1064
Anderson, Mary	27 (1793-1800)	809
Anderson, Mary	49 (1856-62)	598
Anderson, Philip [Androns]	31 (1807-18)	440
Anderson, Stephen	19 (1780-83)	45
Anderson, Thomas	17 (1774-79)	607
Anderson, William	5 (1740-47)	590
Anderson, William	8 (1757-60)	445
Anderson, William	29 (1800-07)	681
Andrew, John	5 (1740-47)	477
Andrew, Joseph	5 (1740-47)	274
Andrew, Joseph Jr.	6 (1747-52)	157
Andrewes, Moses	30 (1800-07)	858
Andrews, Anna C.D.	47 (1851-56)	612

6

Name	Volume	Page
Andrews, John Frederick	49 (1856-62)	716
Andrews, Moses	37 (1826-34)	70
Androns see Anderson		
Annely, Anna Maria	50 (1862-68)	367
Annoto, Therese	39 (1826-34)	986
Anthony, Israel Church	40 (1834-39)	412
Anthony, Mary	41 (1834-39)	864
Appleton, Joseph	29 (1800-07)	423
Archer, James	6 (1747-52)	118
Archibald, George	25 (1793-1800)	200
Arden, Edward	1 (1721-22)	54
Arden, Joseph	9 (1760-67)	278
Arms, Elizabeth	45 (1845-51)	703
Arms, Sarah C.	47 (1851-56)	689
Armstrong, Charles	2 (1722-26)	24
Armstrong, Charles	13 (1767-71)	1052
Armstrong, Emma	49 (1856-62)	883
Armstrong, James	3 (1732-37)	148
Armstrong, James	19 (1780-83)	221
Armstrong, Janet	7 (1752-56)	234
Armstrong, John	24 (1786-93)	809
*Armstrong, Thomas	15 (1771-74)	353
Armstrong, William Henry	22 (1786-93)	110
Arnett, John	18 (1776-84)	312
Arnold, Amos	41 (1834-39)	511
Arnold, Thomas	18 (1776-84)	47
Arnold, Thomas	25 (1793-1800)	110
Arnold, William	13 (1767-71)	858
Arnot, William	23 (1786-93)	716
Arthemale, John Honorey [Arthemalle Jean Honore]	26 (1793-1800)	439
Arthemalle see Arthemale		
Arthur, Bartholomew [Bartholonew]	5 (1740-47)	472

Name	Volume	Page
Arthur, Christopher	2 (1724-25)	61
Arthur, George	20 (1783-86)	308
Arthur, George	34 (1818-26)	87
Arthur, Nathaniel	9 (1760-67)	439
Arthur, Nathaniel	20 (1783-86)	264
Arthur, Peter Simmons	33 (1807-18)	1349
Artope, George Barnard	33 (1807-18)	1357
Ash, Algernoon	5 (1740-47)	602
Ash, James	8 (1757-60)	30
Ash, John	1 (1687-1710)	34
Ash, John (Senr)	20 (1783-86)	67
Ash, John (Junior)	25 (1793-1800)	310
Ash, John	39 (1826-34)	897
Ash, Joseph	11 (1767-71)	198
Ash, Joseph	23 (1786-93)	709
Ash, Richard	10 (1760-67)	771
Ash, Richard Cochran	13 (1767-71)	745
Ash, Samuel	3 (1732-37)	281
Ashbey, John [Ashby]	2 (1727-29)	101
Ashburn, Benjamin	6 (1747-52)	345
Ashby, Anthony	20 (1783-86)	407
Ashby, James A.	44 (1845-51)	66
Ashby, John	8 (1757-60)	164
Ashby, Magdalene	28 (1800-07)	150
Ashby, Thomas	6 (1747-52)	419
Ashby, Thomas	7 (1752-56)	225
Ashby, Thomas	29 (1800-07)	584
Ashby see also Ashbey		
Ashe, Abraham	43 (1839-45)	552
Ashe, Andrew Deveaux	35 (1818-26)	827
Ashe, Colonel	40 (1834-39)	220
Ashe, Colonel	40 (1834-39)	221
Ashe, Elizabeth	34 (1818-26)	359

8

Name	Volume	Page
Ashe, Harriet Ann	48 (1856-62)	84
Ashe, John Sen.	38 (1826-34)	453
Ashe, John (Substitution of Trustee)	40 (1834-39)	353
Ashe, John A.S.	51 (1862-68)	839
Ashmead, Sarah	26 (1793-1800)	489
Ashton, Catherine	29 (1800-07)	719
Asline, John	9 (1760-67)	384
Asteix, Elizabeth	41 (1834-39)	702
Atkin, Edmond (Esqr)	9 (1760-67)	199
Atkins, James	15 (1771-74)	665
Atkins, Jean	13 (1767-71)	851
Atkins, Thomas	6 (1747-52)	468
Atkinson, Anthony	6 (1747-52)	322
Atkinson, Joseph	29 (1800-07)	600
Atkinson, Mary	33 (1807-18)	1162
Atkinson, Thomas	3 (1732-37)	285
Attwell, Ichabod	28 (1800-07)	124
Attwell, Joseph	14 (1771-74)	275
Atwell, Joseph (K. Senr)	1 (1722-24)	26
Atwell, Mary	18 (1776-84)	26
Audebert, Moses	10 (1760-67)	651
Audley, Erasmus	22 (1786-93)	275
Audley, Martha	26 (1793-1800)	441
Aunan, John ⌊Jean⌋	1 (1722-24)	77
Austen, Robert	26 (1793-1800)	605
Austen, William ⌊Austin⌋	33 (1807-18)	968
Austin, Bartholomew	14 (1771-74)	30
Austin, Earles	51 (1862-68)	791
Austin, Elizabeth	47 (1851-56)	811
Austin, George	16 (1774-79)	215
Austin, Margaret B.	47 (1851-56)	773
Austin, William	17 (1774-79)	667
Austin see also Austen		
Auten, Peter W.	50 (1862-68)	109

Name	Volume	Page
Avant, Hannah	17 (1774-79)	516
Avant, John	6 (1747-52)	341
Avant, John	8 (1757-60)	526
Averell, Henry	34 (1818-26)	174
Axson, John	42 (1839-45)	149
Axson, Mary	32 (1807-18)	864
Axson, Samuel, E.	33 (1807-18)	1271
Axson, Susanna ⌐Susannah⌐	25 (1793-1800)	277
Axson, William	28 (1800-07)	59
Axtell, Holland	1 (1692-93)	1
Ayers, Abigaille ⌐Ayres, Abygal⌐	2 (1729-31)	21
Ayrault, Peter	33 (1807-18)	1195
Ayres, Mary	36 (1818-26)	1104
Ayres see also Ayers		
Azuby, Ester	30 (1800-07)	855

B

Name	Volume	Page
Baas, John	34 (1818-26)	168
Baas, Thomas	31 (1807-18)	243
Babin, Catherine	29 (1800-07)	520
Backes, F.	51 (1862-68)	670
Backhouse, Katharine	11 (1767-71)	186
Backshell, William	8 (1757-60)	63
Bacon, Michael	1 (1722-24)	47
Bacot, Elizabeth S. W.	43 (1839-45)	504
Bacot, Henry Harramond	39 (1826-34)	1199
Bacot, Peter	2 (1729-31)	6
Bacot, Peter	3 (1732-37)	150
Bacot, Peter	22 (1786-93)	173
Baddeley, John	22 (1786-93)	35
Badenhop, Jesse	4 (1736-40)	130
Baer, Charles	46 (1851-56)	144
Bafset, John ⌐Bafsett⌐	2 (1727-29)	28

Name	Volume	Page

Bafsett see Bafset, Bassett, Bifsett

Name	Volume	Page
Bagbee, John	4 (1736-40)	137
Bagby, James	9 (1760-67)	42
Bagshaw, Elizabeth	44 (1845-51)	126
Bagshaw, Elizabeth (Codicil)	44 (1845-51)	233
Bagshaw, Robert	36 (1818-26)	1030
Bague, George	28 (1800-07)	181
Bailey, Ann	38 (1826-34)	618
Bailey, Benjn	38 (1826-34)	723
Bailey, Charles	41 (1834-39)	533
Bailey, Charles J.	47 (1851-56)	500
Bailey, Edwd	38 (1826-34)	816
Bailey, Henry	5 (1740-47)	7
Bailey, Henry	10 (1760-67)	591
Bailey, Henry	37 (1826-34)	347
Bailey, Ralph	27 (1793-1800)	810
Bailey, Ralph	48 (1856-62)	310
Bailey, Richard	10 (1760-67)	673
Bailey, Robert S.	49 (1856-62)	729
Bailey, Sarah Grimball	44 (1845-51)	297
Bailey, Sedgwick, M.	49 (1856-62)	975
Bailey, Thomas	48 (1856-62)	204
Baird, Archibald	17 (1774-79)	716
Baird, Christopher	11 (1767-71)	285
Baird, James (Bearde)	8 (1757-60)	254
Baird, Jeremiah	11 (1767-71)	76
Baird, Joshua	15 (1771-74)	595
Baker, Amey	32 (1807-18)	562
Baker, Ann	36 (1818-26)	970
Baker, Ann M.	46 (1851-56)	320
Baker, Benjamin	6 (1747-52)	122
Baker, Benjamin	19 (1780-83)	317
Baker, Benjamin	20 (1783-86)	413

11

Name	Volume	Page
Baker, Elihu	6 (1747-52)	124
Baker, Ellizabeth (Elliott)	18 (1776-84)	297
Baker, Francis	6 (1747-52)	185
Baker, Francis	25 (1793-1800)	120
Baker, Henry	18 (1776-84)	190
Baker, James	7 (1752-56)	325
Baker, John	16 (1774-79)	323
Baker, John	50 (1862-68)	48
Baker, Mary	26 (1793-1800)	490
Baker, Mary Butler	51 (1862-68)	664
Baker, Richard	1 (1687-1710)	15
Baker, Richard	4 (1736-40)	92
Baker, Richard	7 (1752-56)	35
Baker, Richard	12 (1767-71)	618
Baker, Richard Bohun	20 (1783-86)	231
Baker, Richard Bohun	41 (1834-39)	694
Baker, Richard Bohun	50 (1862-68)	379
Baker, Sarah	5 (1740-47)	659
Baker, Sarah	16 (1774-79)	204
Baker, Sarah	17 (1774-79)	733
Baker, Sarah Ann (Anna)	42 (1839-45)	140
Baker, Susannah	35 (1818-26)	582
Baker, Thomas	4 (1736-40)	321
Baker, Thomas	7 (1752-56)	121
Baker, Thomas	16 (1774-79)	35
Baker, Virtue	7 (1752-56)	243
Baker, William	3 (1732-37)	303
Baker, William	5 (1740-47)	363
Baker, William	9 (1760-67)	153
Baker, William	22 (1786-93)	54
Baldwin, Hester	24 (1786-93)	1072
Baldwin, John	4 (1736-40)	88
Baldwin, Joseph T.	36 (1818-26)	942

12

Name	Volume	Page
Balfour, John	19 (1780-83)	297
Balfour, John	20 (1783-86)	287
Ball, Alwyn	40 (1834-39)	267
Ball, Ann	27 (1793-1800)	922
Ball, Ann	42 (1839-45)	155
*Ball, Elias	6 (1747-52)	546
Ball, Elias	8 (1757-60)	200
Ball, Elias	22 (1786-93)	287
Ball, Elias	31 (1807-18)	300
Ball, Elias	40 (1834-39)	109
Ball, Eliza C.	51 (1862-68)	673
Ball, Elizabeth St. J.	45 (1845-51)	646
Ball, George	7 (1752-56)	170
Ball, Hugh Swinton	41 (1834-39)	779
Ball, Isaac	36 (1818-26)	1202
Ball, John	33 (1807-18)	1324
Ball, John	40 (1834-39)	57
Ball, John C.	43 (1839-45)	882
Ball, John Coming	10 (1760-67)	578
Ball, John Coming	24 (1786-93)	1145
Ball, Joseph	12 (1767-71)	630
Ball, Joseph	22 (1786-93)	139
Ball, Judith	14 (1771-74)	307
Ball, Lydia	20 (1783-86)	113
Ball, Martha	35 (1818-26)	551
Ball, Natt Comings	44 (1845-51)	109
Ball, Sampson	11 (1767-71)	219
Ball, Samuel	16 (1774-79)	358
Ball, Samuel	20 (1783-86)	299
Ballard, Elizabeth	51 (1862-68)	696
Ballard, Joseph	49 (1856-62)	1038
Ballantine, James	5 (1740-47)	545
Ballantine, John	10 (1760-67)	523
Ballantine, John	48 (1856-62)	425

Name	Volume	Page
Ballantine, Patrick [Partrick]	1 (1720-21)	35
Ballund, Alexander	42 (1839-45)	172
Bamfield, Rebecca [Bampfield]	29 (1800-07)	394
Bampfield, B. Mara	39 (1826-34)	951
Bampfield, Harriet Hockley	38 (1826-34)	763
Bampfield, James	39 (1826-34)	1165
Bampfield, Sarah	38 (1826-34)	643
Bampfield, William	15 (1771-74)	497
Bampfield, William Hardy	24 (1786-93)	837
Bampfield see also Bamfield		
Banbury, Peter	8 (1757-60)	10
Banbury, William	20 (1783-86)	229
Banks, Charles	32 (1807-18)	582
Banks, Harriett Lowndes	47 (1850-56)	552
Banks, John	29 (1800-07)	713
Banks, William Lee	48 (1856-62)	109
Bankson, Andrew	8 (1757-60)	431
Bannantyne see Bannatyne		
Bannatyne, Frances [Bannantyne; Francis]	9 (1760-67)	196
Barbot, Antoine	47 (1851-56)	654
Bare, Andrew	33 (1807-18)	1309
Barker, Charles	7 (1752-56)	316
Barker, Henrietta C.	48 (1856-62)	300
Barker, Henry L.	43 (1839-45)	684
Barker, Joseph	1 (1692-93)	65
Barker, Mary	1 (1721-22)	16
Barker, Samuel G.	50 (1862-68)	16
Barker, Sarah	2 (G1729-31)	20
Barker, Thomas	4 (1736-40)	313
Barkesdale see Barksdale		
Barksdale, C.D.	49 (1856-62)	1043
Barksdale, Charles	13 (1767-71)	873
Barksdale, George	19 (1780-83)	351
Barksdale, George	20 (1783-86)	8

Name	Volume	Page
Barksdale, George Senr. [Barkesdale]	25 (1793-1800)	144
Barksdale, George	33 (1807-18)	1148
Barksdale, John see Barksdale, Jonathan		
Barksdale, Jonathan [John]	2 (1727-29)	93
Barksdale, Mary	19 (1780-83)	62
Barksdale, Mary	47 (1851-56)	532
Barksdale, Rebecca B.	46 (1851-56)	268
Barksdale, Thomas	28 (1800-07)	16
Barksdale, Thomas	45 (1845-51)	784
Barksdale, Thomas Jones	30 (1800-07)	1065
Barlon, Susannah [Susanna, Susana]	8 (1757-60)	388
Barnard, Alexander	30 (1800-07)	959
Barnes, Edmund	8 (1757-60)	143
Barnes, Isaac	20 (1783-86)	388
Barnes, John [Barns]	12 (1767-71)	431
Barnes, Thomas	4 (1736-40)	275
Barnes, Thomas	46 (1851-56)	257
Barnes, William	19 (1780-83)	368
Barnet, Joseph	15 (1771-74)	490
Barnett, Elisha Sen.	37 (1826-34)	278
Barnett, Elisha	39 (1826-34)	955
Barnett, George	5 (1740-47)	266
Barnett, John	4 (1736-40)	154
Barnett, John	22 (1786-93)	146
Barnett, Samuel J.	42 (1839-45)	234
Barnfield, William	27 (1793-1800)	767
Barns see Barnes		
Barnstine, John Henry	35 (1818-26)	752
Barnwell, Edward M. (P.C.)	46 (1851-56)	22
Barnwell, Collo. John	1 (1722-24)	94
Barnwell, Nathaniel	17 (1774-79)	650
Baron, Alexander	34 (1818-26)	106
Baron, Alexander L.	42 (1839-45)	385

Name	volume	Page
Baron, E. F. L.	43 (1839-45)	824
Baron, Isabel Ann [Isabella]	42 (1839-45)	208
Baron, Robert	10 (1760-67)	493
Baron, Sarah	38 (1826-34)	705
Barquet, Barbara	44 (1845-51)	23
Barr, William	10 (1760-67)	544
Barragan, William	49 (1856-62)	583
Barraque, Jacob	12 (1767-71)	437
Barre, John	47 (1851-56)	860
Barre, William	24 (1786-93)	914
Barret see Barrett		
Barrett, Edward [Barret]	17 (1774-79)	667
Barrett, Rachel	51 (1862-68)	467
Barrett, Solomon I.	45 (1845-51)	741
Barrow, Francis	6 (1747-52)	379
Barten, John	4 (1736-40)	50
Bartlet, James	33 (1807-18)	980
Barton, Elizabeth	33 (1807-18)	1237
Barton, Jane	33 (1807-18)	1003
Barton, Mary Ann	40 (1834-39)	159
Barton, Sarah	32 (1807-18)	675
Barton, Sarah	33 (1807-18)	1386
Barton, Thomas	24 (1786-93)	801
Barton, William, (Senr)	12 (1767-71)	466
Bartram, Thomas	3 (1732-37)	78
Basden, Mary	5 (1740-47)	20
Baskens, John	12 (1767-71)	489
Basquins, Thomas	13 (1767-71)	755
Bassett, George [Bafsett]	2 (1724-25)	33
Bassnett, Mary	1 (1721-22)	35
Bate, Elias	6 (1747-52)	642
Bateman, Isaac	43 (1839-45)	735
Bateman, Robert	2 (1727-29)	75

Name	volume	Page
Bates, Sarah	47 (1851-56)	516
Batsford, Joseph	5 (1740-47)	393
Batterson, James	2 (1726-27)	47
Batton, Isaac (Battoon	14 (1771-74)	197
Battoon, Cornelius	5 (1740-47)	288
Battoon see also Batton		
Batts, John	13 (1767-71)	710
Batty, Thomas	11 (1767-71)	102
Baudoin, George	1 (1692-93)	54
Baxter, James	4 (1736-40)	18
Bay, Elihu Hall	43 (1839-45)	782
Bay, Gracia	51 (1862-68)	605
Bay, John	21 (1783-86)	692
Bay, Margaret	44 (1845-51)	441
Bay, Mary Wainwright	49 (1856-62)	789
Bayly, John	3 (1732-37)	91
Bayly, Peter	21 (1783-86)	700
Baynard, Elizabeth	15 (1771-74)	525
Baynard, William	15 (1771-74)	399
Baynard, William G.	49 (1856-62)	886
Bayne, Daniel	11 (1767-71)	42
Bazil, John	43 (1839-45)	767
Beadon, George	2 (1724-25)	81
Beaird, George	7 (1752-56)	245
Beaird, Margaret	13 (1767-71)	810
Beaird, Matthew	5 (1740-47)	249
Beale, John	31 (1807-18)	15
Beale, Othniel	15 (1771-74)	567
Beale, Othniel	15 (1771-74)	572
Beale, Thomas	5 (1740-47)	164
Beamer, James	1 (1692-93)	25
Beamer, Thomas	9 (1760-67)	60
Beamer see also Beamor		

Name	Volume	Page
Beamor, John [Beamer]	4 (1736-40)	233
Bean, James	41 (1834-39)	574
Bear, John	15 (1771-74)	493
Beard, Dorothy	45 (1845-51)	907
Beard, Robert	26 (1793-1800)	514
Bearde see Baird		
Bearman, Christopher	12 (1767-71)	648
Bearman, Joseph	11 (1767-71)	253
Bearman see also Bearmin		
Bearmin, Mary [Bearman]	12 (1767-71)	674
Beatty, Eleanor	36 (1818-26)	865
Beatty, Francis	17 (1774-79)	533
Beatty, John	9 (1760-67)	261
Beatty, Robert	31 (1807-18)	268
Beaty, William	9 (1760-67)	122
*Beauchamp, Adam	6 (1747-52)	29
Beaud, Rachel	51 (1862-68)	872
Beazley, Martha [Thomas]	5 (1740-47)	630
Beazley, Thomas see Beazley, Martha		
Bebey, Anthony	8 (1757-60)	481
Beckett, John	16 (1774-79)	97
Beckett, William	47 (1851-56)	467
Beckman, Henry	7 (1752-56)	106
Bedggood, Nicholas	16 (1774-79)	168
Bedingfield, Charles	15 (1771-74)	510
Bedon, George	12 (1767-71)	443
Bedon, George	25 (1793-1800)	207
Bedon, Henry	9 (1760-67)	256
Bedon, Martha	10 (1760-67)	893
Bedon, Richard	4 (1736-40)	209
Bedon, Richard	11 (1767-71)	214
Bedon, Ruth	16 (1774-79)	42
Bee, Charles Augusta [Charlotte]	46 (1851-56)	62

18

Name	volume	Page
Bee, Charlotte Augusta see Bee, Charles Augusta		
Bee, Frances Caroline	45 (1845-51)	721
Bee, John	2 (1729-31)	12
Bee, John	6 (1747-52)	160
Bee, Joseph	8 (1757-60)	94
Bee, Joseph	24 (1786-93)	1004
*Bee, Martha	6 (1747-52)	507
Bee, Mary, Mrs.	2 (1729-31)	40
Bee, Mary	33 (1807-18)	1112
Bee, Robert R.	50 (1862-68)	341
Bee, Sarah Waring	28 (1800-07)	213
Bee, Susanna	12 (1767-71)	587
Bee, Susanna	30 (1800-07)	797
Bee, Thomas Junr.	1 (1722-24)	98
Bee, Thomas	2 (1722-26)	17
Bee, Thomas	32 (1807-18)	590
Bee, William	10 (1760-67)	799
Bee, Wm. H.	46 (1851-56)	6
Beekman, Charles	26 (1793-1800)	621
Beekman, Elizabeth	32 (1807-18)	940
Beekman, John	15 (1771-74)	641
Beekman, Samuel	32 (1807-18)	532
Beere, Richard	35 (1818-26)	444
Begbie, Elizabeth	23 (1786-93)	671
Begly, John	24 (1786-93)	1087
Behrens, Heinrich Wilhelm	47 (1851-56)	526
Beil, George	21 (1783-86)	563
Beisner, Henry	46 (1851-56)	56
Belcher, Elijah	36 (1818-26)	882
Belcher, Mary R.	44 (1845-51)	419
Belin. Esther	45 (1845-51)	849
Belin, Esther (Substitution of Trustee)	45 (1845-51)	895

Name	Volume	Page
Belin, James	5 (1740-47)	553
Bell, Andrew	7 (1752-56)	128
Bell, Elizabeth	12 (1767-71)	603
Bell, George	23 (1786-93)	493
Bell, John	24 (1786-93)	1034
Bell, Joseph	23 (1786-93)	558
Bell, Samuel	21 (1783-86)	550
Bell, Walter	5 (1740-47)	235
Bell, William	12 (1767-71)	404
Bell, William	15 (1771-74)	519
Bell, William	46 (1851-56)	302
Bellamy, Esther	35 (1818-26)	494
Bellamy, Timothy	2 (1722-26)	20
Bellingall, Margaret	42 (1839-45)	67
Bellinger, Edmund	22 (1786-93)	159
Bellinger, Edmund, Junior	23 (1786-93)	653
Bellinger, Edmund C.	44 (1845-51)	420
Bellinger, Emily	36 (1818-26)	946
Bellinger, John	49 (1856-62)	720
Bellinger, Joseph	38 (1826-34)	678
Bellinger, Mary Lucia	26 (1793-1800)	499
Bellinger, Mary Rebecca	47 (1851-56)	622
Bellinger, Rebecca	35 (1818-26)	825
Bellinger, William	7 (1752-56)	7
Bellinger, William	13 (1767-71)	687
Bellinger, William, Junior	24 (1786-93)	924
Belser, Christian	32 (1807-18)	565
Belser, John	31 (1807-18)	255
Belton, Jonathan	11 (1767-71)	157
Belton, Peter	4 (1736-40)	111
Benedict, Emily	43 (1839-45)	716
Benison, George	6 (1747-52)	173
Benison, William	6 (1747-52)	488

Name	Volume	Page
Benison, William	21 (1783-86)	802
Bennet, Ann [Bennett; Anne]	9 (1760-67)	175
Bennet, Matthew	21 (1783-86)	464
Bennet, Thomas, Senr. [Bennett]	11 (1767-71)	263
Bennet, William [Bennit]	3 (1731-33)	49
Bennett, Anna Hayes	38 (1826-34)	750
Bennett, Henry	34 (1818-26)	223
Bennett, Joseph B.	38 (1826-34)	649
Bennett, Peter	38 (1826-34)	666
Bennett, Sarah M.	37 (1826-34)	323
Bennett, Thomas	32 (1807-18)	773
Bennett, Thomas	51 (1862-68)	633
Bennett, Thomas B.	51 (1862-68)	523
Bennett, William	15 (1771-74)	504
Bennett, William	18 (1776-84)	325
Bennett, William	20 (1783-86)	412
Bennett, William (Senior)	28 (1800-07)	284
Bennett see also Bennet		
Bennison, Elizabeth	6 (1747-52)	500
Bennit see Bennet		
Benoist, Charles	5 (1740-47)	401
Benoist, James	7 (1752-56)	354
Benoist, John Baptiste	33 (1807-18)	1075
Benoist, John Baptist Achille	44 (1845-51)	346
Benoist, Peter	5 (1740-47)	574
Benoist, Peter [Renoist]	8 (1757-60)	358
Benoist, Peter	27 (1793-1800)	847
Benoist, Samuel	3 (1732-37)	49
Benoist, Samuel	28 (1800-07)	355
Benoist, William	36 (1818-26)	860
Benoist see also Binoist, Boinest		
Bensky see Binsky		
Benson, Lavinia	39 (1826-34)	947
Benson, Lawrence	42 (1839-45)	238

Name	Volume	Page
Bentham, Mary	36 (1818-26)	1218
Bentham, Robert	43 (1839-45)	689
Benton, Samuel	25 (1793-1800)	85
Beresford, Ann	26 (1793-1800)	632
Beresford, Richard	14 (1771-74)	300
Beresford, Richard	50 (1862-68)	1
Beresford, Richard [Berresford] (Reference)	51 (1862-68)	881
Bermon see Birmon		
Bernard, Angelique Girouer Femme	31 (1807-18)	195
Bernard, James	16 (1774-79)	339
Bernard, Martha	26 (1793-1800)	494
Berresford see Beresford		
*Berrie, James	6 (1747-52)	11
Berry, Alex^r	39 (1826-34)	1149
Bert, Claudius Medardus Felix	32 (1807-18)	492
Berterand see Bertrand		
Bertrand, Mary Elizabeth	47 (1851-56)	593
Bertrand, Pierre [Berterand]	1 (1692-93)	68
Berwick, Ann	26 (1793-1800)	328
Bery, William	31 (1807-18)	94
Besley, Richard	21 (1783-86)	806
Bestatt, Abraham	5 (1740-47)	421
Beswicke, John	25 (1793-1800)	176
Betham, Robert	5 (1740-47)	664
Bethune, Angus	32 (1807-18)	888
Betjemann, Henrick [Hanrick]	42 (1839-45)	255
Betson, William	1 (1722-24)	52
Betterson, Jonathan [Bettison]	4 (1736-40)	318
Bettison, Jonathan	8 (1757-60)	219
Bettison see also Betterson		
Beversene, John G.	51 (1862-68)	669
Bianchi, Angelo	51 (1862-68)	470
Bickley, John	51 (1862-68)	441

Name	Volume	Page
Biddell, Ann	1 (1711-18)	56
Biddle, Nicholas	17 (1774-79)	815
Bifset see Bisset		
Bifsett, Mary [Bafsett]	7 (1752-56)	286
Bifsett, William	7 (1752-56)	177
Bigelow, Augusta	43 (1839-45)	550
Bigelow, Cyprian	27 (1793-1800)	839
Bigelow, Sarah	29 (1800-07)	736
Biggs, (M^r) John	30 (1800-07)	1039
Bigler, Barned	17 (1774-79)	617
Biglow, Lyman	42 (1839-45)	159
Bigs, David	17 (1774-79)	729
Bilbeau, James	4 (1736-40)	4
Billing, Zenobia	15 (1771-74)	361
Billings, Rufus	25 (1783-1800)	83
Binoist, Peter [Benoist]	7 (1752-56)	569
Binsky, Martin [Bensky]	8 (1757-60)	180
Birch, Charlotte, A.	50 (1862-68)	381
Bird, Sarah	34 (1818-26)	228
Birmon, Christopher [Bermon]	5 (1740-47)	312
Bishopp, Job	1 (1692-93)	11
Bissell, John H.	44 (1845-51)	435
Bisset, Catherine [Bifset]	9 (1760-67)	300
Bivet, Ann	31 (1807-18)	355
Bixby, Joseph	35 (1818-26)	511
Bize, Hercules Daniel	27 (1793-1800)	964
Black, Alexander	45 (1845-51)	566
Black, Christopher L.	43 (1839-45)	711
Black, Dorothea	48 (1856-62)	37
Black, Frances C. [Francis]	47 (1851-56)	791
Black, Francis C.	49 (1856-62)	1011
Black, Hester	36 (1818-26)	912
Black, James	39 (1826-34)	857

Name	Volume	Page
Black, James W.	38 (1826-34)	623
Black, John	40 (1834-39)	80
Black, William	34 (1818-26)	388
Blackledge, Zachariah	19 (1780-83)	135
Blacklock, William	33 (1807-18)	1046
Blackman, Sarah	28 (1800-07)	143
Blackmon, Benjamin	39 (1826-34)	915
Blackmon, Thomas, Senr	32 (1807-18)	895
Blackwall, William	27 (1793-1800)	920
Blackwood, John	39 (1826-34)	1235
Blackwood, Thomas	41 (1834-39)	480
Blackwood, Thomas (Substitution of Trustee)	49 (1856-62)	822
Blaikie, Elizabeth	31 (1807-18)	67
Blaikie, George	16 (1774-79)	291
Blair, Elizabeth	42 (1839-45)	120
Blair, James	33 (1807-18)	965
Blair, John	30 (1800-07)	1042
Blair, Wade	9 (1760-67)	386
Blake, Charlotte	28 (1800-07)	364
Blake, Daniel	19 (1780-83)	90
Blake, Edward	26 (1793-1800)	361
Blake, Edward	47 (1851-56)	659
Blake, Lady Elizabeth	2 (1726-27)	70
Blake, Elizabeth [Eliza]	24 (1786-93)	1113
Blake, Harriett H.	42 (1839-45)	161
Blake, John	28 (1800-07)	315
Blake, John	29 (1800-07)	754
Blake, John	44 (1845-51)	403
Blake, John	47 (1851-56)	446
Blake, Joseph	1 (1687-1710)	18
*Blake, Joseph	6 (1747-52)	534
Blake, Mary	30 (1800-07)	1079
Blake, Peter	31 (1807-18)	42

Name	volume	Page
Blake, Richard	20 (1783-86)	127
Blake, William	29 (1800-07)	738
Blakeway, Sarah [Blakewey]	25 (1793-1800)	68
Blakeway, William [Blakewey]	2 (1726-27)	49
Blakewey, see Blakeway		
Blamyer, Caroline	51 (1862-68)	855
Blamyer, Harriet	49 (1856-62)	882
Blamyer, John	10 (1760-67)	676
Blamyer, Mary	9 (1760-67)	372
Blamyer see also Blumyer		
Blamyre, Kate	21 (1783-86)	716
Blanchard, Francis	2 (1722-26)	15
Blanck, Martin Daniel	33 (1807-18)	1053
Bland, George	17 (1774-79)	802
Bland, Lancelot	17 (1774-79)	757
* Bland, Richard	18 (1776-84)	39
Blanding, Abram	42 (1839-45)	28
Blanshard, Josiah	16 (1774-79)	212
Blanton, James	45 (1845-51)	881
Blare, James	8 (1757-60)	334
Blasingame, Thomas	14 (1771-74)	311
Bleakly, John [Blekly]	6 (1747-52)	81
Blekly see Bleakly		
Blewer, Elizabeth	36 (1818-26)	1108
Blewer, Washington F.	50 (1862-68)	307
Blome, John	33 (1807-18)	994
Blondeau, Charlotte Regne	51 (1862-68)	594
Blondeau, Etienne	50 (1862-68)	373
Blondeau, Marie Aglae (Boudet fm)	38 (1826-34)	536
Blondel, Pierre	28 (1800-07)	235
Blondell, Thomas [Blundell]	4 (1736-40)	315
Bluit, Hester	41 (1834-39)	604
Blum, Ester	49 (1856-62)	792

Name	Volume	Page
Blum, J. Charles	48 (1856-62)	110
Blum, Mary S.	47 (1851-56)	814
Blumyer, Williams [Blamyer, Blumyres; William]	2 (1724-25)	73
Blumyres see Blumyer		
Blundell, Thomas	24 (1786-93)	944
Blundell see also Blondell		
Bochet, Anthony	16 (1774-79)	150
Bochet, Henry	21 (1783-86)	758
Bochet, John P.	35 (1818-26)	652
Bochet, Nicholas	3 (1732-37)	55
Bochet, Peter	14 (1771-74)	238
*Bochet, Peter	20 (1783-86)	258
Bochet, Samuel	14 (1771-74)	241
Bochet see also Bochett		
Bochett, Mary	29 (1800-07)	608
Bochett, Nicholas [Bochet]	5 (1740-47)	247
Bocken, Christian	45 (1845-51)	618
Bocquet, Elizabeth	31 (1807-18)	110
*Bocquet, Peter [Bocquett]	20 (1783-86)	199
Bocquett see Bocquet		
*Boddicott, Richard	6 (1747-52)	539
Boddington, George	8 (1757-60)	221
Bodell, Ann	14 (1771-74)	32
Bofsard, Henry	13 (1767-71)	976
Bogan, William	9 (1760-67)	294
Boggs, Francis	14 (1771-74)	44
Bohun, Nicholas	1 (1722-24)	11
Boifseau, David	8 (1757-60)	355
Boifseau, James	7 (1752-56)	486
Boifseau see also Boisseau		
Boigard, Mathurin	3 (1732-37)	135
Boineau, Michael	36 (1818-26)	1192
Boinest, Marie Anne Sophie Brunet [Benoist]	42 (1839-45)	246

Name	volume	Page
*Boisseau, James	6 (1747-52)	453
Boisseau, Jane [Boifseau]	10 (1760-67)	615
Bold, John (Senior)	29 (1800-07)	696
Bollard, Moses	25 (1793-1800)	113
Bolles, Abiel	51 (1862-68)	545
Bollough, George	39 (1826-34)	899
Bollough, James (Sener)	20 (1783-86)	119
Bollough, James	32 (1807-18)	650
Bollough, James	35 (1818-26)	633
Bollough, Jesse W., Sr. [Jefse]	42 (1839-45)	333
Bollough, Jessie W., Sr.	51 (1862-68)	683
Bollough, John	20 (1783-86)	182
Bollough, John	29 (1800-07)	574
Bollough, John	29 (1800-07)	647
Bollough, John W.	38 (1826-34)	486
Bolton, Allen	22 (1786-93)	20
Bolton, James	17 (1774-79)	561
Bolton, Thomas	1 (1692-93)	59
Bond, Constantia	7 (1752-56)	236
Bond, Jacob	10 (1760-67)	844
Bond, James	13 (1767-71)	877
Bones, William	48 (1856-62)	260
Bonhoste, Jacob	24 (1786-93)	872
Bonhoste, John	5 (1740-47)	641
Bonneau, Anne	48 (1856-62)	116
Bonneau, Anthony	5 (1740-47)	261
Bonneau, Anthony (Sen.)	8 (1757-60)	56
Bonneau, Anthony	21 (1783-86)	742
Bonneau, Benjamin	28 (1800-07)	144
Bonneau, Eleanor Sarah	33 (1807-18)	1180
Bonneau, Elias	15 (1771-74)	555
Bonneau, Elizabeth	34 (1818-26)	255
Bonneau, Francis	28 (1800-07)	266

Name	Volume	Page
Bonneau, Hannah	43 (1839-45)	916
Bonneau, Henry	9 (1760-67)	61
Bonneau, Henry	18 (1776-84)	31
Bonneau, Jacob	11 (1767-71)	124
Bonneau, John E.	45 (1845-51)	603
Bonneau, John Henry	7 (1752-56)	187
Bonneau, Josiah	19 (1780-83)	303
Bonneau, Josiah	20 (1783-86)	75
Bonneau, Margarite Henritte [Margurite, Henrite]	9 (1760-67)	126
Bonneau, Mary	47 (1851-56)	830
Bonneau, Moses	21 (1783-86)	669
Bonneau, Peter	6 (1747-52)	108
Bonneau, Peter	30 (1800-07)	1114
Bonneau, Samuel	22 (1786-93)	344
Bonneau, Thomas S.	39 (1826-34)	905
Bonneau, William	24 (1786-93)	998
Bonneau, William D.	50 (1862-68)	84
Bonnell, John	47 (1851-56)	489
Bonnell, John	50 (1862-68)	384
Bonnor, Henry [Bonor]	8 (1757-60)	315
Bonny, Thomas	6 (1747-52)	505
Bonor see Bonnor		
Bonthron, John	33 (1807-18)	1258
Booman, Samuel	4 (1736-40)	330
Boomer, John	25 (1793-1800)	160
Boomer, Michael	16 (1774-79)	380
Boon, Charlotte	41 (1834-39)	516
Boon, John [Boone]	25 (1793-1800)	15
*Boone, Ann	6 (1747-52)	550
Boone, James	6 (1747-52)	134
Boone, James	25 (1793-1800)	44
Boone, Jane [Jame]	13 (1767-71)	921
Boone, John	1 (1711-18)	11

Name	volume	Page
Boone, John	17 (1774-79)	517
Boone, Joseph	3 (1732-37)	202
Boone, Joseph W.	50 (1862-68)	264
Boone, Mary	19 (1780-83)	48
Boone, Mary	20 (1783-86)	268
Boone, Sarah	43 (1839-45)	562
Boone, Thomas	6 (1747-52)	285
Boone, Thomas	21 (1783-86)	551
Boone, (Major) William	6 (1747-52)	495
Boone, William Jones	50 (1862-68)	310
Boone, William Jones	51 (1862-68)	539
Boone see also Boon		
Boosley see Bosley		
Booth, John	10 (1760-67)	726
Booth, Margaret [Boothe]	44 (1845-51)	92
Booth, Robert	4 (1736-40)	287
Boothe see Booth		
Borch, Peter	39 (1826-34)	1197
Bordenave, John	48 (1856-62)	207
Bordley, William H.	44 (1845-51)	125
Bordline, John [Borland]	5 (1740-47)	371
Borland, William	5 (1740-47)	55
Borland see also Bordline		
Bosley, Philip [Boosley]	25 (1793-1800)	109
Boswood, James	7 (1752-56)	507
Bothwell, John	18 (1776-84)	293
Bouchonneau, Charles	32 (1807-18)	630
Bouchonneau, Sarah	32 (1807-18)	649
Boudo, Heloise	41 (1834-39)	665
Boudo, Louis	37 (1826-34)	161
Bouman, Peter	31 (1807-18)	308
Bounetheau, E. W.	49 (1856-62)	1005
Bounetheau, Elizabeth	40 (1834-39)	134

Name	Volume	Page

Bourdeaux, Anthoney de [Anthonie de] see Bourdeaux, De Anthony

Bourdeaux, De Anthony [Anthoney de, Anthonie de]	2 (1722-26)	13
Bourdeaux, James	11 (1767-71)	40
Bourdeaux, Mary	27 (1793-1800)	946
Bourdeaux, Nathaniel	29 (1800-07)	550
Bourget, Daniel	13 (1767-71)	693
Bourke, Gibbon	22 (1786-93)	323
Bourne, John	1 (1711-18)	45
Bournonvivier, Gile Pierre	28 (1800-07)	216
Bours, Samuel	19 (1780-83)	292
Boutiton, Margaret	49 (1856-62)	696
Boutwell, Burtenhead	10 (1760-67)	785
Bowden, William	23 (1786-93)	755
Bowen, John	32 (1807-18)	506
Bowen, Margaret Watson	49 (1856-62)	1019
Bowen, William, Senior	21 (1783-86)	629
Bower, Edward	20 (1783-86)	409
Bower, Henry	2 (1722-26)	5
Bower, Patrick	19 (1780-83)	173
Bower, Philip [Phillip]	21 (1783-86)	783
Bowery, Joseph	7 (1752-56)	511
Bowhay, Joseph Proctor	31 (1807-18)	430
Bowler, Charles	10 (1760-67)	813
Bowler, Charles	21 (1783-86)	780
Bowler, William	22 (1786-93)	103
Bowles, Ann	33 (1807-18)	1135
Bowles, Ann C. [Anna]	47 (1851-56)	699
Bowles, John	22 (1786-93)	376
Bowles, Tobias	31 (1807-18)	169
Bowman, John	31 (1807-18)	105
Bowman, Kezia	19 (1780-83)	86
*Bowman, Kezia	20 (1783-86)	256

30

Name	Volume	Page
Bowman, Mary H.	46 (1851-56)	58
Bowman, Thomas, Sr.	15 (1771-74)	521
Bowman, Thomas	16 (1774-79)	330
Bowman, William	25 (1793-1800)	42
Bowrey, William	10 (1760-67)	631
Box, Thomas	16 (1774-79)	61
Boyce, Jeremiah	48 (1856-62)	266
Boyce, Jerome	48 (1856-62)	266
Boyce, Ker	46 (1851-56)	414
Boyce, Patrick J.	47 (1851-56)	833
Boyd, Benjamin	31 (1807-18)	413
Boyd, James B.	49 (1856-62)	1069
Boyd, Wm.	33 (1807-18)	1359
Boyd, William Robert E.	35 (1818-26)	689
Boyden, Mary E.	49 (1856-62)	854
Boyer, Henry	22 (1786-93)	7
Boyer, Jacob Henry	38 (1826-34)	491
Boykin, Fitzgerald Glover	42 (1839-45)	97
Boyle, Hugh	14 (1771-74)	40
Boyle, James	31 (1807-18)	54
Boyle, Mary C.	48 (1856-62)	244
Boyron, Martin (Nuncupative Will)	1 (1711-18)	77
Bradbuery, Thomas	16 (1774-79)	366
Bradley, Elizabeth	33 (1807-18)	1022
Bradley, James	16 (1774-79)	359
Bradley, John	7 (1752-56)	228
Bradley, Lewis	3 (1732-37)	107
Bradley, Martha	48 (1856-62)	364
Bradley, Moses	32 (1807-18)	574
Bradshaw, Deodatus	22 (1786-93)	136
Bradshaw, Henry	14 (1771-74)	298
Bradshaw, James	38 (1826-34)	450
Bradstreet, Simon	19 (1780-83)	192

Name	Volume	Page
Bradwell, Isaac	10 (1760-67)	862
Bradwell, Jacob	5 (1740-47)	365
Bradwell, Lewis	45 (1845-51)	753
Bradwell, Nathaniel	7 (1752-56)	23
Bradwell, Nathaniel	20 (1783-86)	365
Bradwell, Thomas	11 (1767-71)	245
Bradwell, Thomas	48 (1856-62)	180
Brady, John	41 (1834-39)	568
Braggins, William	6 (1747-52)	648
Brailsford, (Mr.) Edward	2 (1729-31)	43
Brailsford, Elizabeth	30 (1800-07)	1102
Brailsford, Elizabeth	36 (1818-26)	1043
Brailsford, John	6 (1747-52)	607
Brailsford, Joseph	8 (1757-60)	514
Brailsford, Mary	35 (1818-26)	679
Brailsford, Mary (Substitution of Trustee)	36 (1818-26)	843
Brailsford, Morton	8 (1757-60)	549
Brailsford, Susan M.	44 (1845-51)	16
Brailsford, Wm. Roper	44 (1845-51)	146
Braithwaite, John	4 (1736-40)	221
Braly, Mary M.	33 (1807-18)	1418
Bramble, John	32 (1807-18)	882
Bramer, James	6 (1747-52)	190
Brandford, Thomas [Branford]	2 (1727-29)	88
Brandon, D.	41 (1834-39)	755
Branfod see Branford		
Branford, Alice	22 (1786-93)	131
Branford, Ann	8 (1757-60)	447
Branford, Elizabeth [Branfod]	28 (1800-07)	137
Branford, Ezekel [Ezikel]	18 (1776-84)	71
Branford, John	1 (1721-22)	41
Branford, William	11 (1767-71)	48

Name	Volume	Page
Branford, William	24 (1786-93)	831
Branford see also Brandford		
Branton, Henry	19 (1780-83)	268
Branton, Henry	20 (1783-86)	235
Bratton, John	18 (1776-84)	304
Brauer, Peter (G.) [Peater]	47 (1851-56)	505
Bready, William	12 (1767-71)	358
Breaker, Charles M.	51 (1862-68)	659
Breaker, John J.	38 (1826-34)	800
Breanon, Patrick	11 (1767-71)	104
Breazeale, Henry	13 (1767-71)	776
Bredenberg, Luder	51 (1862-68)	829
Breen, Philip	37 (1826-34)	91
Bremar, Francis	8 (1757-60)	482
Bremar, Henry	40 (1834-39)	365
Bremer, Frederick Hermon	45 (1845-51)	746
Brenan, Eugene	17 (1774-79)	655
Brenan, Richard	37 (1826-34)	13
Brennan, James	46 (1851-56)	178
Breton, John	4 (1736-40)	215
Bretten, John	2 (1729-31)	45
Bretton, Daniel	6 (1747-52)	242
Bretton see also Britton		
Brewer, Martha	49 (1856-62)	555
Brewer, Theodor [Theodore]	23 (1786-93)	654
Brewton, John	17 (1774-79)	592
Brewton, Mary	9 (1760-67)	17
Brewton, Mary	17 (1774-79)	585
Brewton, Miles	5 (1740-47)	496
Brewton, Miles	16 (1774-79)	405
Brians, John	26 (1793-1800)	356
Brickett, Ann	25 (1793-1800)	9
Brickett, Mathias	14 (1771-74)	117

Name	volume	Page
Brickles, Richard	4 (1736-40)	82
Brickmeyer, August Hermann	51 (1862-68)	616
Brickwedel, John H.	49 (1856-62)	757
Bridgewood, Thomas [Bridgwood]	38 (1826-34)	775
Bridgwood see Bridgewood		
Bridie, Eleanora	39 (1826-34)	983
Bridie, Robert	23 (1786-93)	627
Briegel, Jacob	14 (1771-74)	45
Brifson, Pierce F.	43 (1839-45)	738
Brindley, Stephen	29 (1800-07)	555
Brindley see also Brindly		
Brindly, Frederick [Brindley]	20 (1783-86)	217
Brinkman, Adolph	40 (1834-39)	163
Brinson, John	39 (1826-34)	869
Brisbane, Abbott H.	49 (1856-62)	898
Brisbane, Elizabeth	51 (1862-68)	705
Brisbane, James	26 (1793-1800)	436
Brisbane, John S.	45 (1845-51)	751
Brisbane, Maria	50 (1862-68)	312
Brisbane, Mary	43 (1839-45)	865
Brisbane, Robert	19 (1780-83)	279
*Brisbane, Robert	20 (1783-86)	196
Brisbane, William	14 (1771-74)	101
Brisbane, William	35 (1818-26)	607
Bristow, Elizabeth E.	46 (1851-56)	345
Britt, Miles	33 (1807-18)	1088
Britton, Francis	12 (1767-71)	379
Britton, Jean	8 (1757-60)	240
Britton, Joseph	16 (1774-79)	119
Britton, Moses	16 (1774-79)	121
Britton, Phillip [Bretton]	6 (1747-52)	282
Britton, Timothy	6 (1747-52)	432
Brnot, John	6 (1747-52)	592

Name	volume	Page
Broad, George	40 (1834-39)	428
Broadbelt, Jane	9 (1760-67)	360
Broadbelt, John	10 (1760-67)	691
Broadfoot, William	37 (1826-34)	374
Brobant, James	33 (1807-18)	1333
Brobant, Sarah	39 (1826-34)	997
Brockelbank, Margaret E.	47 (1851-56)	533
Brockinton, Sarah	9 (1760-67)	12
Brockinton, William	5 (1740-47)	386
Brodie, John W.	49 (1856-62)	933
Brodie, Mary	37 (1826-34)	6
Brodie, Thomas	27 (1793-1800)	726
Brodie see also Brody		
Brody, John [Brodie]	8 (1757-60)	91
Broeske, Sarah	34 (1818-26)	296
Brooks, Jacob	16 (1774-79)	86
Brooks, Mary Margaret	40 (1834-39)	424
Bross, Benjamin	51 (1862-68)	876
Broughon- see Broughton		
Broughton, Alexander [Broughon]	10 (1760-67)	556
Broughton, Alexander	25 (1793-1800)	105
Broughton, Andrew	5 (1740-47)	149
Broughton, Andrew	20 (1783-86)	80
Broughton, Ann	23 (1786-93)	474
Broughton, Ann	40 (1834-39)	285
Broughton, Catherine [Catharine]	26 (1793-1800)	631
Broughton, Charlotte	38 (1826-34)	495
Broughton, Daniel	41 (1834-39)	567
Broughton, Elizabeth Damaris	40 (1834-39)	44
Broughton, Henrietta Mary	37 (1826-34)	387
Broughton, John	27 (1793-1800)	820
Broughton, Mary	33 (1807-18)	1211
Broughton, Mary	43 (1839-45)	685

Name	volume	Page
Broughton, Mary Martha	47 (1851-56)	645
Broughton, Nathaniel	7 (1752-56)	280
Broughton, Peter	12 (1767-71)	561
Broughton, Peter	39 (1826-34)	989
Broughton, Philip Porcher	35 (1818-26)	711
Broughton, Thomas	4 (1736-40)	66
Broughton, Thomas	9 (1760-67)	127
Broughton, Thomas	31 (1807-18)	202
Broughton, Thomas	38 (1826-34)	505
Broun, Archibald	27 (1793-1800)	707
Brower, Ann	46 (1851-56)	311
Brown, Ann	38 (1826-34)	524
Brown, Benjamin H.	50 (1862-68)	216
Brown, Clement	1 (1722-24)	56
Brown, Clement C.	29 (1800-07)	386
Brown, Daniel	32 (1807-18)	815
Brown, Daniel	39 (1826-34)	867
Brown, David	10 (1760-67)	678
Brown, Edward	9 (1760-67)	302
Brown, Elizabeth	8 (1757-60)	218
Brown, Elizabeth	10 (1760-67)	756
Brown, Elizabeth	34 (1818-26)	163
Brown, Francis	7 (1752-56)	183
Brown, George	8 (1757-60)	122
Brown, George	18 (1776-84)	319
Brown, George	27 (1793-1800)	716
Brown, George	48 (1856-62)	146
Brown, George W.	49 (1856-62)	1030
Brown, Harriet L.	45 (1845-51)	900
Brown, Hugh	21 (1783-86)	656
Brown, James [Browne]	2 (G1729-31)	31
Brown, James	43 (1839-45)	488
Brown, James W.	51 (1862-68)	501
Brown, John	14 (1771-74)	167

36

Name	Volume	Page
Brown, John	30 (1800-07)	956
Brown, John	30 (1800-07)	1008
Brown, John	36 (1818-26)	881
Brown, John W.	40 (1834-39)	430
Brown, Joseph	32 (1807-18)	854
Brown, Malcom	25 (1793-1800)	309
Brown, Margaret	18 (1776-84)	310
Brown, Mary	13 (1767-71)	1019
Brown, Mary	30 (1800-07)	916
Brown, Mary	37 (1826-34)	250
Brown, Mary	48 (1856-62)	50
Brown, Mary Deas	44 (1845-51)	295
Brown, Mathias	23 (1786-93)	536
Brown, Nathaniel	7 (1752-56)	219
Brown, Patrick	7 (1752-56)	364
Brown, Robert	13 (1767-71)	893
Brown, Samuel T.	48 (1856-62)	253
Brown, Sarah	31 (1807-18)	172
Brown, Sarah	43 (1839-45)	772
Brown, Talbot	5 (1740-47)	565
Brown, Thomas	5 (1740-47)	661
Brown, Thomas	6 (1747-52)	384
Brown, Thomas	15 (1771-74)	407
Brown, William	6 (1747-52)	293
Brown, William	7 (1752-56)	524
Brown, William	32 (1807-18)	792
Browne see Brown		
Brownell, Edmund	45 (1845-51)	863
Browning, John	41 (1834-39)	642
Brownlee, John	37 (1826-34)	309
Brownson, John	1 (1711-18)	49
Broxson, John	24 (1786-93)	911
Brozett, James	5 (1740-47)	213

Name	Volume	Page
Bruce, John	10 (1760-67)	680
Bruce, Robert	23 (1786-93)	616
Bruce, William [Burce]	6 (1747-52)	633
Bruck, John Jacob	5 (1740-47)	571
Bruneau, Paul	1 (1711-18)	84
Brunet, Esaie	8 (1757-60)	118
Brunet, Susanah Mary [Sufana]	8 (1757-60)	473
Brunson, Isaac	13 (1767-71)	807
Brunson, Joseph	4 (1736-40)	231
Brunson, Joseph	5 (1740-47)	209
Brunson, Josiah [Brunston]	8 (1757-60)	499
Brunston see Brunson		
Brunton, John	22 (1786-93)	117
Bryan, Edward Benjamin	49 (1856-62)	839
Bryan, Hugh	7 (1752-56)	154
Bryan, James	19 (1780-83)	230
Bryan, John	29 (1800-07)	582
Bryan, John	44 (1845-51)	333
Bryan, Jonathan	48 (1856-62)	429
Bryan, Joseph	6 (1747-52)	602
Bryan, Julia Grace	51 (1862-68)	650
Bryan, Lydia	43 (1839-45)	553
Bryant, Christian	23 (1786-93)	580
Bryce, Nicol	32 (1807-18)	957
Bryen, James	34 (1818-26)	287
Bryon, John	15 (1771-74)	352
Buchanan, Archibald	36 (1818-26)	919
Buchanan, Dianna	50 (1862-68)	114
Buchanan, Peter	34 (1818-26)	225
Buchanan, William	8 (1757-60)	49
Buchanan, William	8 (1757-60)	205
Buchannan, Robert	2 (1729-31)	100
Bucking, John Henry	49 (1856-62)	949

Name	volume	Page
Buckingham, Elias	22 (1786-93)	361
Buckle, George	29 (1800-07)	425
Buckle, Thomas	22 (1786-93)	187
Buckle, Thomas	26 (1793-1800)	352
Buckley, Grace [Buckly; Grece]	1 (1721-22)	30
Buckly see Buckley		
Buckner, Eliza	40 (1834-39)	382
Budd, John	24 (1786-93)	943
Buer, Thomas	13 (1767-71)	814
Buer, Thomas	26 (1793-1800)	546
Buerhaus, Herman Diedrick	40 (1834-39)	14
Buford, Elizabeth	43 (1839-45)	706
Bufsey see Bussey		
Buist, Mary	43 (1839-45)	850
Buley, Jacob	31 (1807-18)	196
Bulgin, James	29 (1800-07)	511
Bulkley, James	33 (1807-18)	1202
Bulkley, Margaret Maria [Maria M.]	43 (1839-45)	678
Bulkley, Maria M. see Bulkley, Margaret Maria		
Bulkley, Stephen	42 (1839-45)	388
Bull Arthur	8 (1757-60)	295
Bull, Baraby [Barnaby]	7 (1752-56)	277
Bull, Elizabeth	40 (1834-39)	130
Bull, Fenwicke	19 (1780-83)	271
Bull, Fenwicke	20 (1783-86)	190
Bull, Hannah	26 (1793-1800)	612
Bull, John	12 (1767-71)	387
Bull, John	28 (1800-07)	322
Bull, Mary	14 (1771-74)	127
Bull, Stephen [Stev.]	6 (1747-52)	315
Bull, Stephen	13 (1767-71)	752
*Bull, Thomas	15 (1771-74)	355
Bull, Thomas	30 (1800-07)	1005

Name	volume	Page
Bull, William	7 (1752-56)	339
Bull, William	20 (1783-86)	359
*Bull, William	24 (1786-93)	984
Bull, William Stephen	35 (1818-26)	648
Bullard, Edward	11 (1767-71)	142
Bullard, Griffith	6 (1747-52)	319
Bullard, Hopkins (Bullards; Hopkin)	2 (1724-25)	45
Bullard, Sarah	23 (1786-93)	692
Bullards see Bullard		
Bulline, John	9 (1760-67)	251
Bulline, John	14 (1771-74)	217
*Bulline, Thomas	6 (1747-52)	428
Bulline, Thomas	12 (1767-71)	627
Bullock, Stephen Pemmel	26 (1793-1800)	432
Bulman, Daniell	1 (1692-93)	35
Bulow, Charles W.	36 (1818-26)	871
Bulow, Joachim	25 (1793-1800)	318
Bulow, John Joachim	42 (1839-45)	293
Bulow, Thomas Lehre	48 (1856-62)	119
Bunce, Lemuel	32 (1807-18)	882
Bunch, Dennis D.	51 (1862-68)	461
Bunch, Gidian	29 (1800-07)	629
Bunch, Isabella	46 (1851-56)	44
Bunch, John L.	49 (1856-62)	548
Bunch, Laford	39 (1826-34)	1188
Bunch, Mary	50 (1862-68)	280
Bunch, Peter	50 (1862-68)	52
Bunch, Warren	47 (1851-56)	614
Burbage, Daniel	42 (1839-45)	424
Burbage, James	48 (1856-62)	73
Burbage, Thomas	42 (1839-45)	383
Burce see Bruce		
Burch, Edward C.	43 (1839-45)	800

Name	volume	Page
Burckmeyer, Elizabeth	49 (1856-62)	800
Burckmeyer see also Burkmeyer		
Burckmeyer, John	32 (1807-18)	594
Burd, Joseph Vincent	22 (1786-93)	85
Burd, William	8 (1757-60)	291
Burdell, Robert	28 (1800-07)	259
Burden, Kinsey	49 (1856-62)	567
Burden, Kinsey E.	49 (1856-62)	557
Burden, Thomas L.	47 (1851-56)	443
Burgefs, William	21 (1783-86)	626
Burger, Charles	35 (1818-26)	637
Burger, David	29 (1800-07)	700
Burger, Robert	37 (1826-34)	410
Burger, Samuel	44 (1845-51)	3
Burges, James	30 (1800-07)	918
Burges, James S.	45 (1845-51)	647
Burgess, William C.	45 (1845-51)	473
Burick, John	2 (1724-25)	2
Burke, Aedamus [Aedanus]	28 (1800-07)	285
Burke, John	50 (1862-68)	410
Burkmeyer, Charles [Burckmeyer]	26 (1793-1800)	471
Burkmeyer, Daniel [Burkmyer]	16 (1774-79)	178
Burkmyer see Burkmeyer		
Burn, Alexander	20 (1783-86)	215
Burn, Catharine	39 (1826-34)	886
Burn, Samuel	15 (1771-74)	621
Burn, William	47 (1851-56)	463
Burnefs, James	32 (1807-18)	524
Burnet, Edward [Burnett]	3 (1732-37)	204
Burnet, George [Burnett]	1 (1711-18)	8
Burnett, George	2 (1726-27)	43
Burnett, Mary	1 (1721-22)	49
Burnett, Richard	25 (1793-1800)	312

Name	volume	Page
Burnett see also Burnet		
Burnham, Charles	2 (G1729-31)	10
Burnham, Elizabeth	5 (1740-47)	323
Burnham, Nicholass	5 (1740-47)	652
Burnham, Thomas	8 (1757-60)	262
Burnley, William	5 (1740-47)	54
Burnley, William	6 (1747-52)	331
Burns, George	14 (1771-74)	39
Burns, James	42 (1839-45)	321
Burns, John	16 (1774-79)	317
Burrage, John	27 (1793-1800)	873
Burrage, Lawrence	40 (1834-39)	47
Burrell, William	41 (1834-39)	730
Burrows, William	19 (1780-83)	183
Burt, Ann	24 (1786-93)	1026
Burtin, Thomas	8 (1757-60)	28
Burton, Samuel	8 (1757-60)	397
Busch, Stephan	48 (1856-62)	163
Bush, Abraham	22 (1786-93)	291
Bush, Edward	12 (1761-71)	568
Bush, Isaac	28 (1800-07)	307
Bush, Peter	13 (1767-71)	1018
Busing, Mary	42 (1839-45)	371
Bussey, George [Bufsey]	10 (1760-67)	714
Butler, Andrew	51 (1862-68)	790
Butler, Ann	22 (1786-93)	380
Butler, Charles P.	51 (1862-68)	522
Butler, Daniel	31 (1807-18)	450
Butler, Elizabeth	19 (1780-83)	35
Butler, Elizabeth	26 (1793-1800)	402
Butler, George	6 (1747-52)	333
Butler, James	18 (1776-84)	227
Butler, James Henry	22 (1786-93)	149

Name	Volume	Page
Butler, John	30 (1800-07)	903
Butler, Moses	15 (1771-74)	632
Butler, Richard	1 (1692-93)	63
Butler, Sarah	30 (1800-07)	1116
Butler, Shem	1 (1722-24)	51
Butler, Thomas	5 (1740-47)	636
Butler, Thomas	6 (1747-52)	71
Buxbaum, Eliza S.	43 (1839-45)	499
Byden, John	2 (1726-27)	15
Byers, Robert	18 (1776-84)	209
Byers, William	24 (1786-93)	1074
Byrne, B. M.	49 (1856-62)	728
Byrnes, John	49 (1856-62)	905
Byrnes, John P.	50 (1862-68)	83
Bysell, Margareth	21 (1783-86)	467

C

Name	Volume	Page
Cabeuil, Louisa Elizabeth	39 (1826-34)	1134
Caborne, Sarah Esther	25 (1793-1800)	322
Cadwell see Caldwell		
Cafsin, Patrick	33 (1807-18)	1213
Cahusac, Ann C.	41 (1834-39)	583
Cahusac, Daniel	17 (1774-79)	806
Cahusac, Daniel	41 (1834-39)	763
Cahusac, John	9 (1760-67)	91
Cahusac, John	36 (1818-26)	877
Cahusac, Robert	20 (1783-86)	82
Cahusac, Robert	39 (1826-34)	1013
Cain, Daniel	25 (1793-1800)	128
Cain, Daniel	38 (1826-34)	554
Cain, Elizabeth	33 (1807-18)	1205
Cain see also Caine		
Caine, Abraham	6 (1747-52)	21

Name	volume	Page
Caine, Isaac [Cain]	21 (1783-86)	834
Calaghan, Charles	49 (1856-62)	625
Calahan see Callahan		
Calcut, Henry	42 (1839-45)	101
Calder, Alexander	45 (1845-51)	484
Calder, Archibald	17 (1774-79)	572
Calder, Archibald John	29 (1800-07)	631
Calder, Billy	40 (1834-39)	175
Calder, Charles	6 (1747-52)	172
Calder, Henry	34 (1818-26)	307
Calder, James	42 (1839-45)	229
Calder, James	47 (1851-56)	713
Calder, John	11 (1767-71)	116
Calder, William	49 (1856-62)	732
Caldwell, Henry Junior [Calwell]	28 (1800-07)	189
Caldwell, John	50 (1862-68)	150
Caldwell, John W.	51 50 (1862-68)	804
Caldwell, William [Cadwell]	31 (1807-18)	381
Caldwell, William A.	44 (1845-51)	97
Calhoun, Ezekiel	9 (1760-67)	296
Calhoun, John [Colhunn; John]	21 (1783-86)	694
Calhoun see also Colhoun		
Caliote, James	18 (1776-84)	286
Callaghan, John	19 (1780-83)	146
Callaghan, John [Callghan]	20 (1783-86)	238
Callaghan, John	30 (1800-07)	1133
Callahan, Daniel [Calahan; Daniell]	1 (1721-22)	18
Callghan see Callaghan		
Caloff, Henry	31 (1807-18)	462
Caloff, Mary	33 (1807-18)	1425
Calvert, Eliza	47 (1851-56)	858
Calvet, Raymond [Reymond]	10 (1760-67)	815
Calvitt, Samuel E.	46 (1851-56)	142

44

Name	Volume	Page
Calwell see Caldwell		
Cam, William	24 (1786-93)	825
Cambell see Camble		
Camber, Thomas	16 (1774-79)	113
Camble, Hugh [Cambell]	45 (1845-51)	463
Cambridge, Ann M.	51 (1862-68)	495
Cambridge, Elizabeth	35 (1818-26)	531
Cambridge, Tobias	31 (1807-18)	163
Cameron, David	31 (1807-18)	397
Cameron, Samuel	31 (1807-18)	324
Cammer, Francis S.	45 (1845-51)	802
Cammer, Peter	43 (1839-45)	744
Campbell, Ann Loughton	43 (1839-45)	536
Campbell, Archibald	51 (1862-68)	607
Campbell, Collin	20 (1783-86)	390
Campbell, David	24 (1786-93)	820
Campbell, Dougal	13 (1767-71)	960
Campbell, Elizabeth	34 (1818-26)	89
Campbell, Henrietta	40 (1834-39)	181
Campbell, Hugh	5 (1740-47)	147
Campbell, Hugh	5 (1740-47)	269
Campbell, Hugh	22 (1786-93)	167
Campbell, Hugh George	34 (1818-26)	399
Campbell, Isaac Motte	50 (1862-68)	147
Campbell, James	34 (1818-26)	13
Campbell, James	41 (1834-39)	558
Campbell, John	47 (1851-56)	513
Campbell, MaCartan	26 (1793-1800)	565
Campbell, McMillan	32 (1807-18)	741
Campbell, Mary	50 (1862-68)	229
Campbell, Rachel	25 (1793-1800)	41
Campbell, Samuel	15 (1771-74)	520
Campbell, William M.	49 (1856-62)	1048

Name	volume	Page
Campling, William	4 (1736-40)	223
Cannaday, Austin	51 (1862-68)	538
Cannon, Daniel	29 (1800-07)	390
Cannon, Ellinor M.	50 (1862-68)	42
Cannon, George	30 (1800-07)	923
Cannon, Jeremiah	42 (1839-45)	216
Cannon, John	9 (1760-67)	370
Cannon, John	29 (1800-07)	724
Cannon, Martha	32 (1807-18)	851
Cannon, Peter	1 (1721-22)	20
Cannon, William	27 (1793-1800)	917
Cannon, William	32 (1807-18)	555
Canover, Eliza [Conover]	35 (1818-26)	723
Canter, Abraham	48 (1856-62)	238
Canter, Joshua	45 (1845-51)	810
Canter, Rachel	46 (1851-56)	90
Cantey, Josiah	15 (1771-74)	646
Cantey, Margaret	44 (1845-51)	208
Cantey, Samuel	17 (1774-79)	554
Cantley, Roger G.	35 (1818-26)	762
Cantwell, Patrick	45 (1845-51)	545
Cape, Brian	29 (1800-07)	607
Cape, Brian	37 (1826-34)	160
Cape, John	33 (1807-18)	1121
Cape, Jonathan	29 (1800-07)	460
Cape, Mary	35 (1818-26)	502
Capers, Elizabeth Charlotte	48 (1856-62)	296
Capers, Gabriel	28 (1800-07)	330
Capers, John S.	44 (1845-51)	290
Capers, Joseph Ellicott	5 (1740-47)	282
Capers, Martha E.	50 (1862-68)	35
Capers, Richard	7 (1752-56)	287
Capers, Richard	16 (1774-79)	90

Name	Volume	Page
Capers, Thomas	11 (1767-71)	24
Capers, William	21 (1783-86)	745
Capers, William H.	37 (1826-34)	289
Caradeux, T. B.	35 (1818-26)	440
Card, Mary	31 (1807-18)	125
Cardoza, David N.	40 (1834-39)	272
Cardy, Sam¹	16 (1774-79)	60
Care, Adam [John]	36 (1818-26)	952
Care, John see Care, Adam		
Careire see Cariere		
Carew, Esther W.	47 (1851-56)	750
Carew, Thomas	30 (1800-07)	981
Carey, Thomas	31 (1807-18)	358
Cargill, John	17 (1774-79)	779
Cariere, John [Careire]	2 (1724-25)	56
Carivenc, Anthony Alexis Andrew	37 (1826-34)	368
Carivenc, Widow	40 (1834-39)	127
Carman, Andrew	25 (1793-1800)	311
Carmand, Francis	42 (1839-45)	452
Carmand, Francis	46 (1851-56)	88
Carmicael, William	14 (1771-74)	229
Carmichael, John	3 (1732-37)	262
Carmichael, Mary	17 (1774-79)	790
Carne, Samuel	23 (1786-93)	590
Carnes, Lawrence [Laurence]	30 (1800-07)	861
Carpenter, Anna Maria	38 (1826-34)	584
Carpenter, James Edwin	43 (1839-45)	822
Carpentier, M.	36 (1818-26)	1087
Carr, Charity	17 (1774-79)	714
Carr, Isaac	18 (1776-84)	317
Carr, John	28 (1800-07)	169
Carrere, Charles	38 (1826-34)	654
Carrere, Francois	31 (1807-18)	356

Name	Volume	Page
Carrington, Samuel	33 (1807-18)	1264
Carrol see Carroll		
Carroll, Alexander	47 (1851-56)	854
Carroll, Charles [Carroll]	6 (1747-52)	649
Carroll, James Parsons	35 (1818-26)	426
Carroll, Michael	27 (1793-1800)	694
Carse, William	17 (1774-79)	675
Carson, Elizabeth	45 (1845-51)	496
Carson, James	17 (1774-79)	668
Carson, James, Senr	17 (1774-79)	739
Carson, William	33 (1807-18)	1169
Carson, William	39 (1826-34)	896
Carson, Wm. A.	47 (1851-56)	845
Carsten, William F.	49 (1856-62)	709
Cart, Eliza	50 (1862-68)	419
Cart, John	23 (1786-93)	753
Cart, John, Jr.	44 (1845-51)	298
Cart, Susannah	36 (1818-26)	984
Carter, Mayre	30 (1800-07)	1059
Carter, William	22 (1786-93)	156
Carterett, Hugh	1 (1692-93)	6
Cartwright, Hugh	7 (1752-56)	100
Cartwright, Richard	5 (1740-47)	57
Carty, Daniell	1 (1692-93)	5
Carver, William	31 (1807-18)	8
Carwithen, Mary	19 (1780-83)	178
Casey, John	28 (1800-07)	148
Casey, John	44 (1845-51)	447
Caskin, John	26 (1793-1800)	384
Cassovich, Bartolo	49 (1856-62)	684
Castagnou, Bernard	32 (1807-18)	866
Castell, Benjamin	27 (1793-1800)	776
Castell, Sarah (Nuncupative)	28 (1800-07)	128

Name	volume	Page
Castinel, Mark Anthony	28 (1800-07)	193
Cater, Stephen	21 (1783-86)	524
Cater, Thomas	7 (1752-56)	96
Cater, William	6 (1747-52)	198
Catherwood, John James	44 (1845-51)	5
Cator, Thomas	2 (1729-31)	102
Cattel, Sarah [Cattell]	10 (1760-67)	848
Cattell, Benjamin	1 (1721-22)	12
Cattell, Benjamin	19 (1780-83)	348
Cattell, John, (Jun.)	8 (1757-60)	188
Cattell, John	12 (1767-71)	529
Cattell, John	16 (1774-79)	103
Cattell, William	7 (1752-56)	13
Cattell, William	17 (1774-79)	812
Cattell, William	42 (1839-45)	401
Cattell see also Cattel, Cattle		
Catterea see Cutterea		
Cattle, Barsheba	34 (1818-26)	97
Cattle, Benjamin [Cattell]	9 (1760-67)	29
Cattle, John [Cattell]	9 (1760-67)	33
Caught, Mary	34 (1818-26)	153
Caught, Thomas	38 (1826-34)	445
Cavanau, Mary	30 (1800-07)	1099
Cavaneau, James [Caveneau]	27 (1793-1800)	785
Caveneau see Cavaneau		
Caw, David	8 (1757-60)	275
Caw, Jane	46 (1851-56)	137
Caw, Rachel	31 (1807-18)	158
Caw, Thomas	15 (1771-74)	401
Cawood, John, Esq.	2 (1724-25)	105
Ceazer, Hannah	24 (1786-93)	888
Ceser, Doctor	7 (1752-56)	186
Chabociere, Bruneau	1 (1692-93)	31
Chalet, John	44 (1845-51)	204

Name	volume	Page
Chalmers, David	33 (1807-18)	979
Chalmers, Isaac	20 (1783-86)	370
Chalmers see also Chambers		
Chamberlain, Charles V.	51 (1862-68)	646
Chamberlain, Hubbard	21 (1783-86)	822
Chamberlayn, Esther [Chamberlayne]	31 (1807-18)	378
Chamberlayne see Chamberlayn		
Chamberlin, Job	3 (1732-37)	35
Chambers, Henry	1 (1711-18)	90
Chambers, James	9 (1760-67)	265
Chambers, William	23 (1786-93)	594
Chambers, William [Chalmers]	26 (1793-1800)	422
Champignie, Peter	6 (1747-52)	474
Champneys, Amarinthia	33 (1807-18)	1290
Champneys, John	6 (1747-52)	515
Champneys, John	34 (1818-26)	332
Chandler, Elizabeth	17 (1774-79)	503
Chandler, Isaac	6 (1747-52)	257
Chandler, Philip	5 (1740-47)	562
Chandler, Robert	16 (1774-79)	309
Chanet, Anthony	42 (1839-45)	34
Chanler, Isaac	28 (1800-07)	289
Chapeau, Jean Baptiste	45 (1845-51)	639
Chapeau, Mary	48 (1856-62)	301
Chaplin, Benjamin [Benjmain]	12 (1767-71)	356
Chaplin, John, Jr.	18 (1776-84)	147
Chaplin, Sarah	12 (1767-71)	342
Chaplin, William	34 (1818-26)	404
Chapman, Charles	25 (1793-1800)	231
Chapman, Dives [Dwes]	23 (1786-93)	779
Chapman, Dwes	27 (1793-1800)	677
Chapman, Edwin	51 (1862-68)	866
Chapman, James	48 (1856-62)	413

Name	Volume	Page
Chapman, John	12 (1767-71)	661
Chapman, Mary	25 (1793-1800)	228
Chapman, Mary Ellen	46 (1851-56)	23
Chapman, Samuel	31 (1807-18)	24
Chapman, Sarah	7 (1752-56)	213
Chapman, Sarah	28 (1800-07)	9
Chapman, Thomas	43 (1839-45)	615
Chapman, William	1 (1711-18)	33
Chapman, William	17 (1774-79)	580
Chappel, Rebecca	24 (1786-93)	1099
Chardon, Isaac	3 (1732-37)	345
Charlen, Francis Joseph [Charlon]	49 (1856-62)	998
Charles, Andrew	32 (1807-18)	579
Charlon see Charlen		
Charnock, John	4 (1736-40)	160
Chartier, Jean Jacques	28 (1800-07)	106
Chatelain, Mari Loise Chauvereaux [Louise]	31 (1807-18)	184
Chauvet, Paul	22 (1786-93)	124
Chauvin, Isaac [Chouein]	3 (1732-37)	153
Chazal, John P.	37 (1826-34)	190
Cheaves, William	16 (1774-79)	40
Cheesborough, Elizabeth	9 (1760-67)	89
Cheesman, Elizabeth	5 (1740-47)	470
Cheever, Peggy	49 (1856-62)	760
Cheevers, Richard Holmes	28 (1800-07)	379
Cheney, David	11 (1767-71)	242
Chevallier, LePeter [Peter Le]	1 (1711-18)	48
Chevallier, Peter Le see Chevallier, Le Peter		
Chevard, A.	37 (1826-34)	376
Chevillette, John	14 (1771-74)	42
Chicken, George	5 (1740-47)	542
Chicken, William	17 (1774-79)	761

Name	Volume	Page
Child, Ann ‹Anne›	12 (1767-71)	451
Child, Isaac	3 (1732-37)	157
Child, James	1 (1720-21)	55
Child, Margaret	4 (1736-40)	124
Child see also Childe		
Childe, Joseph ‹Child›	2 (1724-25)	54
Childs, Jane	49 (1856-62)	843
Childs, Nathan	22 (1786-93)	285
Chinners, Abraham	8 (1757-60)	363
Chinners, Isaac	11 (1767-71)	206
Chinners, John Sandiford	21 (1783-86)	431
Chion, J. F.	33 (1807-18)	1036
Chisam, Martha	19 (1780-83)	229
Chisholme, William	20 (1783-86)	20
Chisolm, Alexander	31 (1807-18)	402
Chisolm, Alexander Robert	37 (1826-34)	252
Chisolm, George	41 (1834-39)	654
Chisolm, Marianne	42 (1839-45)	357
Chisolm, Providence Hext	49 (1856-62)	766
Chisolm, Robert Trail	35 (1818-26)	602
Chisolm, Thomas	33 (1807-18)	1114
Chisolm, William	35 (1818-26)	565
Chisolme, Alexander	14 (1771-74)	324
Chitty, Charles C.	42 (1839-45)	1
Chouein see Chauvin		
Chouler, Joseph	29 (1800-07)	694
Chovin, Charles	24 (1786-93)	918
Chovin see also Chovine		
Chovine, Alexander ‹Chovin›	7 (1752-56)	567
Chovino, William	21 (1783-86)	810
Chovvino, John	21 (1783-86)	549
Chrichton, George	2 (1727-29)	90
Chrietzburg, Thomas	38 (1826-34)	451

52

Name	volume	Page
Christian, Elizabeth	32 (1807-18)	682
Christie, Alexander	7 (1752-56)	585
Christie, Alexander	36 (1818-26)	908
Christie, David Lamb	47 (1851-56)	731
Christie, Edward	26 (1793-1800)	647
Christie, Joanna, Senior	41 (1834-39)	729
Christie, Mary	12 (1767-71)	402
Chupein, Lewis Y.	46 (1851-56)	305
Chupein, Theodore L.	42 (1839-45)	210
Church, Margaret	46 (1851-56)	342
Clabrook, Richard	29 (1800-07)	459
Claburn see Clayburn		
Clace, Martha	12 (1767-71)	511
Clafs see Class		
Clafson, Christian [Clawson]	33 (1807-18)	985
Claghorn, Robert	6 (1747-52)	556
Claiborne, James H.	42 (1839-45)	162
Clancey, John [Clancy]	8 (1757-60)	332
Clancy see Clancey		
Clapp, Elizabeth	6 (1747-52)	489
Clapp, Gilson [Gillson]	4 (1736-40)	56
Clark, Aaron	42 (1839-45)	392
Clark, Ann	41 (1834-39)	713
Clark, Charles	50 (1862-68)	143
Clark, Daniel	8 (1757-60)	71
Clark, George	34 (1818-26)	300
Clark, James	6 (1747-52)	369
Clark, James	23 (1786-93)	638
Clark, James	34 (1818-26)	385
Clark, James Lardent	15 (1771-74)	411
Clark, Jeremiah [Jeremian]	6 (1747-52)	310
Clark, John	28 (1800-07)	93
Clark, Joseph	31 (1807-18)	161

Name	volume	Page
Clark, Mary Eddy	37 (1826-34)	350
Clark, Mathew	30 (1800-07)	1089
Clark, Patrick ⌐Richd.⌐	7 (1752-56)	447
Clark, Richard	49 (1856-62)	779
Clark, Rich^d see Clark, Patrick		
Clark, Samuel ⌐Samuell⌐	5 (1740-47)	589
Clark, Sarah	36 (1818-26)	885
Clark, Stephen	31 (1807-18)	116
Clark, William	47 (1851-56)	823
Clark, William Mikell	38 (1826-34)	804
Clark see also Clarke		
Clarke, Barnard	44 (1845-51)	252
Clarke, Charles	1 (1692-93)	41
Clarke, Charles	23 (1786-93)	497
Clarke, Charles	44 (1845-51)	86
Clarke, Francis	22 (1786-93)	63
Clarke, Jeremiah	2 (1727-29)	41
Clarke, Joseph	46 (1851-56)	344
Clarke, Mary ⌐Clark⌐	36 (1818-26)	928
Clarke, Samuel	17 (1774-79)	505
Clarke, Solomon	45 (1845-51)	771
Clarkson, Elizabeth Anderson	45 (1845-51)	547
Clarkson, John	45 (1845-51)	589
Clarkson, William	17 (1774-79)	523
Clarkson, William	36 (1818-26)	1181
Class, Margaret ⌐Clafs⌐	10 (1760-67)	471
Clawson see Clafson		
Clay, Elizabeth	5 (1740-47)	295
Clayburn, Frances ⌐Claburn⌐	10 (1760-67)	699
Clayton, Abraham	22 (1786-93)	21
Clayton, David	27 (1793-1800)	657
Clayton, Isham	18 (1776-84)	336
Clayton see also Clyton		
Cleapor, Charles	35 (1818-26)	656

54

Name	Volume	Page
Cleary, Catharine	43 (1839-45)	549
Cleator, John	13 (1767-71)	827
Cleave, Nathan	10 (1760-67)	521
Cleeland see Cleland		
Cleiland, William	9 (1760-67)	281
Cleland, John	8 (1757-60)	489
* Cleland, Robert [Cleeland]	6 (1747-52)	10
Clement, Mary	21 (1783-86)	685
Clement, Sarah	39 (1826-34)	981
Clemmons, Robert	12 (1767-71)	538
Cleveland, Catharine (P.C.)	48 (1856-62)	400
Cleveland, John A.	46 (1851-56)	168
Clifford, Charles	19 (1780-83)	363
Clifford, Elizabeth [Eliza]	19 (1780-83)	199
Clifford, Elizabeth	20 (1783-86)	167
Clifford, Henry	42 (1839-45)	264
Clifford, John	10 (1760-67)	613
Clifford, Martha	1 (1722-24)	8
Clifford, Martha	25 (1793-1800)	67
Clifford, Sarah	8 (1757-60)	263
Clifford, Thomas	9 (1760-67)	290
Clifford, Thomas	11 (1767-71)	169
Clime, Martin [Martain]	22 (1786-93)	200
Clinton, Samuel	25 (1793-1800)	43
Clitherall, James	28 (1800-07)	166
Cloyd, John	3 (1732-37)	117
Clyde, Henry	47 (1851-56)	832
Clyton, John [Clayton]	27 (1793-1800)	675
Coachman, Elizabeth	30 (1800-07)	1123
Coachman, John	6 (1747-52)	321
Coachman, William	13 (1767-71)	711
Coates, Catherine	36 (1818-26)	1075
Coates, Martha	36 (1818-26)	1236

Name	Volume	Page
Coates, William ₍Coats₎	19 (1780-83)	186
Coats see Coates		
Cobham, George	21 (1783-86)	560
Cobia, Ann	43 (1839-45)	726
Cobia, Elizabeth	47 (1851-56)	536
Cobia, Francis Joseph	49 (1856-62)	673
Cobia, Mary	51 (1862-68)	459
Cobia, Nicholas	41 (1834-39)	836
Cobia, Sarah	49 (1856-62)	980
Cobley see Cobly		
Cobly, Eleanor ₍Cobley₎	9 (1760-67)	134
Cobram, John	22 (1786-93)	144
Coburn, Jane M.	40 (1834-39)	292
Coburn, John	34 (1818-26)	121
Cobzy, Charlemagne	34 (1818-26)	171
Cochran, Eliza C.	46 (1851-56)	312
Cochran, James	27 (1793-1800)	683
Cochran, John	31 (1807-18)	133
Cochran, Michael	12 (1767-71)	564
Cochran, Samuel	31 (1807-18)	137
Cochran, Susanna	34 (1818-26)	206
Cochran, Thomas	29 (1800-07)	527
Cochran, William	8 (1757-60)	82
Cochran, William Edwards	6 (1747-52)	166
Cochran, William S.	48 (1856-62)	106
Cochrane, Margaret	41 (1834-39)	612
Cockfield, Barnaby	13 (1767-71)	939
Cockfield, B. W.	42 (1839-45)	354
Cockfield, John	9 (1760-67)	304
Cockfield, John E.	42 (1839-45)	56
Cockfield, Mary	26 (1793-1800)	474
Cockfield, Mary	34 (1818-26)	234
Cockran, Hannah	7 (1752-56)	93

56

Name	Volume	Page
Cockran, Hugh	1 (1711-18)	58
Cockran, John	9 (1760-67)	348
Coffey, Patrick M(ichael)	26 (1793-1800)	635
Coffey, Thomas	3 (1732-37)	92
Coffie, Catherine	30 (1800-07)	994
Coffin, George Matthewes	49 (1856-62)	989
Coffin, Thomas A. (order)	51 (1862-68)	831
Coffin, Thomas Aston	50 (1862-68)	119
Coffy, Marian see Coffy, Mary Ann		
Coffy, Mary Ann (Cofty; Marian)	8 (1757-60)	124
Cofsens, Edmund	17 (1774-79)	684
Cofty see Coffy		
Cogdell, Charles	18 (1776-84)	95
Cogdell, Jane	23 (1786-93)	739
Cogdell, John S.	44 (1845-51)	163
Cogdell, Maria	48 (1856-62)	375
Cogdell, Mary Ann Elizabeth	37 (1826-34)	320
Cogdell, Richard W.	51 (1862-68)	640
Cogswell, Jeremiah (Nuncupative)	1 (1722-24)	32
Cohen, Abraham	31 (1807-18)	294
Cohen, David	21 (1783-86)	435
Cohen, David D.	49 (1856-62)	697
Cohen Eleanor M.	48 (1856-62)	95
Cohen, Isaac	22 (1786-93)	115
Cohen, Jacob	31 (1807-18)	178
Cohen, Jacob (A.)	28 (1800-07)	7
Cohen, Mordecai	44 (1845-51)	356
Cohen, Solomon I	45 (1845-51)	675
Cohrs, H.A.	41 (1834-39)	676
* Coke, Joseph	6 (1747-52)	13
Colburn, James Smith	48 (1856-62)	490
Colburn, William	32 (1807-18)	868
Colcock, Charles Jones	41 (1834-39)	887

Name	Volume	Page
Colcock, Isaac	10 (1760-67)	814
Colcock, John	20 (1783-86)	17
Colcock, Mellifscent (Junr)	32 (1807-18)	638
Colcock, Mellifscent	38 (1826-34)	550
Cole, George F.	50 (1862-68)	22
Cole, James	6 (1747-52)	356
Cole, John	8 (1757-60)	258
Cole, Margaret	51 (1862-68)	685
Cole, Mary	8 (1757-60)	70
Cole, Micaijah [Micaiah]	4 (1736-40)	282
Cole, Ruth	33 (1807-18)	1276
Cole, Thomas	3 (1731-33)	28
Cole, Thomas	14 (1771-74)	109
Cole, William	9 (1760-67)	152
Coleman, Patrick	34 (1818-26)	356
Colhoun, Hugh [Calhoun]	27 (1793-1800)	672
Colhoun, Ifsabella	39 (1826-34)	918
Colhoun, John	37 (1826-34)	157
Colhoun, John Ewing [Erving]	29 (1800-07)	445
Colhoun, Samuel	30 (1800-07)	780
Colhunn see Calhoun		
Collans, Peter	18 (1776-84)	171
Collas, Jean Baptiste	31 (1807-18)	180
Colles, Elizabeth	24 (1786-93)	894
Collet, Charles	31 (1807-18)	454
Colleton, Ann	3 (1732-37)	247
Colleton, Charles (Esq.)	2 (1727-29)	15
* Colleton, John	6 (1747-52)	392
Colleton, Sir John	19 (1780-83)	149
Colleton, Sir John	22 (1786-93)	57
* Colleton, Susannah	6 (1747-52)	435
Colley, Henry	1 (1711-18)	4
Collings, Jonathan	3 (1731-33)	32

Name	volume	Page
Collins, Alexander	2 (1724-25)	10
Collins, Daniel	6 (1747-52)	25
Collins, John	1 (1687-1710)	42
Collins, John	42 (1839-45)	408
Collins, Jonah	6 (1747-52)	150
Collins, Jonah	23 (1786-93)	419
Collins, Jonathan	44 (1845-51)	301
Collins, Margaret	41 (1834-39)	759
Collins, Robert	27 (1793-1800)	824
Collins, Sarah	9 (1760-67)	222
Collins, Susannah	34 (1818-26)	166
Collis, Robert	8 (1757-60)	153
Colson, Abraham	6 (1747-52)	397
Colwell, John	2 (G1729-31)	1
Colyer, Thomas	10 (1760-67)	805
Colzy, Angelique	41 (1834-39)	673
Combafsye see Combassye		
Combassye, Mary ₍Combafsye₎	3 (1732-37)	51
Combe, John	30 (1800-07)	1032
Combe, Philip ₍Phillip₎	4 (1736-40)	16
Coming, Affra	1 (1687-1710)	14
Coming, John	1 (1692-93)	58
Commander, Joseph	14 (1771-74)	226
Commander, Samuel	3 (1732-37)	238
Condy, Thomas D.	48 (1856-62)	268
Coneyars see Conyears		
Conklin, John	36 (1818-26)	1209
Conn, Thomas	11 (1767-71)	313
Connelly, David	22 (1786-93)	133
Conner, Henry W.	49 (1856-62)	773
Conner, Isaac	45 (1845-51)	477
Connin, William ₍Cunning₎	6 (1747-52)	63
Connolly, Catherine ₍Catharine₎	38 (1826-34)	480

Name	volume	Page
Connor, John (Junr) ₁Conor₃	16 (1774-79)	279
Connor, John	18 (1776-84)	271
Connor, Margaret	50 (1862-68)	126
Conor see Connor		
Conover see Canover		
Conrad, John G.	48 (1856-62)	313
Conto, John Peter	36 (1818-26)	951
Conybear see Conybeare		
Conybeare, Thomas ₁Conybear₃	2 (1727-29)	89
Conyears, William ₁Coneyars₃	5 (1740-47)	325
Conyers, Thomas	2 (1722-26)	28
Conyers, William	32 (1807-18)	952
Cook, Augustus	50 (1862-68)	25
Cook, Benjamin	21 (1783-86)	782
Cook, Edward	16 (1774-79)	179
Cook, Elizabeth	28 (1800-07)	95
Cook, John	5 (1740-47)	137
Cook, John	19 (1780-83)	353
Cook, Jonathan	26 (1793-1800)	443
Cook, Mary	33 (1807-18)	1381
Cook, Paul	27 (1793-1800)	962
Cook, Samuel	3 (1731-33)	56
Cook, Samuel	37 (1826-34)	144
Cook, Sarah	25 (1793-1800)	74
Cook, William	19 (1780-83)	55
Cook, William	20 (1783-86)	329
Cook, William C.	40 (1834-39)	55
Cook, Wilson	25 (1793-1800)	95
Cook see also Cooke		
Cooke, Anna ₁Anne₃	2 (1727-29)	23
Cooke, Giles	2 (1729-31)	24
Cooke, John	5 (1740-47)	377
Cooke, John ₁Cook₃	10 (1760-67)	792

Name	volume	Page
Cooke, John	31 (1807-18)	157
Cooke, Thomas	6 (1747-52)	35
Cooke, William	7 (1752-56)	294
Cooke, William	35 (1818-26)	592
Coomer, William	7 (1752-56)	133
Coomer, William	14 (1771-74)	20
Coon, John	27 (1793-1800)	670
Cooper, Charles	34 (1818-26)	99
*Cooper, Eleana	2 (1729-31)	118
Cooper, James	14 (1771-74)	137
Cooper, John	1 (1711-18)	21
Cooper, Lydia J.	45 (1845-51)	486
Cooper, Mary	27 (1793-1800)	923
Cooper, Mary	48 (1856-62)	461
Cooper, Nathaniel	44 (1845-51)	82
Cooper, Peter	20 (1783-86)	309
Cooper, Robert	34 (1818-26)	129
Cooper, Samuel	16 (1774-79)	115
Cooper, Samuel	21 (1783-86)	797
Cooper, Sarah	10 (1760-67)	891
Cooper, Sylvanus	25 (1793-1800)	258
Cooper, Thomas	3 (1732-37)	140
Cooper, Thomas	5 (1740-47)	301
Cooper, Thomas	14 (1771-74)	278
Cooper, Thomas	24 (1786-93)	857
Cooper, William	17 (1774-79)	540
Cooper, William J.	49 (1856-62)	936
Copper, Jacob	12 (1767-71)	612
Coram, Ann	36 (1818-26)	1187
Coram, Charlotte	44 (1845-51)	157
Coram, Edward	9 (1760-67)	263
Coram, Francis	33 (1807-18)	1066
Coram, Henry	20 (1783-86)	59

Name	Volume	Page
Coram, Thomas	31 (1807-18)	435
Corbett, Elizabeth	44 (1845-51)	319
Corbett, John Harleston	47 (1851-56)	617
Corbett, Thomas	32 (1807-18)	856
Corbett, Thomas	45 (1845-51)	731
Corcoram, Jane	39 (1826-34)	1014
Corcoran, Patrick	44 (1845-51)	429
Corcoran, Thomas	49 (1856-62)	857
Cordes, Anthony	1 (1711-18)	37
Cordes, Catherine	30 (1800-07)	898
Cordes, Charlotte	37 (1826-34)	238
Cordes, Elizabeth	30 (1800-07)	1084
Cordes, Frances	47 (1851-56)	564
Cordes, Henrietta Catharine [Catherine]	10 (1760-67)	588
Cordes, Isaac	5 (1740-47)	406
Cordes, James	23 (1786-93)	414
Cordes, James Paul	18 (1776-84)	203
Cordes, Jean [Jane]	1 (1711-18)	88
Cordes, John	7 (1752-56)	582
Cordes, John	27 (1793-1800)	770
Cordes, Lucretia	49 (1856-62)	648
Cordes, Rebecca	43 (1839-45)	680
Cordes, Samuel	26 (1793-1800)	504
Cordes, Samuel	48 (1856-62)	293
Cordes, Thomas	6 (1747-52)	141
Cordes, Thomas	10 (1760-67)	450
Cordes, Thomas (Junior)	27 (1793-1800)	960
Cordier, Filicite Julie Stonestreet [Filicete]	34 (1818-26)	218
Cordier, Peter Augustus Florimond	34 (1818-26)	218
Corfield, Richard	28 (1800-07)	25
Corker, Thomas	13 (1767-71)	995
Cormack, Alexander	15 (1771-74)	596

Name	Volume	Page
Cornelious, Michael	36 (1818-26)	1237
Corosthwaite see Crosthwaite		
Corrie, John	24 (1786-93)	959
Corsan, Lellias	6 (1747-52)	221
Corse, Timothy Hanson	15 (1771-74)	633
Cosby, James	27 (1793-1800)	969
Cossen, Edmond	6 (1747-52)	520
Costa, Francis Philip	34 (1818-26)	10
Coster, John G.	46 (1851-56)	111
Costock, Frederick	30 (1800-07)	1034
Cotes, Christopher	47 (1851-56)	594
Cotes, Christopher	47 (1851-56)	660
Cotten, James Wright	33 (1807-18)	1077
Cottenham, Rebecca	41 (1834-39)	632
Cottingham, John	1 (1692-93)	14
Couliette, Christopher [Coulliette]	14 (1771-74)	160
Coulliette, Thomas	10 (1760-67)	514
Coulliette see also Couliette		
Councell, Agnes	50 (1862-68)	320
Council, James Senior	45 (1845-51)	776
Counsell, Robert	12 (1767-71)	377
Course, Isaac	41 (1834-39)	688
Courtenay, Samuel Gilman	51 (1862-68)	806
Courtenay see also Courtney		
Courtney, Humphrey	36 (1818-26)	1064
Courtney, James C. [Courtenay]	40 (1834-39)	170
Courtonne, Jeremiah	9 (1760-67)	241
Cousins, Thomas	27 (1793-1800)	775
Couturier, Ann	40 (1834-39)	445
Couturier, Eliza M.	44 (1845-51)	121
Couturier, Gideon [Couturirier]	7 (1752-56)	564
Couturier, Gideon	23 (1786-93)	601
Couturier, Isaac	17 (1774-79)	786
Couturier, Isaac	32 (1807-18)	756

Name	Volume	Page
Couturier, Isaac Theodore	39 (1826-34)	1127
Couturier, John	20 (1783-86)	162
Couturier, John J.	40 (1834-39)	117
Couturier, Martha	30 (1800-07)	836
Couturier, Mary R.	45 (1845-51)	620
Couturier, Peter	18 (1776-84)	299
Couturier, Peter (Junior)	20 (1783-86)	177
Couturiere, Isaac	19 (1780-83)	377
Couturirier see Couturier		
Coward, James	48 (1856-62)	423
Coward, Susan Margarett	46 (1851-56)	262
Cowen, Benjamin	8 (1757-60)	320
Cowen, Elizabeth R.	47 (1851-56)	440
Cowen, Joseph R.	44 (1845-51)	128
Cowen, Thomas	15 (1771-74)	449
Cox, Anna M.	50 (1862-68)	220
Cox, Elizabeth	36 (1818-26)	981
Cox, Hannah	26 (1793-1800)	481
Cox, James	32 (1807-18)	534
Cox, John	5 (1740-47)	349
Cox, Joseph	22 (1786-93)	336
Cox, Joseph	37 (1826-34)	44
Cox, Julia	45 (1845-51)	896
Cox, Keturah	32 (1807-18)	571
Cox, Spencer	21 (1783-86)	770
Cox, Thomas	37 (1826-34)	301
Cox, Thomas Campbell	32 (1807-18)	843
Coyle, Patrick [Coyll]	20 (1783-86)	206
Coyll see Coyle		
Coytmore, Richard	9 (1760-67)	18
Crafford, James	17 (1774-79)	614
Crafts, Harriett B. [Harriot]	42 (1839-45)	89
Crafts, William	34 (1818-26)	358

Name	Volume	Page
Cragg, John	6 (1747-52)	43
Craig, Thomas	27 (1793-1800)	899
Cramer, Claas Hermanson [Hermene]	1 (1720-21)	31
Cramer, John	45 (1845-51)	499
Crammer, Margaret	34 (1818-26)	221
Crandal, Ann	43 (1839-45)	785
Crane, John	21 (1783-86)	593
Craven, Alice	30 (1800-07)	926
Craven, Charles	4 (1736-40)	284
Crawford, Daniel	8 (1757-60)	491
Crawford, Daniel	26 (1793-1800)	583
Crawford, George	50 (1862-68)	314
Crawford, James	29 (1800-07)	750
*Crawford, John	6 (1747-52)	7
Crawford, John	9 (1760-67)	74
Crawford, John	31 (1807-18)	325
Crawford, John	44 (1845-51)	198
Crawford, Margaret	48 (1856-62)	384
Crawford, Samuel	9 (1760-67)	299
Crawford, William	28 (1800-07)	271
Crayton, Samuel [Creighton]	30 (1800-07)	1127
Creadick, Richard	15 (1771-74)	495
Cree, David	10 (1760-67)	854
Cree, James, Senior	31 (1807-18)	432
Creighton, Edward	32 (1807-18)	686
Creighton, John	24 (1786-93)	1001
Creighton, Joseph	24 (1786-93)	787
Creighton, Maria	39 (1826-34)	1176
Creighton, Perth	34 (1818-26)	412
Creighton see also Crayton		
Crichton, George	2 (1729-31)	14
Crickton, George	2 (G1729-31)	3
Cripps, Mary	47 (1851-56)	525

Name	volume	Page
Cripps, Robert	16 (1774-79)	94
Crockatt see Crockett		
Crocker, Doddridge	44 (1845-51)	178
Crocker, Francis Shaw	34 (1818-26)	286
Crockett, John [Crockatt]	8 (1757-60)	411
Crofs, Ann	23 (1786-93)	535
Crofs, George	33 (1807-18)	1109
Crofs, John	8 (1757-60)	429
Crofs, John	27 (1793-1800)	845
Crofs, Matthews W.	31 (1807-18)	434
Crofs, Paul	20 (1783-86)	372
*Crofs, Samuel	21 (1783-86)	837
Crofse see Crosse		
Crofskeys, Jemima [Croskeys]	25 (1793-1800)	287
Croft, Catharine	12 (1767-71)	480
Croft, Childermas	9 (1760-67)	147
Croft, Edward	7 (1752-56)	501
Croft, Edward	23 (1786-93)	401
Croft, Hill	3 (1731-33)	25
Croft, John	7 (1752-56)	75
Croft, Peter	34 (1818-26)	305
*Croft, Robert	18 (1776-84)	41
Croft, Sarah	16 (1774-79)	234
Croft, Thomas	3 (1731-33)	66
Croll, Catherine	14 (1771-74)	325
Croll, Thomas	4 (1736-40)	297
Croll, William	2 (1729-31)	51
Croll, William	5 (1740-47)	297
Cromwell, Oliver	32 (1807-18)	627
Cromwell, Samuel	43 (1839-45)	792
Cromwell, Samuel T.	51 (1862-68)	856
Cromwell, Sarah	35 (1818-26)	562
Crook, Dr. William	2 (1724-25)	52

Name	volume	Page
Crosby, Denifs	14 (1771-74)	95
Croskey, William	6 (1747-52)	630
Croskeys, John	2 (1726-27)	31
Croskeys, John	2 (1726-27)	73
Croskeys, John	24 (1786-93)	813
Croskeys, Joseph	1 (1687-1710)	22
Croskeys, Ruth	38 (1826-34)	476
Croskeys, Sarah	25 (1793-1800)	240
Croskeys see also Crofskeys		
Crosley, Leonard	9 (1760-67)	336
Cross, Henry B.	50 (1862-68)	423
Crosse, John ₁Crofse₃	1 (1687-1710)	1
Crosse, Mary ₁Crofse₃	1 (1687-1710)	2
Crosse, Mary ₁Crofse₃	1 (1692-93)	70
Crosthwaite, Thomas ₁Corosthwaite₃	7 (1752-56)	543
Crouch, Henry	19 (1780-83)	391
Croughan, Michael	47 (1851-56)	535
Crovat, Dorothea	37 (1826-34)	95
Crow, John	32 (1807-18)	664
Crow, Margaret B.	48 (1856-62)	112
Crowly, Charles E.	45 (1845-51)	740
Cruger, Elizabeth	33 (1807-18)	1384
Cruger, Elizabeth	38 (1826-34)	737
Cruger, Frederick David	29 (1800-07)	688
Cruikshank, Samuel	49 (1856-62)	546
Cruikshanks, Daniel	41 (1834-39)	698
Cruise, Thedore	46 (1851-56)	324
Crukshanks, Mary	46 (1851-56)	361
Crukshanks, William	40 (1834-39)	124
Cudworth, Benjamin	32 (1807-18)	837
Cufsings, George	7 (1752-56)	163
Cuhun, George	27 (1793-1800)	659
Cuhun, Henry S.	36 (1818-26)	1217
Culbert, John	48 (1856-62)	525

Name	Volume	Page
Culliatt, Adam	12 (1767-71)	420
Culliatt, James	22 (1786-93)	370
Culp, Philip	21 (1783-86)	678
Cuming, Benjamin	18 (1776-84)	51
Cundull, Thomas	7 (1752-56)	160
Cunning see Connin		
Cunningham, Andrew	50 (1862-68)	66
Cunningham, Ann	50 (1862-68)	194
Cunningham, John	44 (1845-51)	224
Cunningham, Sarah A.	44 (1845-51)	341
Cunnington, Elizabeth Sophia ‚Eliza‚	35 (1818-26)	763
Cunnington, William	29 (1800-07)	699
Curling, Thomas	28 (1800-07)	223
Curren, Daniel	44 (1845-51)	289
Curry, James	41 (1834-39)	937
Curtis, William	48 (1856-62)	331
Cusack, Peter	40 (1834-39)	146
Custer, Mary	31 (1807-18)	187
Cutfeild see Cutfield		
Cutfield, Thomas‚Cutfeild‚	2 (G1729-31)	8
Cuthbert, James	41 (1834-39)	828
Cuthbert, James	49 (1856-62)	978
Cutler, Thomas	1 (1722-24)	3
✱ Cutterea, Daniel‚Catterea‚	6 (1747-52)	77
Cyrus (a free Negro)	16 (1774-79)	85

D

Name	Volume	Page
DaCosta, Charles A.	46 (1851-56)	149
DaCosta, Rebecca Mendes	29 (1800-07)	666
DaCosta, Sarah	25 (1793-1800)	89
Dailey, John, Senior	29 (1800-07)	473
Daingerfield, William	37 (1826-34)	37
Daingerfield see also Dangerfield		

Name	Volume	Page
Dakars, Peter	2 (1729-31)	38
Dalaune, John ꜰDelauneꜰ	2 (1727-29)	96
Dalcour see Dalcourt		
Dalcourt, Don FranciscoꜰDalcourꜰ	42 (1839-45)	29
Dale, Hannah	6 (1747-52)	494
Dale, Oliver	16 (1774-79)	196
Dale, Thomas	6 (1747-52)	403
Dalgleish, George	ꜰ 37 (1826-34)	146
Dalgrass, Francis	6 (1747-52)	24
Dallas, FrancisꜰDallisꜰ	8 (1757-60)	313
Dallis see Dallas		
Dalton, Catherine	7 (1752-56)	91
Dalton, Charles	16 (1774-79)	294
Dalton, Frances (C.)	44 (1845-51)	21
Dalton, James	5 (1740-47)	580
Dalton, Mary	20 (1783-86)	286
Dalton, Thomas	1 (1711-18)	12
Dalton, William	7 (1752-56)	303
Daly, Daniel	7 (1752-56)	297
Daly, Henrietta	30 (1800-07)	859
*Daly, James	18 (1776-84)	215
Daly, John	48 (1856-62)	265
Daly, Thomas	26 (1793-1800)	562
Damascke, Martin	41 (1834-39)	506
Dandridge, Elizabeth	14 (1771-74)	124
Dandridge, Francis	8 (1757-60)	178
Dandridge, William	12 (1767-71)	360
Dangerfield, Hannah	48 (1856-62)	179
Dangerfield, William ꜰDaingerfieldꜰ	40 (1834-39)	152
Daniel, John	8 (1757-60)	80
Daniel, John	26 (1793-1800)	530
Daniel, Margaret	33 (1807-18)	1306
Daniel, RobertꜰDaniellꜰ	3 (1731-33)	63

Name	Volume	Page
Daniel, Robert	4 (1736-40)	157
Daniell, Adam	11 (1767-71)	130
Daniell, John	5 (1740-47)	680
Daniell, Robert	1 (1711-18)	94
Daniell, Robert	23 (1786-93)	611
Daniell, Sarah	1 (1721-22)	21
Daniell see also Daniel		
Danjou, Louis	35 (1818-26)	481
Dannelly, Edward	18 (1776-84)	260
Danner, John	36 (1818-26)	961
Danner, Robert Estes	37 (1826-34)	206
Dargan, John	10 (1760-67)	768
Dargan, Timothy	9 (1760-67)	319
Darnell see Darrel		
D'Arques, Robert	6 (1747-52)	72
Darquier, Moses	13 (1767-71)	1027
Darr, Peter	29 (1800-07)	547
Darr, Valentine [Vallentine]	25 (1793-1800)	191
Darrel, Joseph [Darnell, Darrell]	19 (1780-83)	37
Darrell, Edward	37 (1826-34)	298
Darrell, Joseph	20 (1783-86)	27
Darrell see also Darrel		
Darrington, March	38 (1826-34)	749
Dart, Ann H.	46 (1851-56)	139
Dart, Benjamin	23 (1786-93)	529
Dart, Elizabeth Martin	41 (1834-39)	577
Dart, Isaac Motte	35 (1818-26)	835
Dart, John	7 (1752-56)	268
Dart, John	20 (1783-86)	248
Darvell, Ebsworth	5 (1740-47)	656
Darvill, Elizabeth	10 (1760-67)	569
Darymple, Thomas	16 (1774-79)	111
Dash, William	12 (1767-71)	484

Name	volume	Page
Dastas, John	33 (1807-18)	1209
Daubuz, Christiana	31 (1807-18)	410
Dauthereau, Romain Marie	35 (1818-26)	720
✳Davant, John	18 (1776-84)	244
David, Ezekiel	12 (1767-71)	441
David, Peter	7 (1752-56)	221
David see also Davis		
Davidfon see Davidson		
Davidson, Alexander	10 (1760-67)	778
Davidson, Susanna	9 (1760-67)	193
Davidson, Susannah	20 (1783-86)	224
Davidson, Thomas	10 (1760-67)	534
Davidson, William [Davidfon]	5 (1740-47)	432
Davidson, William	50 (1862-68)	396
Davies, Daniel	43 (1839-45)	780
Davies, John S.	50 (1862-68)	95
Davis, Benjamin	39 (1826-34)	903
Davis, Catharine	42 (1839-45)	60
Davis, David	13 (1767-71)	1036
Davis, David, Senr	17 (1774-79)	745
Davis, Francis	38 (1826-34)	713
Davis, Hannah	48 (1856-62)	476
Davis, Jacob [David]	39 (1826-34)	1046
Davis, Jane	49 (1856-62)	840
Davis, Jefse	32 (1807-18)	523
Davis, John	16 (1774-79)	56
Davis, John	41 (1834-39)	946
Davis, Joseph	8 (1757-60)	116
Davis, Mary	16 (1774-79)	336
Davis, Mary	33 (1807-18)	1429
Davis, Mary A.	51 (1862-68)	733
Davis, Mary Ann	44 (1845-51)	405
Davis, Mary Eliza	43 (1839-45)	641

Name	volume	Page
Davis, Pringle A.	40 (1834-39)	173
Davis, Richard	14 (1771-74)	297
Davis, Ross C.	50 (1862-68)	160
Davis, Samuel	4 (1736-40)	266
Davis, Sarah	50 (1862-68)	364
Davis, Thomas	14 (1771-74)	133
Davis, William	15 (1771-74)	580
Davison, Samuel	7 (1752-56)	353
Davison, Samuel	24 (1786-93)	956
Dawes, Hugh P.	45 (1845-51)	654
Dawes, Philip	3 (1732-37)	182
Dawsey, William	38 (1826-34)	721
Dawson, Ann	38 (1826-34)	560
Dawson, Catherine [Catharine, Katherine]	2 (1729-31)	18
Dawson, Charles	19 (1780-83)	108
Dawson, Charles	20 (1783-86)	294
Dawson, Charles P.	47 (1851-56)	874
Dawson, Charlotte M.	48 (1856-62)	143
Dawson, Emma Monk	50 (1862-68)	204
Dawson, J. Drayton	42 (1839-45)	80
Dawson, Jane	36 (1818-26)	967
Dawson, Joanna Septima	44 (1845-51)	328
Dawson, John	32 (1807-18)	576
Dawson, John	36 (1818-26)	883
Dawson, John	39 (1826-34)	1240
Dawson, John , Sr. (Substitution of Trustee)	43 (1839-45)	688
Dawson, John (Substitution of Trustee)	45 (1845-51)	543
Dawson, Mary	36 (1818-26)	1145
Dawson, William	35 (1818-26)	700
Day, Nicholas	3 (1731-33)	10
Day, William	16 (1774-79)	82
D'Azevedo, Rachel D.	43 (1839-45)	556

Name	Volume	Page
Dean, Nathaniel	11 (1767-71)	187
Dean, Thomas	6 (1747-52)	597
Deane, Mary	7 (1752-56)	443
Dear, John	2 (1727-29)	64
Dear see also Deare		
Deare, John [Dear]	2 (1727-29)	66
Dearington, Hannibal (A Slave)	28 (1800-07)	3
Dearington, John	20 (1783-86)	410
Dearington, Richard	22 (1786-93)	357
Dearington, Thomas	11 (1767-71)	98
Dearington, Thomas	25 (1793-1800)	187
Dearmond, Eugenia E.	46 (1851-56)	301
Dearsley, George	1 (1711-18)	80
Deas, Charles D.	46 (1851-56)	435
Deas, David	35 (1818-26)	702
Deas, Elias H.	51 (1862-68)	795
Deas, Eliza K.	49 (1856-62)	811
Deas, Elizabeth	28 (1800-07)	313
Deas, Henry	44 (1845-51)	124
Deas, John	8 (1757-60)	284
Deas, John	23 (1786-93)	721
Deas, John	23 (1786-93)	766
Deas, Margaret Horry	46 (1851-56)	73
Deas, Mary Keating	51 (1862-68)	603
Deas, Robert L.	50 (1862-68)	334
Deas, Seamon	46 (1851-56)	430
Deas, Thomas H.	49 (1856-62)	585
Deas, W. Branford	46 (1851-56)	77
DeBardeleben, F.M.	46 (1851-56)	322
DeBeaufain, Hector Berenger [Berringer]	10 (1760-67)	809
DeBrahm, Mary	30 (1800-07)	952
Deedry, Isaac	16 (1774-79)	77

Name	Volume	Page
Deer, Martin	31 (1807-18)	89
Defausure, Henry [Desaufure; Henery]	9 (1760-67)	248
Dehay, James	38 (1826-34)	668
Dehay, John	31 (1807-18)	237
Dehay, Zachariah	31 (1807-18)	211
Dehon, Francis	24 (1786-93)	818
Dehon, Sarah	48 (1856-62)	92
Dehon, William	50 (1862-68)	34
Deirson, Barnard [Barnerd]	30 (1800-07)	920
Delabere see Delebare		
Delahow see DeLahowe		
DeLahowe, Ann [Delahow]	26 (1793-1800)	485
DeLahoyde, Ann	17 (1774-79)	774
De La Hoyde, Richard	17 (1774-79)	660
Delaire, James	32 (1807-18)	789
Delaize, Ann	37 (1826-34)	135
Delaney, Michael	42 (1839-45)	78
Delange, Jonas Lucas	46 (1851-56)	216
de Larranaga, Vincento Antonio	49 (1856-62)	715
Delaune see Dalaune		
Delavicendiere see Delavincendiere		
Delavincendiere, Etienne Bellumeau [Delavicendiere]	28 (1800-07)	323
de Leaumont, Henry	50 (1862-68)	132
Delebare, George [Delabere]	9 (1760-67)	103
Deleifseline, Amelia M.	39 (1826-34)	1034
Deleifseline see also Deleisline		
Deleisline, Magdalene [Deleifseline]	8 (1757-60)	333
Deleon, M. H., M. D.	44 (1845-51)	416
Delettre, Marie Charlotte	38 (1826-34)	709
Delgar, William B.	46 (1851-56)	160
Deliesselin see Deliesseline		
Deliesseline, John [Deliesselin]	42 (1839-45)	88

Name	volume	Page
Delke, John	23 (1786-93)	559
Della Torre, John C.	50 (1862-68)	361
DeLomenie, Leaumont see De Lomenie, Marie Laurent Therese Leaumont		
DeLomenie, Marie Laurent Therese Leaumont ₍De Lomenie, Leaumont₎	30 (1800-07)	1018
DeMalacare, Cath(erine) De St. Julian	5 (1740-47)	417
Dempsey, Edward	14 (1771-74)	281
Dempsey, James	45 (1845-51)	812
Dempsey, John	33 (1807-18)	1270
Dempsey, Myles	41 (1834-39)	633
Dener, Christianna ₍Christiana₎	47 (1851-56)	785
Dener, (John) Peter	26 (1793-1800)	395
Dener, Laura Ann	44 (1845-51)	151
Dener, Peter see Dener, (John) Peter		
Deneson, Ann Elizabeth ₍Dennifson₎	32 (1807-18)	910
Denison, Henry Mandeville	48 (1856-62)	306
Denley, James	8 (1757-60)	175
Denney, John	7 (1752-56)	92
Dennifson see Deneson		
Dennington, Richard	17 (1774-79)	509
Dennis, Ann	6 (1747-52)	40
Dennis, William J.	46 (1851-56)	436
Dennis, William James	50 (1862-68)	129
Dennison, James	34 (1818-26)	374
Dennistone, George	5 (1740-47)	136
Denny, Charles L.	46 (1851-56)	368
Denny, Mary L.	44 (1845-51)	7
Denny, Mary S.	40 (1834-39)	453
Denoon, David	30 (1800-07)	788
Denoon, John	39 (1826-34)	1045
Denoon, Margaret	36 (1818-26)	1252
DeNorroy see DeNorry		

Name	Volume	Page
DeNorry, John Charles Francis [De Norry, Norroy,	34 (1818-26)	311
Denton, John	10 (1760-67)	795
Derac, Marie Rose	36 (1818-26)	1057
Derdrian see Perdrian		
Dereef, Susan Ann	40 (1834-39)	02
* Derwicke, Henry	6 (1747-52)	432
De St. Julian, Susanna [De St. Julien, St. Julian]	20 (1783-86)	344
De St. Julien, Damaris	4 (1736-40)	43
De St. Julien, James	5 (1740-47)	554
De St. Julien, Joseph	5 (1740-47)	633
De St. Julien, Paul	5 (1740-47)	71
De St. Julien see also De St. Julian		
Desaufsure, Daniel	27 (1793-1800)	772
Desaufsure, Mary	33 (1807-18)	1434
Desaufure see Defausure		
DeSaussure, Henry Alexander	51 (1862-68)	528
DeSaussure, Henry William	42 (1839-45)	44
Desbeaux, Jean	29 (1800-07)	710
Deschamps, Joseph	30 (1800-07)	1003
DesChamps, Saturnin Bagot	29 (1800-07)	684
DesCourdres, Louis P.	41 (1834-39)	628
Desel, Charles	31 (1807-18)	35
Desel, Charles L.	47 (1851-56)	657
Desel, Mary B.	31 (1807-18)	477
Desel, Samuel	32 (1807-18)	859
Desfofses	29 (1800-07)	752
Desgraves, Peter Thomas Chamecaulme	41 (1834-39)	512
Desir, Joseph	44 (1845-51)	152
Desportes, Peter	38 (1826-34)	468
Desrivaux, Boutinot	28 (1800-07)	196
Desriveaux, Melanie	32 (1807-18)	570
Desverneys, Peter	49 (1856-62)	866

Name	Volume	Page

Name-	Volume	Page
Dick, George	15 (1771-74)	609
Dick, James	44 (1845-51)	454
Dick, John	10 (1760-67)	774
Dickinson, Francis	40 (1834-39)	375
Dickinson, John F.	34 (1818-26)	305
Dickinson, Sarah	32 (1807-18)	857
Dicks, Arthur	1 (1720-21)	66
Dickson, Arthur	19 (1780-83)	300
Dickson, John	9 (1760-67)	6
Dickson, John	44 (1845-51)	259
Dickson, Mary	41 (1834-39)	772
Dickson, Samuel	34 (1818-26)	148
Didcott, Elizabeth	19 (1780-83)	22
Didcott, Elizabeth	20 (1783-86)	303
Didcott, John	2 (1724-25)	23
Didcott, John	8 (1757-60)	428
Didcott, Joseph	3 (1732-37)	301
Didcott, Mary	3 (1732-37)	312
Diefenbach, Johann Christoph	50 (1862-68)	155
Dierssen, William	51 (1862-68)	678
Dietrick, Hans	12 (1767-71)	517
Dill, Jane Eliza	47 (1851-56)	497
Dill, John	22 (1786-93)	351
Dill, Joseph	5 (1740-47)	464
Dill, Joseph	26 (1793-1800)	414
Dill, Sarah	29 (1800-07)	558
Dillingham, James	50 (1862-68)	248
Dingle, Alexander	8 (1757-60)	286
Dinin, Elisha	27 (1793-1800)	652
Disher, Elizabeth	48 (1856-62)	427
Diston, Charles	2 (1729-31)	97
Diston, Martha	6 (1747-52)	614
Diston, Sarah	6 (1747-52)	139

Name	Volume	Page
Diston, Thomas	6 (1747-52)	136
Divver, James	44 (1845-51)	291
Dixey, William	4 (1736-40)	95
Dixon, Hennery	16 (1774-79)	342
Dixon, Thomas ⌐Dixson⌐	12 (1767-71)	526
Dixson see Dixon		
D'Jough, Joseph	36 (1818-26)	888
Doar, John	29 (1800-07)	577
Doar, Josiah	46 (1851-56)	3
Doar, Thomas	41 (1834-39)	622
Doar, Thomas	48 (1856-62)	231
Dobbin, Hugh	14 (1771-74)	184
Dobson, Oliver, L.	45 (1845-51)	655
Dodd, John	13 (1767-71)	822
Dogett, Elizabeth	7 (1752-56)	499
Domom see Donom		
Donaldson, James	31 (1807-18)	218
Donaldson, William	8 (1757-60)	351
Doning, William ⌐Donning⌐	3 (1731-33)	74
Doniphan, Joseph G.	51 (1862-68)	867
Donnavan, John	11 (1767-71)	212
Donneley, John	50 (1862-68)	324
Donning, Frances	7 (1752-56)	418
Donning, George	5 (1740-47)	504
Donning, William	5 (1740-47)	206
Donning see also Doning		
Donnom, James	18 (1776-84)	13
Donnom, Jane	45 (1845-51)	839
Donnom, Jonathan	16 (1774-79)	248
Donnom, Joseph	23 (1786-93)	402
Donom, Jacob ⌐Domom⌐	5 (1740-47)	493
Donovan, Daniel	2 (1727-29)	87
✻Donovan, James	20 (1783-86)	273

Name	volume	Page
Donovan, John	16 (1774-79)	128
Donovan, John Cattell	22 (1786-93)	172
Donovan, Mary Ann	21 (1783-86)	803
Dooley, William	50 (1862-68)	289
Dore, Anthony	22 (1786-93)	383
Dorouseau see Durouseau		
Dorr, John	24 (1786-93)	945
Dorrill, James	45 (1845-51)	733
Dorrill, Jonathan	22 (1786-93)	283
Dorrill, Melliceant Mary	49 (1856-62)	699
Dorrill, Robert	17 (1774-79)	736
Dorrill, Robert	39 (1826-34)	1245
Dorsey, Providence	4 (1736-40)	273
Dortch, Thomas	17 (1774-79)	800
Dotterer, Thomas	44 (1845-51)	115
Dougherty, John	43 (1839-45)	812
Dougherty, Joseph	46 (1851-56)	189
Dougherty, Patrick	26 (1793-1800)	543
Doughty, Charles	34 (1818-26)	31
Doughty, Elizabeth	33 (1807-18)	1156
Doughty, James	39 (1826-34)	944
Doughty, Mary	33 (1807-18)	1422
Doughty, Thomas	32 (1807-18)	951
Doughty, William	33 (1807-18)	1412
Doughty, William C.	40 (1834-39)	436
Douglafs, Samuel	27 (1793-1800)	808
Douglas, James	33 (1807-18)	1107
Douglas, Margaret [Douglass]	49 (1856-62)	965
Douglass see Douglas		
Dounken see Dunkan		
Doux Saint, William [Douxsaint]	26 (1793-1800)	399
Douxsaint, Mary Hester [E.]	24 (1786-93)	887
Douxsaint see also Doux Saint		

80

Name	Volume	Page
Dow, Alexander	36 (1818-26)	1021
Dow, John	15 (1771-74)	427
Dow, John	21 (1783-86)	734
Dowd, Martin	51 (1862-68)	760
Dowfe see Dowse		
Dowling, Edward	34 (1818-26)	312
Down, James	25 (1793-1800)	223
Downer, Thomas	31 (1807-18)	41
Downes, Arthur	21 (1783-86)	535
Downes, Richard (Junr)	14 (1771-74)	246
Downes, Richard	19 (1780-83)	370
Downes, William	22 (1786-93)	253
Downie, Robert	48 (1856-62)	9
Dowse, Gideon [Dowfe]	5 (1740-47)	646
Dowse, Hugh	9 (1760-67)	24
Dowse, Stephen	5 (1740-47)	238
Doyen, John Baptiste Gabriel	34 (1818-26)	96
Doyle, Edward	43 (1839-45)	730
Doyle, Grace	35 (1818-26)	590
Doyle, Patrick	34 (1818-26)	109
Doyle, Thomas	34 (1818-26)	136
Doyley, Daniel	13 (1767-71)	778
D'Oyley, Daniel	34 (1818-26)	342
Dozier, Leonar	17 (1774-79)	519
Drage, Theodorus Swaine	16 (1774-79)	332
Drake, Charles Cantey	25 (1793-1800)	263
Drake, Jonathan	3 (1731-33)	42
Drake, Jonathan	13 (1767-71)	742
Drake, Mary	12 (1767-71)	371
Drake, Matilda Sophia	44 (1845-51)	338
Drayton, Alfred Rose	49 (1856-62)	584
Drayton, Ann	5 (1740-47)	103
Drayton, Charles	34 (1818-26)	344

Name	Volume	Page
Drayton, Emma	46 (1851-56)	8
Drayton, Hannah	39 (1826-34)	1228
Drayton, Henrietta A.	49 (1856-62)	795
Drayton, Hester Rose	33 (1807-18)	1125
Drayton, John (Junr)	16 (1774-79)	6
Drayton, John	35 (1818-26)	767
Drayton, Maria C.	49 (1856-62)	541
Drayton, Mary M.	47 (1851-56)	705
Drayton, Rebecca	42 (1839-45)	185
Drayton, Sarah Maria	42 (1839-45)	359
Drayton, Stephen Fox	3 (1732-37)	128
Drayton, Thomas	1 (1722-24)	99
Drayton, Thomas	9 (1760-67)	76
Drayton, Thomas	37 (1826-34)	75
Drayton, William	23 (1786-93)	651
Drayton, William Henry	37 (1826-34)	64
Drayton, William (Heyward)	46 (1851-56)	25
Dreffill see Drifell		
Drefsler, Hans Jockin (Dresler; Jochim)	34 (1818-26)	69
Dreher, Fredierieck	37 (1826-34)	115
Drennes, Martha	43 (1839-45)	746
Dresler see Drefsler		
Drew, Margaret	9 (1760-67)	359
Drew, Nathaniel	6 (1747-52)	476
Drewes, Henry	38 (1826-34)	589
Drhan see Durham		
Drifell, John (Dreffill)	23 (1786-93)	410
Driggers, Jonas	48 (1856-62)	337
Dring, Azariah	7 (1752-56)	495
Droze, Daniel	19 (1780-83)	119
Droze, John F. (John L.)	48 (1856-62)	276
Droze, John L. see Droze John F.		
Droze, Stephen	26 (1793-1800)	380

Name	volume	Page
Drysdale, John	33 (1807-18)	1129
Dubari, Etienne	31 (1807-18)	420
Dubert, Godfrey [Godfry]	28 (1800-07)	104
Dubois, John	18 (1776-84)	72
DuBois, Louis	37 (1826-34)	394
Dubois, Robert (A)	36 (1818-26)	983
Dubois, Samuel	19 (1780-83)	126
Dubois, Samuel	20 (1783-86)	323
Dubois, Susanna	8 (1757-60)	133
Dubose, Ann Susan	49 (1856-62)	947
Dubose, Edwin	50 (1862-68)	404
Du Bose, Edwin C.	50 (1862-68)	99
Dubose, Esther	10 (1760-67)	458
Dubose, Isaac	5 (1740-47)	141
Dubose, Isaac	15 (1771-74)	458
Dubose, Jonathan	14 (1771-74)	74
Dubose, Joseph	28 (1800-07)	374
Dubose, Samuel [Dibose]	31 (1807-18)	424
Dubose, Samuel	48 (1856-62)	448
Dubose, William	47 (1851-56)	576
Duc, Francis	42 (1839-45)	176
Ducat, George	8 (1757-60)	437
Duckles, Richard	10 (1760-67)	660
Duff, James	5 (1740-47)	560
Duff, Mary Elizabeth	5 (1740-47)	660
Duffy, Andrew	26 (1793-1800)	394
Duffy, Bernard	26 (1793-1800)	559
Dufort, John	39 (1826-34)	1078
Dufsen, Alexander Vander	13 (1767-71)	915
Dugard, Benjamin	11 (1767-71)	287
Dugats, Elizabeth	30 (1800-07)	834
Duke, Nicholas	3 (1731-33)	47
Dukes, Babara	16 (1774-79)	186

Name	Volume	Page
Dukes, Joan	14 (1771-74)	139
Dulles, Joseph	33 (1807-18)	1366
Dumay, Ettienne	3 (1732-37)	168
Dumay, Jane	11 (1767-71)	73
Dumonchet, Elizabeth	39 (1826-34)	1044
Dumont, Guillaume	30 (1800-07)	961
Dumont, M.A.R.	39 (1826-34)	1232
Dunbar, E.	33 (1807-18)	1182
Dunbar, William	31 (1807-18)	354
Duncan, Archibald	29 (1800-07)	747
Duncan, John	37 (1826-34)	351
Duncan, Patrick	42 (1839-45)	103
Dunham, John	2 (1727-29)	10
Dunham, Stephen	32 (1807-18)	802
Dunkan, William [Dounken]	26 (1793-1800)	610
Dunkley, Carleton	29 (1800-07)	495
Dunklin, Joseph [Dunkline]	20 (1783-86)	335
Dunkline see Dunklin		
Dunlap, Benjamin F.	20 (1783-86)	94
Dunlap, Robert [Dunlop]	29 (1800-07)	633
Dunlop, Patrick	11 (1767-71)	31
Dunlop see also Dunlap		
Dunn, Catherine	44 (1845-51)	119
Dunn, John	4 (1736-40)	192
Dunn, John	24 (1786-93)	808
Dunn, John	38 (1826-34)	442
Dunneman, Carol [Carl]	50 (1862-68)	24
Dunning, Thomas	31 (1807-18)	100
Duperet, George	33 (1807-18)	1231
DuPoid D'or, James [Du Poid's]	2 (1724-25)	83
DuPoid's D'or see Dupoid D'or		
Dupont, Abraham	9 (1760-67)	36
Dupont, Abraham	51 (1862-68)	711

Name	Volume	Page
Dupont, Cornelius	43 (1839-45)	666
Dupont, Francis	49 (1856-62)	901
Dupont, Gideon	23 (1786-93)	617
Dupont, John	10 (1760-67)	573
Dupont, Joseph	42 (1839-45)	433
Dupont, Maria	47 (1851-56)	481
DuPont, Mary C.	33 (1807-18)	1130
Duprat, Raymond	37 (1826-34)	231
DuPre, Cornelius [Corneline]	5 (1740-47)	674
Dupre, Daniel	24 (1786-93)	1081
Dupre, Daniel A.	50 (1862-68)	36
Dupre, Jean	6 (1747-52)	305
DuPré see also DuPree		
Dupree, Francis	43 (1839-45)	791
DuPree, Samuel [Du Pré]	27 (1793-1800)	950
Dupuy, Andrew [André]	1 (1721-22)	56
Duquercron, Pamela	49 (1856-62)	955
Durand, Levi	10 (1760-67)	670
Durand, Susannah	27 (1793-1800)	667
Durant, Margaret [Durat; Margret]	37 (1826-34)	405
Durant, Paul	45 (1845-51)	890
Durat see Durant		
Durborow, Benjamin	20 (1783-86)	341
Durborow see also Durburow		
Durburow, Benjamin [Durborow]	19 (1780-83)	120
Durffey, Anstis	19 (1780-83)	212
Durham, Lydia [Drhan]	3 (1731-33)	20
Durouseau, Susanne [Dorouseau, Susannah]	6 (1747-52)	168
Durr, John	34 (1818-26)	402
Durr, Michal [Michael]	25 (1793-1800)	171
Durrett, Margaret	44 (1845-51)	302
Dutarque, John	10 (1760-67)	866
Dutarque, Lewis	6 (1747-52)	97

Name	Volume	Page
Dutarque, Mary	11 (1767-71)	189
Dutart, Daniel	3 (1732-37)	318
Dutart, Moses	6 (1747-52)	51
Dutrieux, Casimir	44 (1845-51)	331
Duva, Mary	16 (1774-79)	99
Duval, Louis	44 (1845-51)	400
Duval, Peter	41 (1834-39)	773
Duvall, Catharine	35 (1818-26)	496
Duvall, Lewis	2 (1724-25)	1
Duynmier, Albert	20 (1783-86)	9
Duynmier, William	36 (1818-26)	1122
Dwight, Daniel	6 (1747-52)	59
Dwight, Emily Louisa	37 (1826-34)	406
Dwight, Isaac Broughton	24 (1786-93)	1102
Dwight, John	13 (1767-71)	685
Dwight, Samuel	36 (1818-26)	1196
✱ Dwight, Thomas Broughton	9 (1760-67)	400
Dymes, Robert	8 (1757-60)	433
Dymes, Thomas	2 (1729-31)	3
Dyott, John	37 (1826-34)	303

E

Name	Volume	Page
Eadon, James (Senr)	9 (1760-67)	286
Eady, Daniel	40 (1834-39)	266
Eady, Susannah	33 (1807-18)	972
Eady, Jonathan	49 (1856-62)	562
Eakerman, Richard	5 (1740-47)	620
Earl, James	26 (1793-1800)	488
Earle, Oswald	41 (1834-39)	711
Earnest, Barnet	35 (1818-26)	658
Earnest, John B.	50 (1862-68)	296
Eason, Dorothea	48 (1856-62)	165
Easton, Caleb	14 (1771-74)	262

Name	Volume	Page
Easton, Christopher	8 (1757-60)	471
Easton, Thomas	7 (1752-56)	415
Eaton, Jeremiah	21 (1783-86)	433
Eaton, Joshua	21 (1783-86)	791
Eaton, Samuel	8 (1757-60)	60
Eberley, Barbara	33 (1807-18)	1251
Eberley, John	27 (1793-1800)	878
Eberson, Thomas	10 (1760-67)	611
Eberson, William	11 (1767-71)	201
Eckert, Robert D.	31 (1807-18)	429
Eckhard, George B.	43 (1839-45)	836
Eckhard, Jacob, Senr	39 (1826-34)	1214
Eckhard, Priscilla B.	44 (1845-51)	29
Eddy, John	30 (1800-07)	800
Eddy, Jonathan	49 (1856-62)	562
Eddy, William	11 (1767-71)	257
Eden, Edward	41 (1834-39)	863
Eden, Jeremiah	20 (1783-86)	38
Eden, Joshua	28 (1800-07)	276
Edes, Daniel	32 (1807-18)	655
Edes, James	8 (1757-60)	173
Edes, Sarah	10 (1760-67)	810
Edgar, Samuel	6 (1747-52)	604
Edgell, Richard	3 (1731-33)	30
Edings, Abraham	6 (1747-52)	317
Edings, Joseph Sen,	23 (1786-93)	564
Edings, Joseph D.	50 (1862-68)	266
Edings, Mary	38 (1826-34)	447
Edings, Mary (Substitution of Trustee)	43 (1839-45)	668
Edings, Theodora	8 (1757-60)	518
Edings, William	11 (1767-71)	4
Edings, William	40 (1834-39)	400
Edings, William	48 (1856-62)	351

Name	Volume	Page
Edings, William M.	45 (1845-51)	761
Edkins, John	29 (1800-07)	487
Edmandson, Mary ⌐Edmanson⌐	19 (1780-83)	88
Edmanson see Edmandson		
Edmonds, Sarah	16 (1774-79)	190
Edmondston, Charles	49 (1856-62)	875
Edward, William	15 (1771-74)	652
Edwards, Alexander	31 (1807-18)	457
Edwards, Charles L.	42 (1839-45)	59
Edwards, Charles Lee	50 (1862-68)	40
Edwards, Edward Holmes	43 (1839-45)	613
Edwards, Evan	27 (1793-1800)	700
Edwards, Frances Brewton	50 (1862-68)	41
Edwards, George	48 (1856-62)	446
Edwards, Hannah	3 (1732-37)	187
Edwards, Hannah	36 (1818-26)	1005
Edwards, Henrietta	44 (1845-51)	412
Edwards, Henry B.	45 (1845-51)	556
Edwards, Jacob	47 (1851-56)	702
Edwards, James	26 (1793-1800)	495
Edwards, James Fisher	43 (1839-45)	713
Edwards, James Fisher	49 (1856-62)	1006
Edwards, John	6 (1747-52)	243
Edwards, John	13 (1767-71)	786
Edwards, John	20 (1783-86)	147
Edwards, John, Jun.	22 (1786-93)	216
Edwards, John	27 (1793-1800)	799
Edwards, John	34 (1818-26)	289
Edwards, John Jones	49 (1856-62)	986
Edwards, Joseph	1 (1692-93)	22
Edwards, Mary	32 (1807-18)	807
Edwards, Mary Cochran	24 (1786-93)	935
Edwards, Mary E.	43 (1839-45)	828

Name	Volume	Page
Edwards, Mary M.	33 (1807-18)	1071
Edwards, Mathew [Matthew]	17 (1774-79)	709
Edwards, Dr. P. G.	44 (1845-51)	253
Edwards, Rebekah	35 (1818-26)	474
Edwards, Sarah	19 (1780-83)	286
Edwards, Sarah	20 (1783-86)	78
Edwards, Wiell see Edwards, William		
Edwards, William	19 (1780-83)	101
Edwards, William	19 (1780-83)	293
Edwards, William	20 (1783-86)	288
Edwards, William [Wiell]	20 (1783-86)	311
Efswein, Theodore	39 (1826-34)	934
Egan, Catherine	8 (1758-63)	10
Egan, Dennis [Denis]	26 (1793-1800)	512
Egan, Edmund	22 (1786-93)	164
Egan, John	25 (1793-1800)	133
Egan, Thomas	22 (1786-93)	227
Eggart, Juliet	40 (1834-39)	138
Egleston, John	35 (1818-26)	733
Egleston, Sarah	38 (1826-34)	635
Ehney, Peter M.	46 (1851-56)	51
Ehney, Ulrick	10 (1760-67)	512
Ehny, Christina	17 (1774-79)	638
Ehrhard, Abraham	8 (1757-60)	211
Ehrhardt, Francis	17 (1774-79)	661
Ehrick, John M.	42 (1839-45)	235
Ekells, John	14 (1771-74)	232
Ekells, Robert	12 (1767-71)	535
Elbert, Hannah	12 (1767-71)	447
Elder, James	45 (1845-51)	65]
Elders, John	14 (1771-74)	24
Elders, Mary	17 (1774-79)	752
Elfe, Benjamin	38 (1826-34)	436

Name	volume	Page
Elfe, Deborah	39 (1826-34)	1029
Elfe, Eleanor S.	47 (1851-56)	454
Elfe, Eliza	51 (1862-68)	527
Elfe, Thomas	18 (1776-84)	88 ⎫ Duplic.
*Elfe, Thomas	18 (1776-84)	145 ⎭
Elicott, Joseph	1 (1711-18)	74
Ellery, Thomas	4 (1736-40)	115
Ellington, Edward	26 (1793-1800)	368
Elliot, Catharine O. [Elliott]	47 (1851-56)	610
Elliot, Charles [Elliott]	19 (1780-83)	332
Elliot, Joseph [Elliott]	4 (1736-40)	140
Elliot, Joseph [Elliott]	4 (1736-40)	328
Elliot, Robert	36 (1818-26)	1249
Elliot, Samuel P. [Elliott]	36 (1818-26)	1161
Elliot, Thomas	4 (1736-40)	101
Elliot, Thomas Law [Elliott]	8 (1757-60)	31
Elliot, William [Elliott]	4 (1736-40)	104
Elliot see also Elliott		
Elliott, Amerinthea	35 (1818-26)	743
Elliott, Ann	29 (1800-07)	625
Elliott, Artimus	9 (1760-67)	111
Elliott, Barnard	8 (1757-60)	272
Elliott, Barnard	30 (1800-07)	1016
Elliott, Benjamin	24 (1786-93)	786
Elliott, Charles	29 (1800-07)	562
*Elliott, Elizabeth	25 (1793-1800)	2
Elliott, Elizabeth (B.)	7 (1752-56)	63
Elliott, Esther	5 (1740-47)	98
Elliott, Gibbes L.	49 (1856-62)	612
Elliott, Jehu	9 (1760-67)	227
*Elliott, John	25 (1793-1800)	6
Elliott, Joseph	20 (1783-86)	73
Elliott, Juliet G.	45 (1845-51)	705

Name	Volume	Page
Elliott, Maria	37 (1826-34)	11
Elliott, Mary M.	37 (1826-34)	112
Elliott, Robert	2 (1727-29)	1
Elliott, Sabina	25 (1793-1800)	103
Elliott, Samuel	17 (1774-79)	622
Elliott, Sarah	16 (1774-79)	253
Elliott, Stephen	6 (1747-52)	469
Elliott, Thomas	3 (1731-33)	13
Elliott, Thomas	9 (1760-67)	52
Elliott, Thomas	12 (1767-71)	389
Elliott, Thomas	13 (1767-71)	806
Elliott, Thomas	22 (1786-93)	305
Elliott, Thomas John	3 (1732-37)	31
Elliott, William [Elliot]	3 (1731-33)	11
Elliott, William	11 (1767-71)	171
Elliott, William	17 (1774-79)	575
Elliott, William	17 (1774-79)	763
Elliott, William	31 (1807-18)	451
Elliott, William S.	42 (1839-45)	123
Elliott, William S.	51 (1862-68)	483
Elliott see also Elliot		
Ellis, Benjamin	35 (1818-26)	789
Ellis, Edmond	16 (1774-79)	320
Ellis, James	2 (1724-25)	14
Ellis, John	7 (1752-56)	579
Ellis, Judith	14 (1771-74)	330
Ellis, Mary	19 (1780-83)	164
*Ellis, Mary	20 (1783-86)	186
Ellis, Samuel	31 (1807-18)	59
Ellis, Thomas	1 (1722-24)	23
Ellis, William	15 (1771-74)	419
Ellison, Robert	14 (1771-74)	215
Elmes, Anna	7 (1752-56)	390

Name	Volume	Page
Elmes, Samuel	13 (1767-71)	864
Elmes, Thomas	2 (1724-25)	39
Elmes, Thomas	5 (1740-47)	474
Elmes, William	1 (1721-22)	8
Elmore, Dorcas	37 (1826-34)	155
Elmore, Jefse	28 (1800-07)	293
Elmore, John	27 (1793-1800)	790
Elmore, Mathias	11 (1767-71)	297
Elsinore, James	24 (1786-93)	839
Elsworth, John T.	50 (1862-68)	110
Elsworth, Theophilus	41 (1834-39)	751
Emanuel, Sylvia	36 (1818-26)	989
Emerry see Emery		
Emerson, Jones	32 (1807-18)	794
Emery, Jonathan	37 (1826-34)	88
Emery, Robert [Emerry]	23 (1786-93)	626
Emms, Hezekiah	5 (1740-47)	234
Emperor, Amerentia	5 (1740-47)	374
Emperor, John, Capt. (Memorandum)	1 (1711-18)	101
Engevin, Jane	23 (1786-93)	513
England, Alexander	45 (1845-51)	586
England, Elizabeth	48 (1856-62)	248
England, John (Bishop)	42 (1839-45)	409
English, Henry	44 (1845-51)	55
English, James	47 (1851-56)	841
English, John	27 (1793-1800)	939
English, William	33 (1807-18)	1379
English, William	46 (1851-56)	297
Enston, William	49 (1856-62)	628
Epser, Gottleibe [Gottleib]	48 (1856-62)	145
Ernst, John	19 (1780-83)	257
Ernst, John	20 (1783-86)	103
Ervin, Robert	16 (1774-79)	246

Name	volume	Page
Ervin, Samuel	29 (1800-07)	413
Esnard, Ann Pebarte	50 (1862-68)	37
Esnard, Peter	49 (1856-62)	802
Ethridge, Sarah	28 (1800-07)	306
Eude, Louis	41 (1834-39)	647
Eustace, Thomas	21 (1783-86)	772
Euston, William	29 (1800-07)	721
Evans, Ann	27 (1793-1800)	854
Evans, Daniel	3 (1731-33)	5
Evans, Daniel	23 (1786-93)	770
Evans, Elias	22 (1786-93)	373
Evans, Elizabeth	26 (1793-1800)	447
Evans, George	1 (1711-18)	78
Evans, James	44 (1845-51)	433
Evans, Johanna Christian	8 (1757-60)	391
Evans, John	12 (1767-71)	670
Evans, John	13 (1767-71)	714
Evans, John	16 (1774-79)	208
Evans, John	21 (1783-86)	631
Evans, John	44 (1845-51)	250
Evans, Jonah	36 (1818-26)	965
Evans, Jonathan	5 (1740-47)	618
Evans, Leaycraft	43 (1839-45)	936
Evans, Martha	51 (1862-68)	537
Evans, Mary	9 (1760-67)	194
Evans, Mary	32 (1807-18)	503
Evans, Phillip	7 (1752-56)	179
Evans, Richard Rippon	31 (1807-18)	383
Evans, Rowland	3 (1732-37)	45
Evans, Samuel	7 (1752-56)	391
Evans, Susan	41 (1834-39)	852
Evans, Thomas	6 (1747-52)	598
Evans, Thomas	22 (1786-93)	158

Name	volume	Page
Eve, Abraham	1 (1722-24)	42
Eveleigh, George	24 (1786-93)	1126
Eveleigh, Nicholas	24 (1786-93)	936
Eveleigh, Samuel	4 (1736-40)	235-A
Everard, Richard	5 (1740-47)	117
Everingham, John	45 (1845-51)	614
Everingham, Rebecca	45 (1845-51)	615
Evon, Louisa	50 (1862-68)	215
Ewing, Adam	28 (1800-07)	71
Ewing, Robt W.	33 (1807-18)	1147
Eycott, John	6 (1747-52)	512
Eyland, James	40 (1834-39)	295
Eylman, Christian	41 (1834-39)	540

F

Name	volume	Page
Faber, Christian Henry	37 (1826-34)	354
Faber, Christian Henry (Substitution of Trustee)	43 (1839-45)	644
Faber, Henry F.	41 (1834-39)	916
Faber, John C. Junr	34 (1818-26)	291
Faber, John Christopher	34 (1818-26)	22
Faber, Joseph W.	49 (1856-62)	788
Faber, Mary M.	49 (1856-62)	913
Fabian, Ann Sanders	41 (1834-39)	808
Fabian, James	12 (1767-71)	381
Fabian, John	5 (1740-47)	308
Fabian, John	5 (1740-47)	488
Fabian, Jonathan	18 (1776-84)	2
*Fabian, Joseph	15 (1771-74)	438
Fabian, Joseph	22 (1786-93)	166
Fabian, Mary	6 (1747-52)	418
Fabian, William	14 (1771-74)	158
Fable, John	39 (1826-34)	860

Name	Volume	Page
Fabre, John	28 (1800-07)	129
Faesch, Sarah ₍Faesh₎	33 (1807-18)	1030
Faesh see Faesch		
Fair, William	40 (1834-39)	28
Fairchild, Anne	1 (1721-22)	38
Fairchild, Daniel	50 (1862-68)	191
Fairchild, Leander	24 (1786-93)	975
Fairchild, Thomas	3 (1732-37)	113
Fairweather, Robert	9 (1760-67)	380
Falcke, Frederick Adolph	33 (1807-18)	1302
Falconnet, John Baptiste	31 (1807-18)	4
Falkingham, Joseph	3 (1732-37)	59
Falling see Faulling		
Fallon, James	22 (1786-93)	286
Fallows, James	19 (1780-83)	298
Fallows, James	20 (1783-86)	53
Fancheraud, Gideon ₍Faucheraud, Fauchereaud₎	7 (1752-56)	108
Farasteau see Forresteau		
Farewel see Farewell		
Farewell, Henry ₍Farewel₎	2 (1726-27)	25
Fargison, Cathrine ₍Cathany₎	6 (1747-52)	565
*Farguson, William	6 (1747-52)	571
Farlefs see Farless		
Farless, Thomas ₍Farlefs₎	3 (1732-37)	174
Farley, James	1 (1721-22)	7
Farquhar, Robert	20 (1783-86)	337
Farquharson, James	19 (1780-83)	52
Farquharson, Joseph	25 (1793-1800)	21
Farr, Elizabeth	35 (1818-26)	803
Farr, John	3 (1732-37)	90
Farr, John Emperor	36 (1818-26)	930
Farr, Nathaniel	25 (1793-1800)	121
Farr, Phebe	18 (1776-84)	338

Name	Volume	Page
Farr, Sarah	32 (1807-18)	804
Farr, Thomas	18 (1776-84)	224
Farr, Thomas	22 (1786-93)	260
Farr, William Branford	27 (1793-1800)	778
Farr see also FFarr		
Farrall, William [Farrell]	34 (1818-26)	187
Farrar, Samuel S.	49 (1856-62)	827
Farrell, B.	36 (1818-26)	1042
Farrell see also Farrall		
Farrignton see Farrington		
Farrington, Thomas [Farrignton]	3 (1732-37)	269
Farrow, Thomas M.	49 (1856-62)	693
Farwell, Henry	14 (1771-74)	299
Farwell, Thomas	5 (1740-47)	242
Fash, Leonard	41 (1834-39)	724
Fastbender, Catherine [Cathrine]	31 (1807-18)	387
Faucheraud see Fancheraud		
Fauchereaud, Charles	11 (1767-71)	216
Fauchereaud, Mary	13 (1767-71)	770
Fauchereaud see also Fancheraud		
Faulling, Thomas	41 (1834-39)	525
Faulling, William [Falling]	33 (1807-18)	1015
Faures, S. Ve	32 (1807-18)	708
Favell, Thomas	5 (1740-47)	621
Fawshaw, Edward	31 (1807-18)	121
Fayett, Louisa	50 (1862-68)	215
Fayfsoux, Ann	31 (1807-18)	342
Fayfsoux, Peter	25 (1793-1800)	264
Fayolle, Peter	41 (1834-39)	608
Fayolle, Theodore B.	41 (1834-39)	908
Fayssoux, Elizabeth	43 (1839-45)	823
Fcott see Scott		
Feay, Obadiah, M.	33 (1807-18)	1374

Name	Volume	Page
Feemster, John	9 (1760-67)	85
Felderin, Ursula	4 (1736-40)	205
Felmore, Peter	30 (1800-07)	1015
Felsted see Taylor		
Fendell see Fendin		
Fendin, John	8 (1757-60)	308
Fendin, Richard [Fendell]	17 (1774-79)	480
Fenny, John [Finney]	7 (1752-56)	222
Fenwick, Robert	2 (1726-27)	21
Fenwick, Sarah	2 (1726-27)	55
Fenwicke, Edward, Senior	16 (1774-79)	386
Fenwicke, John	12 (1767-71)	543
Feraud, Claude Alexandre [Alexander]	29 (1800-07)	704
Ferguson, Ann	40 (1834-39)	326
Ferguson, Catherine [Katherine]	9 (1760-67)	404
*Ferguson, Charles	9 (1760-67)	397
Ferguson, Charles	23 (1786-93)	524
Ferguson, David	17 (1774-79)	771
Ferguson, Eliza M.	43 (1839-45)	509
Ferguson, Henry	5 (1740-47)	460
Ferguson, Hugh	11 (1767-71)	261
Ferguson, Hugh	23 (1786-93)	600
Ferguson, Mary	15 (1771-74)	577
Ferguson, Samuel Wragg	35 (1818-26)	714
Ferguson, Thomas	22 (1786-93)	11
Ferguson, William	5 (1740-47)	516
Ferguson, William, Sr.	15 (1771-74)	576
Ferguson, William	20 (1783-86)	358
Ferguson see also Furguson		
Ferrell, Mary Ann	50 (1862-68)	61
Ferret, Rosalie	32 (1807-18)	787
Ferrette, Josephine	48 (1856-62)	53
Ferrette, Marie Louise [Louisa]	36 (1818-26)	944

Name	Volume	Page
Ferrini, William E.	48 (1856-62)	117
Ferris, Henry	42 (1839-45)	135
Ferris, Sarah [Reid]	40 (1834-39)	18
Fesch, Andrew	9 (1760-67)	208
Fewox, Jemima	26 (1793-1800)	602
Fewthy see Futhey		
Ffarr, Thomas (Senr)[Farr]	2 (1729-31)	71
Ffirth, Hutchinson D.	47 (1851-56)	675
Ffitch see Fitch		
Fflood see Flood		
Ffolansby see Folansby		
Ffrost see Frost		
Ffuller see Fuller		
Fick, Charles	36 (1818-26)	901
Ficken, John F.	50 (1862-68)	321
Ficken, Rebecca	51 (1862-68)	723
Ficklin see Fickling		
Fickling, Anne	24 (1786-93)	806
Fickling, George	24 (1786-93)	1024
Fickling, George [Ficklin]	25 (1793-1800)	267
Fickling, George	28 (1800-07)	214
Fickling, Isaac	40 (1834-39)	64
Fickling, James	26 (1793-1800)	553
Fickling, Jeremiah	10 (1760-67)	563
Fickling, Jeremiah	28 (1800-07)	12
Fickling, Jeremiah	28 (1800-07)	311
Fickling, Joseph	27 (1793-1800)	818
Fickling, Mary	31 (1807-18)	176
Fickling, Samuel	29 (1800-07)	720
Fidler, Joseph	5 (1740-47)	79
Fidling, Ann (A)	1 (1711-18)	3
Field, Charles	7 (1752-56)	200
Field, John	10 (1760-67)	536

Name	volume	Page
Field, Richard	9 (1760-67)	346
Field, William	11 (1767-71)	22
Fife, Isabel Mary [Isabella]	44 (1845-51)	106
Fife, James	30 (1800-09)	783
Fife, James	43 (1839-45)	847
Figuers, Peter B.	35 (1818-26)	534
Figuiere, Francois	32 (1807-18)	685
Filben, John	5 (1740-47)	643
Filben see also Filbin		
Filbin, Charles	28 (1800-07)	317
Filbin, John [Filben]	16 (1774-79)	1
Filbin, John	32 (1807-18)	713
Fillette, Augustine Frances	50 (1862-68)	164
Filley, John	28 (1800-07)	130
Fillhauer, George [Vialhauer]	26 (1793-1800)	435
Finch, Isabella	9 (1760-67)	162
Finch, Joseph	33 (1807-18)	970
Finck, Henry	51 (1862-68)	601
Findlay, Alexander	20 (1783-86)	321
Findley, Jemima	48 (1856-62)	366
Findley, Sarah	12 (1767-71)	649
Findly, John	17 (1774-79)	511
Findly, Jemima	48 (1856-62)	366
Finlayson, John	30 (1800-07)	1078
Finley, Mary	46 (1851-56)	57
Finley, Thomas	27 (1793-1800)	826
Finley, William	20 (1783-86)	105
Finney see Fenny		
Firth, Samuel	3 (1731-33)	34
Fishborn, William	7 (1752-56)	578
Fishburn, William	8 (1757-60)	553
Fisher, Catharine	25 (1793-1800)	180
Fisher, Daniel	24 (1786-93)	953

Name	volume	Page
Fisher, George	24 (1786-93)	987
Fisher, Henrietta	6 (1747-52)	416
Fisher, Hugh	3 (1732-37)	122 ⎫ Dupliaat
Fisher, Hugh	3 (1732-37)	131 ⎭
Fisher, James	33 (1807-18)	1196
Fisher, Jane Macintosh	44 (1845-51)	431
Fisher, Prudence	13 (1767-71)	813
Fisher, Samuel	48 (1856-62)	527
Fisher, Susan	45 (1845-51)	795
Fisher, Thomas	3 (1732-37)	233
Fisk, Rasmus Nelson [Frisk]	32 (1807-18)	609
Fiske, William	7 (1752-56)	12
Fitch, Elizabeth	6 (1747-52)	493
Fitch, John, Jr.	5 (1740-47)	286
Fitch, Jonathan [Ffitch]	2 (1724-25)	77
Fitch, Stephen	6 (1747-52)	70
Fitch, Susannah	3 (1732-37)	37
Fitch, Thomas	5 (1740-47)	219
Fitchet see Fitchett		
Fitchett, John [Fitchet]	5 (1740-47)	434
Fittig, Nicholas	16 (1774-79)	182
Fitzgerald, Alexander	15 (1771-74)	359
Fitzgerald, Luke	6 (1747-52)	119
Fitzgerald, Tho(mas)	1 (1720-21)	21
Fitzgerald, Thomas	22 (1786-93)	339
Fitzgerrold, James	5 (1740-47)	495
Fitzjareld, James	27 (1793-1800)	852
Fitzpatrick, Anne	51 (1862-68)	720
Fitzsimons, Bernard	49 (1856-62)	580
Fitz Simons, Christopher	20 (1783-86)	198
Fitzsimons, Christopher	39 (1826-34)	1130
Flagg, George	36 (1818-26)	975
Flagg, George (Substitution of Trustee)	36 (1818-26)	1059

Name	Volume	Page
Flagg, Henry Collins	28 (1800-07)	138
Flagg, Rachel	42 (1839-45)	63
Flanigan, Emma [Flaninga; Elme]	39 (1826-34)	900
Flanigan, John [Flanigen]	18 (1776-84)	249
Flanigen see Flanigan		
Flaninga see Flanigan		
Flavel, Rebecca	5 (1740-47)	344
Fleeming, Sarah	8 (1757-60)	373
Fleming, Elizabeth	18 (1776-84)	9
Fleming, James	36 (1818-26)	1063
Fleming, John	6 (1747-52)	470
Fleming, John	12 (1767-71)	406
Fleming, Matthew	32 (1807-18)	893
Fleming, Robert [Flemming]	43 (1839-45)	902
Fleming, Thomas	6 (1747-52)	561
Fleming, Thomas	8 (1757-60)	166
Fleming, Thomas	47 (1851-56)	630
Fleming, William	6 (1747-52)	398
Flemming see Fleming		
Fletcher, John	34 (1818-26)	65
Flin, William	16 (1774-79)	98
Flinn, Andrew	34 (1818-26)	281
Flinn, Charles	24 (1786-93)	1043
Flinn, Eliza	43 (1839-45)	788
Flint, William	23 (1786-93)	629
Flood, George [Fflood]	2 (1724-25)	85
Florin, Henry	34 (1818-26)	406
Florin, Lucas	31 (1807-18)	456
Flower, J. C. see Flower, Joseph Edward		
Flower, Joseph Edward [J. C.]	8 (1757-60)	17
Floyd, Edward	33 (1807-18)	1399
Flud, James	10 (1760-67)	717
Flud, William	7 (1752-56)	240

Name	Volume	Page
Flude, John	18 (1776-84)	239
Flyn, Thos.	33 (1807-18)	1073
Fobes, Thomas	34 (1818-26)	244
Fogartie, Christian	38 (1826-34)	711
Fogartie, David	12 (1767-71)	658
Fogartie, Francis	28 (1800-07)	320
Fogartie, Martha	33 (1807-18)	1215
Fogartie, Mary	31 (1807-18)	87
Fogartie, Sarah	23 (1786-93)	662
Fogartie, Stephen	8 (1757-60)	22
Foifsin, Elias	11 (1767-71)	14
Foifsin, Esther	35 (1818-26)	819
Foifsin, Peter	31 (1807-18)	123
Foissin, Martha	49 (1856-62)	678
Folansby, William [Ffolansby]	1 (1721-22)	14
Folck, Jacob	17 (1774-79)	506
Folger, Edward J.	51 (1862-68)	627
Follin, Auguste	40 (1834-39)	178
Follin, Joseph	47 (1851-56)	592
Follin, Marie Josephe Heberte	45 (1845-51)	649
Follin, Mathew Firmin	45 (1845-51)	488
Foord, Joseph [Foords]	1 (1720-21)	48
Foords see Foord		
Footell, Ann	2 (1727-29)	98
Fopell, Elizabeth	11 (1767-71)	168
Forbes, Alexander	32 (1807-18)	738
Forbes, Roberts	50 (1862-68)	298
Forbes, S. W.	45 (1845-51)	804
Force, Lewis Miller	45 (1845-51)	612
Ford, George	18 (1776-84)	80
Ford, Hannah	38 (1826-34)	470
Ford, Isaac	27 (1793-1800)	671
Ford, Jacob	40 (1834-39)	67

Name	Volume	Page
Ford, Joyce	5 (1740-47)	67
Ford, Mary	7 (1752-56)	403
Ford, Mary M.	39 (1826-34)	998
Ford, Stephen	7 (1752-56)	584
Ford, Thomas	11 (1767-71)	26
Ford, Timothy	38 (1826-34)	823
Ford, Tobias	23 (1786-93)	648
Ford, William Richard	12 (1767-71)	370
Fordyce, John	6 (1747-52)	517
Forester, William	16 (1774-79)	32
Forgison, William	5 (1740-47)	519
Forrest, Charity	39 (1826-34)	1229
Forrest, James	50 (1862-68)	242
Forrest, Joanna	26 (1793-1800)	571
Forresteau, Anthony [Farasteau]	22 (1786-93)	37
Forrester, Alexander	46 (1851-56)	280
Forrester, James [Samuel]	5 (1740-47)	420
Forrester, Samuel see Forrester, James		
Fort, Arthur	15 (1771-74)	537
Fort, Dariues [Darines]	50 (1862-68)	117
Fort, Elias	19 (1780-83)	349
Fort, Elias	20 (1783-86)	91
Fort, John	43 (1839-45)	900
Fort, Moses	7 (1752-56)	554
Foskey, Brian [Bryan]	25 (1793-1800)	39
Foster, Andrew	1 (1720-21)	64
Foster, Christopher	27 (1793-1800)	858
Foster, Hannah	30 (1800-07)	844
Foster, John	21 (1783-86)	714
Foster, John Robert	28 (1800-07)	294
Foster, Sarah	35 (1818-26)	579
Fothringham see Fothringhame		
Fothringhame, Allexander [Fothringham; Alexander]	17 (1774-79)	535

Name	Volume	Page
Fouche, Seulette	31 (1807-18)	139
Fougeres, Le Marquis de	40 (1834-39)	371
Foulke, Joseph	26 (1793-1800)	627
Foust, Casper	18 (1776-84)	210
Fowke, Chandler Dinwiddle [Dinwiddie]	26 (1793-1800)	423
Fowke, Mary	32 (1807-18)	800
Fowler, Andrew	45 (1845-51)	844
Fowler, Ann	22 (1786-93)	56
Fowler, Edward	6 (1747-52)	542
Fowler, Gilbert	9 (1760-67)	244
Fowler, James	7 (1752-56)	88
Fowler, James	14 (1771-74)	332
Fowler, John	27 (1793-1800)	796
Fowler, Jonathan	15 (1771-74)	559
Fowler, Michael	31 (1807-18)	265
Fowler, Richard	32 (1807-18)	684
Fowler, Thomas	12 (1767-71)	566
Fox, Joseph	7 (1752-56)	439
Fox, Margaret [Margeret]	3 (1732-37)	189
Fox, Patt	36 (1818-26)	870
Foxworth, Abram	37 (1826-34)	93
Foxworth, Robert	39 (1826-34)	935
Foxworth, Samuel	51 (1862-68)	621
Frampton, Jonathan	11 (1767-71)	89
Franchomme, Charles	2 (1724-25)	42
Francis, Edward	42 (1839-45)	51
Francis, John L.	51 (1862-68)	588
Francisco, Caroline	44 (1845-51)	62
Francish, Joseph	31 (1807-18)	381
Francklyn, John	3 (1732-37)	133
Frank, William, M.D.	47 (1851-56)	865
Franks, Lawrence [Laurence]	30 (1800-07)	874

Name	Volume	Page
Fraser, Alexander	24 (1786-93)	882
Fraser, Charles	49 (1856-62)	736
Fraser, Elizabeth	44 (1845-51)	77
Fraser, James	43 (1839-45)	548
Fraser, John	7 (1752-56)	190
Fraser, John	23 (1786-93)	422
Fraser, John	33 (1807-18)	1047
Fraser, John	46 (1851-56)	347
Fraser, John L.	33 (1807-18)	1207
Fraser, Judith	14 (1771-74)	211
Fraser, Judith [Judtih]	34 (1818-26)	186
Fraser, Mary	46 (1851-56)	318
Fraser, Mary Allston	45 (1845-51)	592
Fraser, Peter William	45 (1845-51)	507
Fraser, Rebecca L. D.	51 (1862-68)	491
Fraser, Susan	43 (1839-45)	909
Frazer, Isaac	17 (1774-79)	538
Freare, Sarah	28 (1800-07)	162
Freatas, Joseph	45 (1845-51)	732
Freazer, John Ladson	29 (1800-07)	497
Freazer, Sarah	33 (1807-18)	1369
Frederick, John	6 (1747-52)	544
Freeman, Benjamin	50 (1862-68)	107
Freeman, Eliz^th M^t	34 (1818-26)	137
Freeman, Henry R.	45 (1845-51)	754
Freeman, John	9 (1760-67)	375
Freeman, Joseph	17 (1774-79)	609
Freeman, Richard	41 (1834-39)	555
Freeman, William	32 (1807-18)	535
Freer, Ann	26 (1793-1800)	345
Freer, Charles	31 (1807-18)	209
Freer, Charles	38 (1826-34)	608
Freer, Edward	29 (1800-07)	388

Name	volume	Page
Freer, George Hext	31 (1807-18)	65
Freer, John, Jr.	12 (1767-71)	531
Freer, John	22 (1786-93)	231
Freer, John I.	39 (1826-34)	987
Freer, Maria Augusta	42 (1839-45)	18
Freer, Solomon ⌐Solom⌐	19 (1780-83)	245
Freer, Solomon	20 (1783-86)	414
Freer, Susan	33 (1807-18)	1278
Freeze, Frederick	51 (1862-68)	617
Freneau, Peter	32 (1807-18)	769
Fresquet, Paulin	26 (1793-1800)	513
Freuin, Francis	2 (1726-27)	10
Friday, William, Senr	39 (1826-34)	1011
Frierfon see Frierson		
Frierson, James (E. Senr)	18 (1776-84)	322
Frierson, John ⌐Frierfon⌐	9 (1760-67)	124
Frierson, Thomas	13 (1767-71)	966
Frierson, William	15 (1771-74)	622
Frifsell see Frissell		
Frink, John	14 (1771-74)	37
Frink, Thomas Bloget ⌐Blodget⌐	34 (1818-26)	249
Fripp, Charles E.	43 (1839-45)	717
Fripp, John	5 (1740-47)	305
Fripp, John	19 (1780-83'	250
Fripp, Sarah Harriet	50 (1862-68)	417
Frisbie see Phrisbey		
Frisch, Charles (Wilhelm) ⌐Frish; Carl⌐	35 (1818-26)	463
Frisch, Elizabeth	35 (1818-26)	796
Frisel, Alexander	5 (1740-47)	139
Frisel, Mary	14 (1771-74)	14
Frish see Frisch		
Frisk see Fisk		
Frissell, Eli ⌐Frifsell⌐	8 (1757-60)	416

Name	Volume	Page
Frizer, Elizabeth	29 (1800-07)	451
Frizer, Joseph	22 (1786-93)	268
Frizer, Joseph	24 (1786-93)	1016
Frogatt, Addin	24 (1786-93)	829
Frogatt, Adin	10 (1760-67)	452
Frogatt, Elizabeth	24 (1786-93)	829
Fronty, Mary	39 (1826-34)	956
Fronty, Michael	39 (1826-34)	926
Frost, Edward	51 (1862-68)	877
Frost, Elizabeth	43 (1839-45)	760
Frost, George [Ffrost]	1 (1711-18)	43
Frost, Henry R.	51 (1862-68)	485
Frost, Mary	10 (1760-67)	832
Frost, Mary C.	36 (1818-26)	1180
Fry, Baynard	8 (1757-60)	92
Fry, Thomas	1 (1716-21)	3
Fryer, John	8 (1757-60)	161
Fryer, John	27 (1793-1800)	856
Fryer, Julia	44 (1845-51)	28
Fullarton, George	1 (1687-1710)	45
Fuller, Ann	24 (1786-93)	981
Fuller, Benjamin	6 (1747-52)	472
Fuller, Benjamin	21 (1783-86)	503
Fuller, Benjamin	22 (1786-93)	298
Fuller, Catharine Ann	45 (1845-51)	680
Fuller, Elizabeth	13 (1767-71)	898
Fuller, Janet [Jannet]	34 (1818-26)	77
Fuller, Judith	29 (1800-07)	457
Fuller, Katherine [Katharine]	33 (1807-18)	1079
Fuller, Mary	6 (1747-52)	498
Fuller, Nathaniel	6 (1747-52)	290
Fuller, Nathaniel	19 (1780-83)	67
Fuller, Nathaniel	20 (1783-86)	252

Name	Volume	Page
Fuller, Oliver	45 (1845-51)	624
Fuller, Richard	6 (1747-52)	179
Fuller, Sarah	7 (1752-56)	138
Fuller, Tacheus	27 (1793-1800)	662
Fuller, Thomas	23 (1786-93)	392
Fuller, Whitmarsh	13 (1767-71)	720
Fuller, William ⌈Ffuller⌉	3 (1731-33)	37
Fuller, William	10 (1760-67)	781
Fuller, William	26 (1793-1800)	400
Fullerton, Elizabeth	35 (1818-26)	549
Fullton, David	5 (1740-47)	511
Fulmart, Martin	8 (1757-60)	392
Fulton, Paul	5 (1740-47)	278
Fultz, William	32 (1807-18)	917
Furguson, Elizabeth ⌈Ferguson⌉	7 (1752-56)	290
Furman, Richard	36 (1818-26)	1155
Futerell, Catherine	39 (1826-34)	870
Futhey, James ⌈Fewthy⌉	4 (1736-40)	22
Futhey, Samuel	14 (1771-74)	91
Futhy, Francis	7 (1752-56)	78
Futhy, Robert	7 (1752-56)	73
Fyffe, William	14 (1771-74)	169

G

Name	Volume	Page
Gabeau, Dorothea ⌈Dorothy⌉	42 (1839-45)	338
Gadsden, Alexander Edward	50 (1862-68)	277
Gadsden, Ann	30 (1800-07)	939
Gadsden, Ann Margaret	40 (1834-39)	156
Gadsden, Benjamin C.	51 (1862-68)	743
Gadsden, Christopher	30 (1800-07)	869
Gadsden, Rt. Revd. Christopher Edward D D⌈Edwards⌉	46 (1851-56)	104
Gadsden, Emma Georgianna	47 (1851-56)	733
Gadsden, James (Genl.)	48 (1856-62)	386

Name	Volume	Page
Gadsden, James W.	46 (1851-56)	234
Gadsden, James W^m	34 (1818-26)	85
Gadsden, John	38 (1826-34)	826
Gadsden, Rebecca	41 (1834-39)	857
Gadsden, Rebecca	42 (1839-45)	4
Gadsden, Thos.	5 (1740-47)	37
Gadsden, Thomas	13 (1767-71)	717
Gadsden, Thomas	24 (1786-93)	950
Gadsden, Thomas	35 (1818-26)	487
Gadsden, W. S.	48 (1856-62)	312
Gaillard, Arthur P.	48 (1856-62)	148
Gaillard, Augustus Theodore	41 (1834-39)	661
Gaillard, Bartholomew	45 (1845-51)	489
Gaillard, Charles, Senr	32 (1807-18)	598
Gaillard, Cornelia	45 (1845-51)	912
Gaillard, Edwin	40 (1834-39)	324
Gaillard, Ellinor	31 (1807-18)	188
Gaillard, Harriet	42 (1839-45)	380
Gaillard, Harriet G.	46 (1851-56)	79
Gaillard, Henrietta P.	45 (1845-51)	774
Gaillard, James	12 (1767-71)	449
Gaillard, John	28 (1800-07)	47
Gaillard, Peter, Senr	39 (1826-34)	1119
Gaillard, Peter C.	48 (1856-62)	398
Gaillard, Peyre	30 (1800-07)	1058
Gaillard, Theodore	19 (1780-83)	187
Gaillard, Theodore	20 (1783-86)	135
Gaillard, Theodore, Senior	30 (1800-07)	849
Gaillard, Theodore, Jun.	36 (1818-26)	1006
Gaillard, Theodore Samuel	47 (1851-56)	708
Galaspee, John	2 (1729-31)	57
Galaven, James [Galavnen]	16 (1774-79)	281

Galavnen see Galaven

Name	volume	Page
Gale, Daniel	2 (1724-25)	94
Gale, Hannah	4 (1736-40)	168
Gale, Samuel	33 (1807-18)	1356
Galibo, Francis	37 (1826-34)	117
Gallman, Henry	11 (1767-71)	289
Gallman, Henry	17 (1774-79)	513
Gallman, John	8 (1757-60)	246
Galluchat, Joseph	36 (1818-26)	1136
Galluchat, Marie	29 (1800-07)	488
Gandouin, Izidore	40 (1834-39)	297
Ganes, Henry	14 (1771-74)	83
Gantt, Susan A.	50 (1862-68)	273
Garbon, Gabriel	47 (1851-56)	529
Garden, Alexander	7 (1752-56)	559
Garden, Alexander	20 (1783-86)	63
Garden, Alexander	24 (1786-93)	926
Garden, Alexander	38 (1826-34)	532
Garden, Elias W.	45 (1845-51)	898
Garden, Elizabeth Susan	46 (1851-56)	16
Garden, John	20 (1783-86)	404
Garden, John	44 (1845-51)	166
Gardner, James B.	50 (1862-68)	198
Gardner, John	5 (1740-47)	419
Gardner, John	35 (1818-26)	671
Gardner, Mary Ann	51 (1862-68)	489
Gardner, Susan	44 (1845-51)	452
Gardner see also Garner		
Gardon, Judith [Judy]	2 (1724-25)	75
Garland, Mary Ann	45 (1845-51)	641
Garner, Eliza	42 (1839-45)	319
Garner, Henry [Gardner]	37 (1826-34)	367
Garner, Melcher	10 (1760-67)	749
Garner, Melcher	23 (1786-93)	496

Name	Volume	Page
Garner, William	20 (1783-86)	259
Garnier see Gernier		
Garring, Francis	2 (1729-31)	10
Garvey, John	11 (1767-71)	303
Garvey, Michael	21 (1783-86)	811
Gatchell, Eli M.	45 (1845-51)	611
Gatenbe, William	9 (1760-67)	160
Gates, John	42 (1839-45)	139
Gates, Thomas, D. D.	39 (1826-34)	1182
Gates, Thomas	46 (1851-56)	209
Gatewood, William C.	49 (1856-62)	806
Gaujan, Ann E(trenne)	46 (1851-56)	82
Gaujan, Marie Rosalie	44 (1845-51)	326
Gaujan, Theodore	44 (1845-51)	219
Gaultier, Mary	6 (1747-52)	400
Gayer, W.J.	46 (1851-56)	5
Geddes, Gilbert C.	44 (1845-51)	340
Geddes, Henry	34 (1818-26)	102
Geddes, Peter	51 (1862-68)	624
Gefkin, Christiana	41 (1834-39)	479
Gefkin, Henry C.	47 (1851-56)	691
Geigelman, Ralph	14 (1771-74)	162
*Geiger, Harman (Herman)	6 (1747-52)	537
Geiger, Jacob	12 (1767-71)	620
Geiger, Jacob	14 (1771-74)	314
Geiger, John Jacob	25 (1793-1800)	25
Geiger, William	19 (1780-83)	130
Geiger, William	21 (1783-86)	429
Gell, John	36 (1818-26)	1023
Gelzer, Daniel	8 (1757-60)	39
Gelzer, Daniel	19 (1780-83)	57
Gelzer, John	16 (1774-79)	206
Gelzer, Sarah	44 (1845-51)	48

Name	volume	Page
Gendron, John	7 (1752-56)	408
Gendron, John	7 (1752-56)	411
Gendron, Philip	1 (1722-24)	86
Gennerick, Amelia	37 (1826-34)	245
Gennerick, John Frederick	31 (1807-18)	11
Gensel, John	34 (1818-26)	213
Gentil, Auguste	36 (1818-26)	1139
George, Rachel	39 (1826-34)	1180
Gerard, Peter G.	47 (1851-56)	828
Gerken, Henry	50 (1862-68)	26
German, Ralph	6 (1747-52)	303
Germont, Peter	34 (1818-26)	130
Gernier, John [Garnier; Jean]	18 (1776-84)	291
Gerrald, Mildred	10 (1760-67)	766
Gervais, Harriet Lowndes [Loundes]	47 (1851-56)	764
Gervais, John Lewis	27 (1793-1800)	756
Gervais, John Lewis J.	31 (1807-18)	232
Gervais, Mary	30 (1800-07)	1061
Gervais, Paul T.	47 (1851-56)	838
Gervais, Paul T. (Substitution of Trustee)	48 (1856-62)	19
Gervais, Rawlins Lowndes	30 (1800-07)	1119
Geury see Guery		
Geyer, Mary	43 (1839-45)	486
Gianinni, Jacob	41 (1834-39)	786
Giball, Knight	16 (1774-79)	173
Gibbes, Anne	13 (1767-71)	964
Gibbes, Benjamin	1 (1722-24)	6
Gibbes, Charlotte	43 (1839-45)	920
Gibbes, Culcheth	17 (1774-79)	612
Gibbes, Elizabeth	13 (1767-71)	886
Gibbes, John, Sen[r]	10 (1760-67)	639
Gibbes, John	14 (1771-74)	18

112

Name	Volume	Page
Gibbes, John Walter [Gibbs; Walters]	23 (1786-93)	449
Gibbes, Mary	27 (1793-1800)	901
Gibbes, Mary P.	43 (1839-45)	759
Gibbes, Robert	6 (1747-52)	640
Gibbes, Robert	25 (1793-1800)	184
Gibbes, Sarah	36 (1818-26)	1093
Gibbes, Sarah Middleton	44 (1845-51)	59
Gibbes, William, Junior	23 (1786-93)	399
Gibbes, W^m H(asell)	40 (1834-39)	1
Gibbins, Michael [Gibbons]	7 (1752-56)	132
Gibbon, George	51 (1862-68)	857
Gibbons, Joseph	6 (1747-52)	609
Gibbons see also Gibbins		
Gibbs, Benjamin	30 (1800-07)	885
Gibbs, George	38 (1826-34)	660
Gibbs, George (Substitution of Trustee)	41 (1834-39)	620
*Gibbs, Peter	15 (1771-74)	410
Gibbs, William	22 (1786-93)	389
Gibbs, William	31 (1807-18)	370
Gibbs see also Gibbes		
Gibbson, William [Gibson]	20 (1783-86)	263
Gibson, Daniel	3 (1732-37)	177
Gibson, David C.	51 (1862-68)	793
Gibson, James	40 (1834-39)	113
Gibson, John	18 (1776-84)	228
Gibson, John	34 (1818-26)	68
*Gibson, William	6 (1747-52)	9
Gibson, William	19 (1780-83)	249
Gibson, William, Jr.	44 (1845-51)	313
Gibson see also Gibbson		
Giese, Charles	44 (1845-51)	205
Gigleman, Margaret	24 (1786-93)	821

Name	Volume	Page
Gignilliat, Benjamin	27 (1793-1800)	849
Gignilliat, Gabriel	20 (1783-86)	85
Gignilliat, John	6 (1747-52)	346
Gilbert, Andre	29 (1800-07)	706
Gilbertson, James	1 (1720-21)	49
Gilchrist, Mary	51 (1862-68)	741
Gilchrist, Robert B.	47 (1851-56)	793
Gilchrist see also Gillchrist		
Giles, Abraham	13 (1767-71)	1014
Giles, Jean	23 (1786-93)	570
Giles, Mary	25 (1793-1800)	235
Giles, Robert	28 (1800-07)	381
Giles, Robert F.	51 (1862-68)	487
Giles, Thomas	23 (1786-93)	412
Gill, John	33 (1807-18)	976
Gill, William	41 (1834-39)	762
Gilland, George	46 (1851-56)	93
Gillchrist, Patrick	2 (1729-31)	30
Gillchrist, Robert [Gilchrist]	3 (1732-37)	108
Gilledeau, Mary	23 (1786-93)	488
Gillerd, John	23 (1786-93)	423
Gilles, Francis	50 (1862-68)	199
Gilliland, William D.	46 (1851-56)	402
Gillon, Alexander	25 (1793-1800)	252
Gilman, Samuel	48 (1856-62)	246
Gilmore, Dennis	39 (1826-34)	874
Gilmore, James	14 (1771-74)	243
Gindra, Abraham	11 (1767-71)	57
Girardeau, James	8 (1757-60)	9
Girardeau, John	1 (1720-21)	69
Girardeau, John	41 (1834-39)	617
Girardeau, John B.	46 (1851-56)	49
Gist, Juba	50 (1862-68)	166

Name	Volume	Page
Gist, Mordecai	24 (1786-93)	1124
Gist, States	35 (1818-26)	645
Gist, William	28 (1800-07)	347
Given, William	49 (1856-62)	895
Givens, Philip [Phillip]	7 (1752-56)	224
Glast, Robert	7 (1752-56)	244
Glaze, Gabriel	1 (1711-18)	54
Glaze, James	12 (1767-71)	510
Glaze, Malachi	9 (1760-67)	273
Glaze, Sarah	6 (1747-52)	74
Glaze, William	2 (1729-31)	36
Glemet, Marieen Veuve	38 (1826-34)	799
Glen, Daniel [Glenn]	8 (1757-60)	168
Glen, Daniel	24 (1786-93)	1132
Glen, Jane	44 (1845-51)	258
Glen, John	31 (1807-18)	70
Glen, John	46 (1851-56)	100
Glen, Margaret	42 (1839-45)	5
Glen, Tenah	38 (1826-34)	736
Glenn see Glen		
Glindkamp, Henry	36 (1818-26)	985
Glover, Anne	31 (1807-18)	95
Glover, Charles Worth	5 (1740-47)	631
Glover, Charlesworth	3 (1732-37)	8
Glover, Hannah	10 (1760-67)	540
Glover, John	9 (1760-67)	40
Glover, Joseph	20 (1783-86)	219
Glover, Joseph (Dr.)	42 (1839-45)	143
Glover, Mary Witter	48 (1856-62)	208
Glover, Moses	31 (1807-18)	439
Glover, Sanders	33 (1807-18)	973
Glover, William	12 (1767-71)	486
Glover, Wilson	35 (1818-26)	777

Name	Volume	Page
Gnech, Maria E.	43 (1839-45)	743
Godard, René, Senior	21 (1783-86)	724
Godard, René	43 (1839-45)	873
Godber, Melvin S. H.	51 (1862-68)	438
Godber, William S.	45 (1845-51)	619
Goddard, Francis	5 (1740-47)	551
Goddard, Francis	18 (1776-84)	302
Goddard, Mary	7 (1752-56)	295
Goddard, Peter Cuttino	49 (1856-62)	981
Goddard, William	8 (1757-60)	282
Godet, David	5 (1740-47)	672
Godfrey, Benjamin	3 (1732-37)	144
Godfrey, Benjamin	46 (1851-56)	107
Godfrey, Elizabeth	29 (1800-07)	462
Godfrey, Elizabeth, Mrs. (Substitution of Trustee)	36 (1818-26)	1019
Godfrey, John	1 (1722-24)	44
Godfrey, John	21 (1783-86)	536
Godfrey, John	23 (1786-93)	745
Godfrey, Thomas	18 (1776-84)	75
Godfrey, William	13 (1767-71)	819
Godin, Benjamin	6 (1747-52)	85
Godin, David	7 (1752-56)	330
Godin, Isaac	17 (1774-79)	700
Godin, Marianne [Marrianne]	7 (1752-56)	357
Godin, Martha	22 (1786-93)	41
Godwin, Elizabeth	6 (1747-52)	577
Godwin, John	5 (1740-47)	522
Goldberg, David	42 (1839-45)	391
Golden, Stephen	15 (1771-74)	663
Goldtrap, William	27 (1793-1800)	705
Golightly, Cultcheth [Culch]	6 (1747-52)	276

Gomm see Gomme

Name	Volume	Page
Gomme, James (Gomm)	21 (1783-86)	766
Gonfreville, Theodore	43 (1839-45)	728
Gonzales, Basilio	48 (1856-62)	387
Good, Francis	37 (1826-34)	42
Good, Francis	42 (1839-45)	220
Good, Sarah	36 (1818-26)	1027
Goodall, James	26 (1793-1800)	411
Goodbe, Hannah	9 (1760-67)	276
Goodbe, James	3 (1732-37)	273
Goodbe, John	5 (1740-47)	276
Goodbee, Alexander	6 (1747-52)	613
Goodbee, Joseph	2 (1727-29)	104
Goodby, John	1 (1720-21)	39
Goodrich, Ann	41 (1834-39)	697
Goodwyn, Jefse	11 (1767-71)	61
Goodwyn, John	17 (1774-79)	462
Goodwyn, Martha	17 (1774-79)	767
Goorgen, Hans	8 (1757-60)	16
Gordon, Alexander	3 (1731-33)	50
Gordon, Alexander	7 (1752-56)	255
Gordon, Catherine Ann	45 (1845-51)	551
Gordon, Charles	18 (1776-84)	44
Gordon, George	12 (1767-71)	511
Gordon, James	4 (1736-40)	217
Gordon, James (Indenture)	32 (1807-18)	847
Gordon, James	33 (1807-18)	1246
Gordon, Jane C.	50 (1862-68)	283
Gordon, John	9 (1760-67)	223
Gordon, John	21 (1783-86)	792
Gordon, John (Indenture)	32 (1807-18)	847
Gordon, John	40 (1834-39)	176
Gordon, Martha	39 (1826-34)	1204
Gordon, Mary	11 (1767-71)	210

Name	Volume	Page
Gordon, Mary	24 (1786-93)	1108
Gordon, Rachel	36 (1818-26)	1147
*Gordon, Roger	6 (1747-52)	523
Gordon, Thomas	11 (1767-71)	191
Gordon, William	33 (1807-18)	1346
Goslee, Robert	43 (1839-45)	620
Gotsman, John	14 (1771-74)	293
Gotsman, Margaretha	14 (1771-74)	16
Gotten, Mary [Gotton]	40 (1834-39)	219
Gottier, Francis	21 (1783-86)	465
Gottier, Isabella	27 (1793-1800)	747
Gottier, Isabella	27 (1793-1800)	768
Gotton see Gotten		
Goudy, Robert	17 (1774-79)	413
*Gough, Edward	6 (1747-52)	560
Gough, Emma	46 (1851-56)	427
Gough, Francis	6 (1747-52)	407
Gough, John	4 (1736-40)	316
Gough, John	22 (1786-93)	33
Gough, John Parker	34 (1818-26)	120
*Gough, O'Neal	6 (1747-52)	570
Gough, Rebecca E.	44 (1845-51)	39
Gough, Richard	7 (1752-56)	83
Gough, Richard	26 (1793-1800)	408
Goulding, John	3 (1732-37)	234
Goulding, Peter	8 (1757-60)	441
Gourden, Lewis [Gourdin]	7 (1752-56)	311
Gourdin, Elizabeth	40 (1834-39)	281
Gourdin, Elizabeth (Codicil)	40 (1834-39)	323(Du
Gourdin, Elizabeth (Codicil)	40 (1834-39)	333(Du
Gourdin, Louisa Martha	38 (1826-34)	651
Gourdin, Peter	16 (1774-79)	296
Gourdin, Samuel	35 (1818-26)	446

Name	Volume	Page
Gourdin, Samuel	38 (1826-34)	603
Gourdin, Samuel T.	47 (1851-56)	448
Gourdin, Theodore Louis	51 (1862-68)	612
Gourdin, Theodore, Senior	36 (1818-26)	1222
Gourdin, Theodore T.	50 (1862-68)	202
Gourdin, William Allston	50 (1862-68)	243
Gourdin, William D. (M.D.)	40 (1834-39)	449
Gourdin see also Gourden		
Gourdine, Theodore	15 (1771-74)	618
Gouré, André	33 (1807-18)	1375
Gourlay, John	26 (1793-1800)	376
Govan, Andrew	14 (1771-74)	151
Govan, John	11 (1767-71)	265
Gower, Thomas	1 (1711-18)	63
Grady, James	33 (1807-18)	984
Graeme, Anne	24 (1786-93)	1149
Graham, Abraham	4 (1736-40)	280
Graham, Daniel E.	33 (1807-18)	971
Graham, Hugh	45 (1845-51)	789
Graham, Margaret	44 (1845-51)	161
Graham, Susanna	33 (1807-18)	982
Graham, William	14 (1771-74)	309
Graham, William	37 (1826-34)	340
Grainger see Granger		
Gralton, Michail	51 (1862-68)	648
Gramann, Augustus Ernst	48 (1856-62)	252
Gramann, Sophia	45 (1845-51)	735
Grand, James Le see Grand, Le James		
Grand, L.I.B.	31 (1807-18)	276
Grand, LeJames (De Lomboy) [James Le]	2 (1726-27)	53
Grandclos, Bigrel de	28 (1800-07)	295
Grange, Hugh	5 (1740-47)	604
Grange, Jane	7 (1752-56)	378
Grenger, Caleb [Grainger]	22 (1786-93)	266

Name	volume	Page
Grant, Alexander	24 (1786-93)	1048
Grant, Eleanor D.	49 (1856-62)	953
Grant, Hary	32 (1807-18)	938
Grant, Hugh	30 (1800-07)	774
Grant, John	5 (1740-47)	430
Grant, Robert	33 (1807-18)	1143
Grantt, Ann	43 (1839-45)	861
Gratia see Gratis		
Gratis, Elizabeth [Gratia]	10 (1760-67)	708
Gratzel, (Von Gratz), Johann Friederick Wilhelm [Friedrick]	23 (1786-93)	677
Graumiller, Henry	22 (1786-93)	304
Gravenstine, Ursula	31 (1807-18)	175
Graves, A. Duncan	47 (1851-56)	517
Graves, Agnes	11 (1767-71)	269
Graves, Charles	43 (1839-45)	871
Graves, Daniel De Saussure	51 (1862-68)	628
Graves, Humphrey	25 (1793-1800)	230
Graves, J. Boonen	38 (1826-34)	528
Graves, Leonard	11 (1767-71)	71
Graves, Moses	3 (1732-37)	229
Graves, Sarah	41 (1834-39)	580
Graves, Thomas	10 (1760-67)	548
Graves, William	7 (1752-56)	334
Gray, Andrew	47 (1851-56)	782
Gray, Henry	36 (1818-26)	1039
Gray, Nicholas	21 (1783-86)	492
Gray, Patrick	49 (1856-62)	908
Gray, Ruth Ann	48 (1856-62)	44
Grayson, John	17 (1774-79)	731
Grayson, Sarah M.	51 (1862-68)	439
Grayson, Sarah M. (order)	51 (1862-68)	653
Grayson, William J.	50 (1862-68)	153
Gready, James	24 (1786-93)	803

Name	Volume	Page
Grear, Joseph	6 (1747-52)	284
Greatbeach, Thomas	1 (1692-93)	43
Greeland, Ann [Greenland]	17 (1774-79)	719
Greeme, David	17 (1774-79)	726
Green, Daniel	4 (1736-40)	132
Green, Edmund	32 (1807-18)	702
Green, Elizabeth	10 (1760-67)	798
Green, Elizabeth B.	47 (1851-56)	703
Green, Isaac	14 (1771-74)	245
Green, James	5 (1740-47)	39
Green, James	5 (1740-47)	313
Green, John	1 (1722-24)	61
Green, John	24 (1786-93)	915
*Green, John (C.)	6 (1747-52)	463
Green, Joshua	4 (1736-40)	52
Green, Judith	49 (1856-62)	964
Green, Keatty	51 (1862-68)	792
Green, Samuel	13 (1767-71)	828
Green, Sarah	19 (1780-83)	255
Green, Sophia	51 (1862-68)	547
Green, Susannah [Sufanna]	5 (1740-47)	669
Green, Thomas P.	50 (1862-68)	166
Greene, Mary Ann	38 (1826-34)	425
Greene, Mary Ann	43 (1839-45)	655
Greenhill, Elizabeth Farr	48 (1856-62)	397
Greenhill, Hume	35 (1818-26)	787
*Greening, Mason	18 (1776-84)	220
Greenland, Catherine	9 (1760-67)	201
Greenland, Elizabeth [Eliza]	41 (1834-39)	898
Greenland, John	2 (1724-25)	76
Greenland, John	18 (1776-84)	261
Greenland, Joseph	20 (1783-86)	357
Greenland, Washington C.	36 (1818-26)	1247

Name	Volume	Page
Greenland, William P. (Sub- stitution of Trustee)	39 (1826-34)	996
Greenland see also Greeland		
Greenwood, John	12 (1767-71)	639
Greenwood, Timothy	22 (1786-93)	122
Greenwood, William	35 (1818-26)	717
Greer, Benjamin	46 (1851-56)	155
Greer, William	50 (1862-68)	102
Greeves, Adam ⌐Greves⌐	4 (1736-40)	89
Gregg, John	18 (1776-84)	152
Gregorie, James	31 (1807-18)	25
Gregorie, James (Substitution of Trustee)	35 (1818-26)	505
Gregorie, Mary Christiana	35 (1818-26)	829
Gregory, James (Substitution of Trustee)	40 (1834-39)	137
Gregory, Theophilus	3 (1732-37)	125
Gregson, Thomas	38 (1826-34)	691
Greignier, Andrew ⌐Grenier⌐	6 (1747-52)	573
Grelee, Joseph	27 (1793-1800)	704
Grene, John	14 (1771-74)	310
Grenier see Greignier		
Greves see Greeves		
Grier, Andrew (Senr)	10 (1760-67)	802
Grier, Andrew	17 (1774-79)	423
*Grier, Andrew	18 (1776-84)	142
Grier, Joseph, Junr	12 (1767-71)	401
Grier, Patrick	12 (1767-71)	423
Grier, Samuel	14 (1771-74)	222
Grierson, Elizabeth T.	49 (1856-62)	719
Griffen see Griffin		
Griffin, Benjamin	1 (1721-22)	51
Griffin, Joyce	6 (1747-52)	181
Griffin, Susanna ⌐Griffen⌐	2 (1727-29)	55
Griffin, Susanna ⌐Susanne⌐	2 (1727-29)	79

Name	Volume	Page
Griffith, Edward	22 (1786-93)	315
Griffith, Margaret	46 (1851-56)	99
Griger see Mc Gregor		
Grigor, Alexander	31 (1807-18)	331
Grimball, Charles	13 (1767-71)	782
Grimball, Charles Isaac	25 (1793-1800)	118
Grimball, Isaac	7 (1752-56)	25
Grimball, John	1 (1722-24)	38
Grimball, John	30 (1800-07)	974
Grimball, Joshua	8 (1757-60)	140
Grimball, Paul	1 (1692-93)	75
*Grimball, Paul	6 (1747-52)	448
Grimball, Paul	11 (1767-71)	20
Grimball, Paul Chaplin	50 (1862-68)	270
Grimball, Rebekah	11 (1767-71)	8
Grimball, Thomas	1 (1722-24)	17
Grimball, Thomas	2 (1722-26)	1
Grimball, Thomas, Jr.	20 (1783-86)	31
Grimke, Benjamin S.	37 (1826-34)	284
Grimké, Henry	46 (1851-56)	182
Grimke, James M.	44 (1845-51)	197
Grimke, John	50 (1862-68)	269
Grimke, John Fauchereaud	34 (1818-26)	199
Grimke, John Paul	24 (1786-93)	833
Grimke, Mary	24 (1786-93)	1006
Grimke, Mary (S.)	42 (1839-45)	14
Grimke, Sarah D.	51 (1862-68)	784
Grimké, Thomas S.	40 (1834-39)	131
Grimstone, Richard	5 (1740-47)	625
Grindlay, James	10 (1760-67)	695
Grininger, John Christian	29 (1800-07)	441
Grininger, Martha	30 (1800-07)	771
Griswold, William F(rederick)	32 (1807-18)	876
Grooms, John	46 (1851-56)	217

Name	Volume	Page
Gros, John	46 (1851-56)	255
Grove, Samuel	18 (1776-84)	60
Grove, Samuel	19 (1780-83)	132
Groves, Elizabeth	49 (1856-62)	1073
Gruber, Catharina	33 (1807-18)	1059
Gruber, Christian	19 (1780-83)	15
Gruber, Christian	21 (1783-86)	553
Gruber, Margaret B.	44 (1845-51)	175
Grume, James	7 (1752-56)	152
Grume, John	17 (1774-79)	500
Grumes, George	44 (1845-51)	406
Grunzweig, Frederick	27 (1793-1800)	706
Gué, John Francis	36 (1818-26)	1036
Guerard, Alice C.	48 (1856-62)	321
Guerard, Ann	46 (1851-56)	238
Guerard, Mrs. Ann (Codicil)	46 (1851-56)	261
Guerard, Benjamin	23 (1786-93)	427
Guerard, David	8 (1758-63)	1
Guerard, Hannah	3 (1732-37)	266
Guerard, Jacob	36 (1818-26)	904
Guerard, John	1 (1711-18)	65
Guerard, John	10 (1760-67)	481
Guerard, Mary Anne	18 (1776-84)	240
Guerard, Peter	2 (1724-25)	9
Guerin, Esther	28 (1800-07)	134
Guerin, Francis	31 (1807-18)	352
Guerin, Henry	32 (1807-18)	499
Guerin, Jeane Veuve	33 (1807-18)	1408
Guerin, John	7 (1752-56)	580
*Guerin, Mary	14 (1771-74)	335
Guerin, Mary	18 (1776-84)	294
Guerin, Mary	21 (1783-86)	454
Guerin, Mathurin	19 (1780-83)	74
Guerin, Mattheurin [Mathurin]	25 (1793-1800)	250

Name	volume	Page
Guerin, Peter	25 (1793-1800)	45
Guerin, Robt	32 (1807-18)	509
Guerin, Samuel	17 (1774-79)	747
Guerin, Vincent	25 (1793-1800)	13
Guerin, William	11 (1767-71)	323
Guerrin, Isaac	8 (1757-60)	137
Guerry, Andrew Caleb	30 (1800-07)	782
Guerry, James (Senr)	41 (1834-39)	949
Guerry, James	47 (1851-56)	810
Guerry, Jean	21 (1783-86)	788
Guerry, Peter [Gurry]	4 (1736-40)	27
Guerry, Peter	20 (1783-86)	374
Guerry, Peter	32 (1807-18)	894
Guerry, Stephen	14 (1771-74)	233
Guerry, Stephen	21 (1783-86)	598
Guerry, Theo.	31 (1807-18)	234
Guery, James [Geury; Jaques]	3 (1732-37)	164
Gufsendaner, John	9 (1760-67)	150
Guichard, Levi (Mr.)	2 (1729-31)	49
Guignard, Gabriel	8 (1757-60)	97
Guilbert, Andre Louis Eugene [Eugene Andre Louis]	41 (1834-39)	891
Guilbert, Eugene Andre Louis see Guilbert, Andre Louis Eugene		
Guild, Thomas	4 (1736-40)	271
Guillandeau, James	22 (1786-93)	202
Guillot, John	33 (1807-18)	1217
Guilou, Saml	32 (1807-18)	726
Guinefs, John	17 (1774-79)	658
Guinn, Alexander	32 (1807-18)	901
Guiraud, Pierre	24 (1786-93)	919
Gulden, Christina	46 (1851-56)	18
Gunn, Philip	49 (1856-62)	689
Gunn, William	32 (1807-18)	690
Gunter, Edward	18 (1776-84)	165

Name	volume	Page
Gunther, Phillis	43 (1839-45)	899
Gurard see Gureard		
Gureard, Ester [Gurard]	23 (1786-93)	448
Gurry see Guerry		
Guy, Christ^r	7 (1752-56)	346
Guy, Jane see Guy, John		
Guy, John [Jane]	23 (1786-93)	446
Guy, Margaret	1 (1720-21)	68
* Guy, William	6 (1747-52)	440
Gyles, Mary Ann	41 (1834-39)	663
Gyles, Mary R.	49 (1856-62)	581
Gyles, Rosina	40 (1834-39)	415

H

Name	volume	Page
Habernicht, John D.	46 (1851-56)	228
Hacket, Elizabeth	12 (1767-71)	594
*Haddon, Michael	6 (1747-52)	452
Haddrell, Susanah	8 (1757-60)	513
Hafell see Hasell		
Hafer, Julia	42 (1839-45)	292
Hafsell see Hasell		
Haggard, John	18 (1776-84)	298
Haggat, Nanny	28 (1800-07)	202
Haig, David	39 (1826-34)	1003
Haig, E.M.	47 (1851-56)	684
Haig, George	23 (1786-93)	702
Haig, H.M.	40 (1834-39)	393
Haig, Robert	35 (1818-26)	451
Haig, Susan Singleton [Singlleton]	34 (1818-26)	118
Haige, Lillia	5 (1740-47)	127
Hails, Thomas	9 (1760-67)	173
Haily, James	9 (1760-67)	239
Hains, Willis	44 (1845-51)	267
Hainsworth see Haynesworth		

Name	Volume	Page
Hale, John	2 (1726-27)	41
Hale, William	19 (1780-83)	170
Hale, William	20 (1783-86)	208
Hales, Elender	17 (1774-79)	645
Hall, Arthur	3 (1732-37)	21
Hall, Benjamin	5 (1740-47)	462
Hall, Daniel	31 (1807-18)	422
Hall, George	7 (1752-56)	247
Hall, George Abbott	24 (1786-93)	922
Hall, Harriet	38 (1826-34)	430
Hall, James	36 (1818-26)	850
Hall, John	11 (1767-71)	2
Hall, John	21 (1783-86)	596
Hall, Maria Theresa	44 (1845-51)	160
Hall, Martha	3 (1732-37)	63
Hall, Mary	22 (1786-93)	145
Hall, Sabina	37 (1826-34)	187
Hall, Samuel D.	41 (1834-39)	711
Hall, Sarah	42 (1839-45)	124
Hall, Susan	38 (1826-34)	778
Hall, Susanne [Susanna]	44 (1845-51)	104
Hall, Thomas	8 (1757-60)	1
Hall, Thomas	32 (1807-18)	826
Hall, William	12 (1767-71)	348
Hall, William	32 (1807-18)	810
Hall, William	51 (1862-68)	745
Hallom, Mary	34 (1818-26)	315
Halsey, Elisha L.	43 (1839-45)	819
Halsey, Lucy	43 (1839-45)	919
Halsted, Job S., Jr.	44 (1845-51)	34
Haly, John	17 (1774-79)	456
Haly, Mary	38 (1826-34)	602
Ham, Samuel	30 (1800-07)	1045
Ham, Sarah	31 (1807-18)	359

Name	Volume	Page
Ham, Thomas (Senr)	23 (1786-93)	749
Hambleton, Rachel	21 (1783-86)	655
Hambleton, Robert	30 (1800-07)	1040
Hambleton see also Hamilton		
Hamilton, Anna Agatha	48 (1856-62)	262
Hamilton, Archibald	6 (1747-52)	54
Hamilton, Archibald	11 (1767-71)	126
Hamilton, Charles	10 (1760-67)	677
Hamilton, David	26 (1793-1800)	551
Hamilton, Elizabeth M.	42 (1839-45)	90
Hamilton, Elizabeth Mathews	50 (1862-68)	27
Hamilton, George	7 (1752-56)	229
Hamilton, Harriott Cleland	42 (1839-45)	94
Hamilton, James	6 (1747-52)	104
Hamilton, James	26 (1793-1800)	420
Hamilton, James	42 (1839-45)	340
Hamilton, Jane	45 (1845-51)	886
Hamilton, John	2 (1727-29)	78
Hamilton, John ⌈Hambleton⌉	5 (1740-47)	35
Hamilton, John	5 (1740-47)	339
Hamilton, John	23 (1786-93)	528
Hamilton, John R.	41 (1834-39)	692
Hamilton, Margaret	42 (1839-45)	463
Hamilton, Paul	4 (1736-40)	226
Hamilton, Paul	27 (1793-1800)	804
Hamilton, Pringle	9 (1760-67)	8
Hamilton, Robert	7 (1752-56)	362
Hamilton, Rosianna	16 (1774-79)	273
Hamilton, William	18 (1776-84)	282
Hamilton, William N.	49 (1856-62)	675
Hamlim see Hamlin		
Hamlin, Cornelius	44 (1845-51)	309
Hamlin, Frances	36 (1818-26)	1235
Hamlin, George ⌊Hamlim⌋	5 (1740-47)	523

Name	Volume	Page
Hamlin, George	22 (1786-93)	148
* Hamlin, Samuel	18 (1776-84)	132
Hamlin, Samuel	44 (1845-51)	396
Hamlin, Sarah	42 (1839-45)	73
Hamlin, Thomas	11 (1767-71)	146
Hamlin, Thomas	33 (1807-18)	1382
Hamlin, Thomas	45 (1845-51)	487
Hamlin, William	30 (1800-07)	985
Hammerton, William	3 (1731-33)	31
Hanahan, Elizabeth Mary	50 (1762-68)	17
Hanahan, James C.	49 (1756-62)	102
Hanahan, John	11 (1767-71)	97
Hanahan, John	29 (1800-07)	728
Hanahan, John	47 (1851-56)	806
Hanahan, Martha	31 (1807-18)	208
Hanahan, Mary	35 (1818-26)	421
Hanahan, William	33 (1807-18)	1287
Hanahan, William (Substitution of Trustee)	36 (1818-26)	1020
Hanbury, John	1 (1694-1704)	6
Hancock, Elias	2 (G1729-31)	45
Hancock, Henry	47 (1851-56)	669
Hancock, William	6 (1747-52)	65
Handlen, Champernown	8 (1757-60)	511
Handlen, Edward	5 (1740-47)	623
Handlen, John [Handlin]	7 (1752-56)	198
Handlin see Handlen		
Hanks, Louis B.	51 (1862-68)	817
Hanley, John	35 (1818-26)	742
Hannah, Alexander	38 (1826-34)	727
Hannay, Hannah	42 (1839-45)	416
Hanscom, Mofes	14 (1771-74)	146
Hanscome, Aaron [Hunfcome; Aron]	9 (1760-67)	108
Hanscome, Joseph	41 (1834-39)	809
Hanscome, Thomas	22 (1786-93)	177

Name	volume	Page
Hanscome, Thomas	39 (1826-34)	960
Happoldt, Christian David	42 (1839-45)	324
Happoldt, Christian David	49 (1856-62)	963
Happoldt, John George	35 (1818-26)	545
Harbert, Philip [Herbert]	5 (1740-47)	62
Harbeson, Robert	46 (1851-56)	375
Harbison, John	22 (1786-93)	251
Harby, A. Tobias	49 (1856-62)	650
Harby, Henry J.	45 (1845-51)	909
Hardcastle, Elizabeth, Mrs.	31 (1807-18)	238
Harden, Sarah	23 (1786-93)	726
Harden, William	21 (1783-86)	768
Hardin, Thomas	6 (1747-52)	622
Harding, Hugh [Hardy]	2 (1726-27)	62
Hardy, George	7 (1752-56)	59
Hardy, Matthew	12 (1767-71)	642
Hardy, Thomas	44 (1845-51)	299
Hardy see also Harding		
Hargrave, Henry	3 (1731-33)	58
Hargrave, Jonathan	2 (1729-31)	111
Hargrove, Joseph	17 (1774-79)	637
Harigol, Christian	31 (1807-18)	249
Harleston, Anna Bella	41 (1834-39)	756
Harleston, Edward	20 (1783-86)	362
Harleston, Edward	36 (1818-26)	1214
Harleston, Elizabeth	7 (1752-56)	533
Harleston, Elizabeth	29 (1800-07)	756
Harleston, Elizabeth	38 (1826-34)	782
Harleston, John	11 (1767-71)	329
* Harleston, John (Junr)	20 (1783-86)	225
Harleston, John	25 (1793-1800)	147
Harleston, Nicholas	11 (1767-71)	317
Harleston, Nicholas, Senr	39 (1826-34)	1063
Harleston, Nicholes [Nicholas]	46 (1851-56)	340

Name	Volume	Page
Harleston, Sarah	35 (1818-26)	569
* Harley, James	20 (1783-86)	275
Harley, Sarah	5 (1740-47)	245
Harrell, Jacob	22 (1786-93)	119
Harrifon see Harrison		
Harrinton, Whitmel	5 (1740-47)	583
Harris, Charles	27 (1793-1800)	710
Harris, Francis	3 (1732-37)	245
Harris, John	1 (1692-93)	24
Harris, Richard	1 (1711-18)	40
Harris, Robert D.	31 (1807-18)	56
* Harris, Sarah	6 (1747-52)	521
Harris, Simpson	19 (1780-83)	325
Harris, Tucker	35 (1818-26)	516
Harris, Tucker (Petition)	35 (1818-26)	575
Harris, Tucker (Petition)	35 (1818-26)	576
Harris, Tucker (Petition)	35 (1818-26)	577
Harris, W. A. I.	50 (1862-68)	434
Harris, William	7 (1752-56)	551
Harris, William	45 (1845-51)	672
Harrison, Carolina	27 (1793-1800)	685
Harrison, Daniel Wheeler	47 (1851-56.)	572
Harrison, Josiah	24 (1786-93)	1100
Harrison, Richard ⌐Harrifon⌐	5 (1740-47)	431
Harrison, Thomas	7 (1752-56)	429
Harrison, William	16 (1774-79)	123
Harrison, William	16 (1774-79)	125
Harrison, William	25 (1793-1800)	249
Harry, David	18 (1776-84)	105
Harry, Joseph	23 (1786-93)	690
Harry, Thomas	38 (1826-34)	424
Hart, Alexander M(oses)	26 (1793-1800)	607
Hart, Arthur	17 (1774-79)	593
Hart, Bella	46 (1851-56)	21

Name	Volume	Page
Hart, Daniel	31 (1807-18)	441
Hart, Hamelton	37 (1826-34)	142
Hart, Hymon (Hyman)	24 (1786-93)	946
Hart, Moses Hart	25 (1793-1800)	317
Hart, Philip	26 (1793-1800)	397
Hart, Solomon	30 (1800-07)	863
Hartee, Elijah	12 (1767-71)	390
Hartley, George Harland	24 (1786-93)	1086
Hartley, James	8 (1757-60)	339
*Hartley, Thomas	15 (1771-74)	443
Hartly, Henry	11 (1767-71)	295
Hartman, John	20 (1783-86)	406
Hartman, John	27 (1793-1800)	739
Hartman, Justus	42 (1839-45)	24
Hartman, Ruth	11 (1767-71)	144
Hartman, Sarah	16 (1774-79)	141
Hartman, William	22 (1786-93)	303
Harvey, Arnold	10 (1760-67)	526
Harvey, Arnold	40 (1834-39)	144
Harvey, Benjamin	7 (1752-56)	520
Harvey, Benjamin	9 (1760-67)	309
Harvey, Benjamin	32 (1807-18)	805
Harvey, Catharine (Thornhill)	39 (1826-34)	864
Harvey, Childermas	12 (1767-71)	478
Harvey, Dorcas	28 (1800-07)	350
Harvey, Edward	44 (1845-51)	200
Harvey, Elizabeth	17 (1774-79)	525
Harvey, Elizabeth	31 (1807-18)	118
Harvey, Elizabeth	32 (1807-18)	808
Harvey, Isabella	48 (1856-62)	40
Harvey, John	24 (1786-93)	800
Harvey, John	35 (1818-26)	806
Harvey, John A.	50 (1862-68)	98
Harvey, Josiah R.	41 (1834-39)	832

Name	Volume	Page
Harvey, Martha	46 (1851-56)	45
Harvey, Mary	4 (1736-40)	283
Harvey, Thomas	22 (1786-93)	69
Harvey, William	11 (1767-71)	161
Harvey, William	20 (1783-86)	377
Harward, Martha	4 (1736-40)	276
* Hasell, Andrew	9 (1760-67)	416
Hasell, Andrew	23 (1786-93)	538
Hasell, Andrew	35 (1818-26)	571
Hasell, Elizabeth	25 (1793-1800)	225
Hasell, John	7 (1752-56)	48
Hasell, Sarah	30 (1800-07)	792
Hasell, Thomas	5 (1740-47)	361
Hasell, Thomas [Hafsell, Hafell]	7 (1752-56)	556
Haselwood, Hannah	14 (1771-74)	319
Hasfort, Joseph	6 (1747-52)	100
Hasfort, Joseph	15 (1771-74)	561
Haskell, Elnathan	37 (1826-34)	8
Haskins, Benoney Peter	14 (1771-74)	51
Haskins, James Benoni Peter	29 (1800-07)	636
Haskins, Peter	10 (1760-67)	857
Haslett, John	41 (1834-39)	928
Hatch, Mary M.	45 (1845-51)	883
Hatch, Robert	32 (1807-18)	770
Hatcher, James	18 (1776-84)	270
Hatcher, Thomas	48 (1856-62)	82
Hatfield, Sarah	33 (1807-18)	1105
Hatley, Roger Peter Handasyde	15 (1771-74)	368
Hatt, James F.	48 (1856-62)	173
Hatter, Elizabeth	19 (1780-83)	365
Hatter, Elizabeth Blanch	33 (1807-18)	1342
Hatter, John	22 (1786-93)	362
Hatton, William	3 (1732-37)	211
Hauck, Mary	39 (1826-34)	1239

Name	Volume	Page
Hawkes, Moses	3 (1732-37)	286
Hawkins, Edward	18 (1776-84)	115
Hawkins, Phillip [Philip]	21 (1783-86)	436
Hawkins, Robert	18 (1776-84)	201
Hay, John	3 (1732-37)	73
Hay, Peter	14 (1771-74)	43
Hay, Susannah	14 (1771-74)	191
Hayden, Jane	42 (1839-45)	61
Haydon, John	7 (1752-56)	337
Haydon, Thomas	2 (1729-31)	70
Hayes, Charles	4 (1736-40)	20
Hayes, John	3 (1732-37)	69
Hayes, John	8 (1757-60)	508
Hayn see Haynes		
Hayne, Anna P.	48 (1856-62)	162
Hayne, Arthur P.	51 (1862-68)	630
Hayne, Elizabeth	42 (1839-45)	362
Hayne, Isaac	6 (1747-52)	593
Hayne, Isaac	20 (1783-86)	46
Hayne, Rebecca Brewton	50 (1862-68)	76
Hayne, Robert Y.	42 (1839-45)	42
Hayne, Sarah	25 (1793-1800)	80
Hayne, Sarah	47 (1851-56)	574
Hayne, Susan S.	51 (1862-68)	808
Hayne, William A.	42 (1839-45)	269
Hayne, William Edward	43 (1839-45)	820
Haynes, John	4 (1736-40)	259
Haynes, Mathew [Hayn, Matthew]	4 (1736-40)	304
*Haynes, Nicholas	6 (1747-52)	1
Haynesworth, Richard [Hainsworth, Haynsworth]	9 (1760-67)	245
Haynsworth see Haynesworth		
Hayward, Samuel	35 (1818-26)	558
Hazard, William	48 (1856-62)	57

Name	Volume	Page
Hazelton, Richard, Junior	23 (1786-93)	551
Hazzard, William	8 (1757-60)	53
Healy, John	29 (1800-07)	735
Heape, Mary Ann	17 (1774-79)	629
Heard, John (Senr)	17 (1774-79)	640
✝Hearne, Andrew	21 (1783-86)	836
Hearne, John	5 (1740-47)	435
Hearne, John	21 (1783-86)	687
Hearne, John	22 (1786-93)	197
Heath, Henrietta	51 (1862-68)	682
Heath, John D.	45 (1845-51)	500
Heathly, William	5 (1740-47)	199
Hebberd, Martin	25 (1793-1800)	244
Hedley, John Lucius [Lucuis]	47 (1851-56)	546
Heffing, Henry	28 (1800-07)	45
Hefseling, Jouwke Henderick	27 (1793-1800)	857
Heiert see Heirert		
Heigler, Nicholas	17 (1774-79)	620
Heilbron, Harriet	46 (1851-56)	382
Heilbron, James	41 (1834-39)	934
Heilbron, James	49 (1856-62)	976
Heirert, Michael [Heiert]	14 (1771-74)	171
Heitt, Anthony [Hiett]	11 (1767-71)	19
Heitt, Robert	11 (1767-71)	280
Heixt, Elizabeth	23 (1786-93)	512
Helfrid, Ann	36 (1818-26)	988
Hendcock, Elizabeth	27 (1793-1800)	842
Henderson, David	14 (1771-74)	80
Henderson, James	15 (1771-74)	485
Henderson, John	6 (1747-52)	473
Henderson, Robert	31 (1807-18)	64
Henderson, Robert Pierie [Peirie, Peiru]	8 (1757-60)	20
Henderson, William	22 (1786-93)	264
Henderson, William Harcourt	6 (1747-52)	540

Name	volume	Page
Hendlen, Thomas	25 (1793-1800)	143
Hendrick, James	8 (1757-60)	88
Hendrick, John	3 (1732-37)	243
Hendrick, William	6 (1747-52)	251
Hendrickson see Henrickson		
Hendrie, Andrew	10 (1760-67)	753
Hennesy, Thomas ⌜Hennessy⌝	49 (1856-62)	858
Henning, Grace	16 (1774-79)	170
Henri, Marguerite Jean	15 (1771-74)	553
Henrickson, Betje	37 (1826-34)	163
Henrickson, Jacob⌜Hendrickson⌝	25 (1793-1800)	219
Henry, Amelia	36 (1818-26)	1134
Henry, Archibald	8 (1757-60)	427
Henry, George	41 (1834-39)	638
Henry, John	31 (1807-18)	215
Henry, Judith J.	40 (1834-39)	364
Henry, Peter	25 (1793-1800)	211
Henry, R.F.	44 (1845-51)	343
Henshaw, Vivion	40 (1834-39)	451
Henvill, Richard	8 (1757-60)	314
Henzey, Bigoe D.	31 (1807-18)	417
Hepburn, Susannah	33 (1807-18)	1122
Hepworth, Thomas	2 (1727-29)	50
Herbert see Harbert		
Herbet, Phoebe	51 (1862-68)	868
Herckenrath, Leonardus Johannis	51 (1862-68)	443
Hericks, Anna Catharina	26 (1793-1800)	532
Heringdine, Siles	13 (1767-71)	765
Heriot, Benjamin D.	50 (1862-68)	257
Heriot, Eliza F.	51 (1862-68)	765
Herman, Henry	35 (1818-26)	458
Hernandes, Rafel	27 (1793-1800)	968
Herren, Stephen	46 (1851-56)	151
Herring, Esther	32 (1807-18)	653

Name	volume	Page
Hertz, Hendel Moses	42 (1839-45)	187
Hesket, Mary	11 (1767-71)	64
Hesket see also Heskett		
Heskett, George [Hesket]	5 (1740-47)	684
Heskett, John	19 (1780-83)	214
*Heskett, Joseph	6 (1747-52)	456
Heskett, Martha	21 (1783-86)	437
Heslpp, Thomas [Hislop]	5 (1740-47)	426
Heulan, John James	39 (1826-34)	993
Hevey, Frances	50 (1862-68)	308
Hewett, Sussanah	33 (1807-18)	1417
Hewett see also Hewitt		
Hewitt, Sarah [Hewett, Jackson]	46 (1851-56)	277
Hewitt, Thomas	41 (1834-39)	644
Hewitt, William	9 (1760-67)	358
Hext, Alexander	5 (1740-47)	23
Hext, Alexander	13 (1767-71)	951
Hext, Amias	1 (1722-24)	71
Hext, David	7 (1752-56)	265
Hext, David	8 (1757-60)	381
Hext, Edward	5 (1740-47)	82
Hext, Edward	12 (1767-71)	344
Hext, Francis [Ffrancis]	5 (1740-47)	539
Hext, Francis [Ffrancis]	5 (1740-47)	578
Hext, George	8 (1757-60)	540
Hext, Hugh	3 (1732-37)	12
Hext, Hugh	5 (1740-47)	355
Hext, John	5 (1740-47)	100
Hext, John	22 (1786-93)	60
Hext, Joseph	7 (1752-56)	366
Hext, Sarah	7 (1752-56)	320
Hext, Thomas	11 (1767-71)	193
Hext, Thomas	24 (1786-93)	893
Hext, Thomas	34 (1818-26)	157

137

Name	volume	Page
Hext, William	7 (1752-56)	189
Hext, William	23 (1786-93)	744
Heyward, Alice S.	50 (1862-68)	168
Heyward, Charles	51 (1862-68)	481
Heyward, Daniel	17 (1774-79)	690
Heyward, Elizabeth	22 (1786-93)	276
Heyward, Hannah	38 (1826-34)	542
Heyward, Hannah (Substitution of Trustee)	41 (1834-39)	597
Heyward, James	9 (1760-67)	112
Heyward, James	26 (1793-1800)	567
Heyward, Jane V(anderhorst)	48 (1856-62)	519
Heyward, John	15 (1771-74)	447
Heyward, John	34 (1818-26)	347
Heyward, Maria Louisa	46 (1851-56)	395
Heyward, Nathaniel	45 (1845-51)	823
Heyward, Nathaniel (Substitution of Trustee)	45 (1845-51)	904
Heyward, Thomas	5 (1740-47)	243
Heyward, William C.	50 (1862-68)	139
Heywood, Henry	7 (1752-56)	376
Hibben, Andrew	21 (1783-86)	468
Hibben, James	40 (1834-39)	160
Hibben, James (Substitution of Trustee)	45 (1845-51)	836
Hichborn, Elizabeth [Eliza]	34 (1818-26)	251
Hickey, Catherine	29 (1800-07)	693
Hickin, J.	3 (1731-33)	75
Hickman, Joshua	41 (1834-39)	649
Hicks, George	9 (1760-67)	287
Hicks, John	34 (1818-26)	190
Hicks, Robert	10 (1760-67)	715
Hier, Barbare [Barbary]	26 (1793-1800)	379
Hiet, Robert	6 (1747-52)	340
Hiett see Heitt		

Name	Volume	Page
Hill, Asa	31 (1807-18)	278
*Hill., Charles	6 (1747-52)	566
Hill, Duncan	27 (1793-1800)	846
Hill, Elizabeth	28 (1800-07)	288
Hill, Francis	20 (1783-86)	236
Hill, Henry Duncan	34 (1818-26)	260
Hill, John	2 (1729-31)	17
Hill, John	7 (1752-56)	249
Hill, John	47 (1851-56)	866
Hill, Mary	43 (1839-45)	544
Hill, Richard	5 (1740-47)	649
Hillbrun, Thomas [Hillburn]	10 (1760-67)	623
Hillburn see Hillbrun		
Hilliard, James	6 (1747-52)	240
Hillman, Ann	42 (1839-45)	386
Hilson, John	49 (1856-62)	595
Hilton, Dowson	18 (1776-84)	29
Hilton, Nathaniel	48 (1856-62)	377
Himeli, Bartholomew Henry	23 (1786-93)	493
Hinchy, Michael (Nuncupative)	46 (1851-56)	269
Hinckley, William	19 (1780-83)	10
*Hinckley, William	20 (1783-86)	240
Hinds, Patrick	27 (1793-1800)	697
Hinds, Thomas	33 (1807-18)	1165
Hines, David	39 (1826-34)	858
Hinson, Benjamin	1 (1711-18)	36
Hinson, Susan	48 (1856-62)	478
Hippers, Peter	31 (1807-18)	281
Hippolite, Paul	31 (1807-18)	452
Hirschinger, John	6 (1747-52)	651
Hisfort, Joseph	12 (1767-71)	590
Hisfort, Joseph	13 (1767-71)	725
Hislop see Heslpp		
Hix, Joseph	40 (1834-39)	320

Name	Volume	Page
Hixt, Joseph	21 (1783-86)	576
Hoats, Michael	24 (1786-93)	1008
Hobson, Joshua	1 (1692-93)	12
Hodge, Sarah	14 (1771-74)	154
Hodges, Henry	8 (1757-60)	156
* Hodges, Richard	6 (1747-52)	652
Hodgson, Elizabeth	48 (1856-62)	455
Hodgson, Mary	29 (1800-07)	641
Hodsden, John	18 (1776-84)	69
Hodson, Thomas [Hoffon]	8 (1757-60)	250
Hoff, Philip	46 (1851-56)	75
Hoffon see Hodson		
Hogg, Alexander	30 (1800-07)	857
Hogg, George, Sr.	11 (1767-71)	208
Hogg, George	14 (1771-74)	110
Hogg, John	8 (1757-60)	321
Hohn, Charles F.	40 (1834-39)	222
Holbeatch, Joseph	1 (1720-21)	53
Holbrook, Harriott Pinckney	50 (1862-68)	151
Holder, Mary	17 (1774-79)	634
Holiday, Charles	3 (1731-33)	57
Holiday, William	19 (1780-83)	174
Holiday, William	20 (1783-86)	207
Holland, Jane	41 (1834-39)	904
Holland, John	36 (1818-26)	935
Holland, John, Senr	41 (1834-39)	907
Hollensbee, James	36 (1818-26)	1044
Holley see Holly		
Holliday, Elizabeth	5 (1740-47)	335
Holliday, Giles	4 (1736-40)	128
Hollingsbee see Hollingsby		
Hollingsby, Elizabeth [Hollinsbee; Hollingsbee]	33 (1807-18)	1013
Hollingsworth, Elizabeth	15 (1771-74)	396
Hollingsworth, Samuel	7 (1752-56)	216

Name	Volume	Page
Hollinsbee, George W.	38 (1826-34	541
Hollinsbee see also Hollingsby		
Hollinshead, Sarah	34 (1818-26)	394
Hollinshead, William	33 (1807-18)	1227
Hollinshed, Zachariah ⌐Sachariah⌐	15 (1771-74)	650
Holloway, Richard	43 (1839-45)	891
Holly, John ⌐Holley⌐	47 (1851-56)	451
Hollybush, Elizabeth	12 (1767-71)	645
Hollybush, John	1 (1721-22)	47
Hollybush, John	6 (1747-52)	363
Hollybush, Sarah	10 (1760-67)	705
Holman, Conrad	14 (1771-74)	188
Holman, John	24 (1786-93)	908
Holman, John	24 (1786-93)	1076
Holman, John	36 (1818-26)	920
Holman, Mary	27 (1793-1800)	788
Holman, Thomas	2 (1729-31)	60
Holman, Thomas	7 (1752-56)	478
Holman, Thomas	15 (1771-74)	668
Holmes, Andrew	31 (1807-18)	1
Holmes, Ann Eliza Legare	48 (1856-62)	107
Holmes, Anna Maria	49 (1856-62)	544
Holmes, Daniel	21 (1783-86)	577
Holmes, Edgar H.	50 (1862-68)	203
Holmes, Eliza C.	46 (1851-56)	85
Holmes, Elizabeth	15 (1771-74)	454
Holmes, Elizabeth	32 (1807-18)	585
Holmes, Elizabeth	41 (1834-39)	521
Holmes, Elizabeth Elliott	31 (1807-18)	127
Holmes, Elizabeth O.	34 (1818-26)	215
Holmes, Francis	2 (1726-27)	4
Holmes, Francis	2 (1727-29)	58
Holmes, Harriet A.	38 (1826-34)	664
Holmes, Henry M.	46 (1851-56)	396

Name	Volume	Page
Holmes, Isaac	6 (1747-52)	583
Holmes, Isaac	8 (1757-60)	386
* Holmes, Isaac	9 (1760-67)	424
Holmes, Isaac Edward	51 (1862-68)	655
Holmes, James	34 (1818-26)	354
Holmes, James F.	36 (1818-26)	1227
Holmes, John	21 (1783-86)	760
Holmes, John (Senior)	25 (1793-1800)	238
Holmes, John	30 (1800-07)	820
Holmes, John	35 (1818-26)	504
Holmes, John	36 (1818-26)	902
Holmes, John L.	48 (1856-62)	516
Holmes, Joseph Bee	36 (1818-26)	991
Holmes, Mary B.	44 (1845-51)	330
Holmes, Peter	25 (1793-1800)	54
Holmes, Ralph	6 (1747-52)	207
Holmes, Ralph	26 (1793-1800)	479
Holmes, Rebecca	49 (1856-62)	1032
Holmes, Thomas	18 (1776-84)	207
Holmes, William	2 (1724-25)	50
Holmes, William	4 (1736-40)	109
Holmes, William	4 (1736-40)	269
Holmes, William	19 (1780-83)	106
Holmes, William A.	40 (1834-39)	373
Holson, Christopher	17 (1774-79)	777
Holton, Margaret Sharps	49 (1856-62)	1049
Holzendorf, Frederick	7 (1752-56)	157
Holzendorf, Rosanna [Holzendorff]	9 (1760-67)	145
Holzendorff see Holzendorf		
Homafsel, Charles	30 (1800-07)	102"
Hood, Catherine	13 (1767-71)	958
Hood, Robin	44 (1845-51)	18
Hood, Thomas Clarke	48 (1856-62)	46
Hook, Conrod	30 (1800-07)	814
Hooper, David	32 (1807-18)	901

Name	volume	Page
Horry, Elias	40 (1834-39)	88
Horry, Elias L. (Codicil)	39 (1826-34)	862
Horry, Elias L. (Codicil)	39 (1826-34)	873
Horry, Elias Lynch	39 (1826-34)	854
Horry, Elizabeth	21 (1783-86)	676
Horry, Harriott	38 (1826-34)	809
Horry, John	13 (1767-71)	793
Horry, Jonah	32 (1807-18)	613
Horry, Lucretia	40 (1834-39)	305
Horry, Mary S.	46 (1851-56)	54
Horry, Peter [Horrey]	4 (1736-40)	257
Horry, Pickney [Pinckney]	37 (1826-34)	385
Horry, Thomas	34 (1818-26)	241
Horsburgh, William	9 (1760-67)	161
Horsey, Miranda W.	49 (1856-62)	770
Horsey, Thomas	29 (1800-07)	485
Hort, Benjamin S.	36 (1818-26)	1166
Hort, Robert Smith	37 (1826-34)	148
Hort, Sarah Mary	43 (1839-45)	582
Hort, Sarah Mary (Substitution of Trustee)	43 (1839-45)	715
Hort, Sarah Rutledge	50 (1862-68)	328
Hort, William	36 (1818-26)	1231
Hort, William C.	34 (1818-26)	245
Horton, Thomas A.P.	51 (1862-68)	726
Hoster, Edmond	27 (1793-1800)	945
Houfer see Houser		
Houghf, Daniel	45 (1845-51)	652
Houghton, John	5 (1740-47)	336
Houghton, John	8 (1758-63)	8
Houlton, Jas.	32 (1807-18)	728
House, John	19 (1780-83)	142
House, John	20 (1783-86)	277
Houser, Henry [Houfer]	2 (1726-27)	20
How, Henry	23 (1786-93)	657

Name	Volume	Page
How, Thomas	40 (1834-39)	79
Howard, Henry M.	48 (1856-62)	303
Howard, Joseph	16 (1774-79)	348
Howard, Joseph L.	51 (1862-68)	608
Howard, Rachel	12 (1767-71)	591
Howard, Robert	16 (1774-79)	361
Howard, Robert	17 (1774-79)	465
Howard, Robert	27 (1793-1800)	831
Howard, Thomas	47 (1851-56)	674
Howe, Mary	41 (1834-39)	598
Howell, Arthur	7 (1752-56)	80
Howell, John	17 (1774-79)	804
Howell, (John) Thomas	8 (1757-60)	501
Howell, William	8 (1757-60)	74
Hoy, Daniel	21 (1783-86)	490
Hoyland, Anna Maria	33 (1807-18)	1027
Hoyler, Michael	15 (1771-74)	435
Huard, Stanislas	41 (1834-39)	823
Hubbard, J. E.	47 (1851-56)	644
Hubbard, Thomas (Hubburd)	1 (1687-1710)	47
Hubburd see Hubbard		
Hutchinson, John	11 (1767-71)	283
Huddy, Charles	3 (1731-33)	73
Hudson, William	22 (1786-93)	271
Hues, Patrick	27 (1793-1800)	880
Huff, Abbygail	37 (1826-34)	370
Huff, Samuel	33 (1807-18)	1200
Hufman, Daniel	50 (1862-68)	349
Huger, Ann	40 (1834-39)	240
Huger, Anna H.	42 (1839-45)	72
Huger, Binkey	28 (1800-07)	238
Huger, Carlos ⌐Charlos⌐	35 (1818-26)	438
Huger, Charlotte	41 (1834-39)	493
Huger, Daniel	7 (1752-56)	271

Name	Volume	Page
Huger, Daniel	27 (1793-1800)	972
Huger, Daniel	48 (1856-62)	369
Huger, Daniel E.	47 (1851-56)	474
Huger, Elizabeth ₍Eliza₎	37 (1826-34)	360
Huger, Francis	28 (1800-07)	161
Huger, Francis	45 (1845-51)	498
Huger, Francis Kinloch	47 (1851-56)	559
Huger, Isabella Johannes (M)	51 (1862-68)	458
Huger, John	29 (1800-07)	589
Huger, John	46 (1851-56)	272
Huger, John (Substitution of Trustee)	46 (1851-56)	394
Huger, John (Order)	46 (1851-56)	399
Huger, Martha	34 (1818-26)	150
Huger, Mary	41 (1834-39)	791
Huger, Sarah	39 (1826-34)	1006
Huget, (Widow) Mary ₍Huguet₎	40 (1834-39)	417
Huggins, Eli	30 (1800-07)	831
Huggins, George	15 (1771-74)	676
Huggins, Hester	35 (1818-26)	490
Huggins, Jacob Bonhost	35 (1818-26)	492
Huggins, John	5 (1740-47)	200
Huggins, Joseph	9 (1760-67)	237
Huggins, William	40 (1834-39)	380
Hughes, Beulah	45 (1845-51)	820
Hughes, Caleb ₍Hughs₎	27 (1793-1800)	835
Hughes, Edward	14 (1771-74)	296
Hughes, Henry	21 (1783-86)	710
Hughes, John	20 (1783-86)	88
Hughes, Mary	7 (1752-56)	214
Hughes, Richard	1 (1711-18)	25
Hughes, Sarah	26 (1793-1800)	378
Hughes, Thomas	22 (1786-93)	228
Hughs, Caleb	27 (1793-1800)	792
Hughs, Thomas	8 (1757-60)	270

Name	Volume	Page
Hughs see also Hughes		
Huguenin, Anna M. (Order)	48 (1856-62)	247
Huguenin, Anna Maria	46 (1851-56)	385
Huguet see Huget		
Hull, Samuel J.	51 (1862-68)	499
Hull, William	15 (1771-74)	545
Humbert, David	12 (1767-71)	524
Humbert, Elizabeth	35 (1818-26)	675
Hume, Alexander	44 (1845-51)	349
Hume, John	42 (1839-45)	268
Hume, Peter	5 (1740-47)	600
Hume, Robert	4 (1736-40)	46
Hume, Robert	10 (1760-67)	816
Hume, Thomas M.	49 (1856-62)	812
Humphrey, William	16 (1774-79)	351
Humphreys, Benjamin	28 (1800-07)	127
Humphreys, John [Humphrys]	21 (1783-86)	651
Humphreys, Mary B.	50 (1862-68)	7
Humphreys see also Humphris		
Humphris, David [Humphreys]	21 (1783-86)	442
Humphryes, Thomas	21 (1783-86)	708
Humphrys, Ann	24 (1786-93)	791
Humphrys see also Humphreys		
Humpt, Christopher	28 (1800-07)	274
Hunfcome see Hanscome		
Hunt, Benjamin F(aneuel)	47 (1851-56)	626
Hunt, Daniel	3 (1732-37)	101
Hunt, Daniel	9 (1760-67)	302
Hunt, Elizabeth	11 (1767-71)	119
Hunt, George Bethune	48 (1856-62)	390
Hunt, Hannah	39 (1826-34)	1070
Hunt, Joseph	12 (1767-71)	606
Hunt, Joseph	35 (1818-26)	631
Hunt, Robert	7 (1752-56)	527

Name	volume	Page
Hunt, Thomas	38 (1826-34)	812
Hunt, William M.	50 (1862-68)	420
Hunter, (Of Mortimer Berks Baronet), Sir Claudius Stephen	46 (1851-56)	404
Hunter, George	7 (1752-56)	356
Hunter, James	15 (1771-74)	656
* Hunter, James	21 (1783-86)	587
Hunter, John	44 (1845-51)	138
Hunter, Joseph	6 (1747-52)	232
Hunter, Margaret	41 (1834-39)	674
Hunter, Margaret	41 (1834-39)	789
Hunter, Mary	11 (1767-71)	291
Hunter, William	10 (1760-67)	738
Hurd, Sarah	44 (1845-51)	192
Hurly, John	23 (1786-93)	682
Hurst, James	31 (1807-18)	320
Hurst, Joseph	8 (1757-60)	265
Hurst, Robert	25 (1793-1800)	12
Husemeyer, William	44 (1845-51)	8
Huston, James	34 (1818-26)	219
Hutchins, Elizabeth	16 (1774-79)	14
Hutchins, John	7 (1752-56)	283
Hutchins, Nathaniel	2 (1729-31)	9
Hutchinson, Ann	32 (1807-18)	622
Hutchinson, Elizabeth Love	40 (1834-39)	26
Hutchinson, Esther	35 (1818-26)	574
Hutchinson, James	5 (1740-47)	399
Hutchinson, (Doctor) John	2 (G1729-31)	43
Hutchinson, John	8 (1757-60)	310
Hutchinson, John Elias	24 (1786-93)	811
Hutchinson, Lydia	47 (1851-56)	848
Hutchinson, Mary	35 (1818-26)	460
Hutchinson, Providence	7 (1752-56)	468
Hutchinson, Ribton	8 (1757-60)	84
Hutchinson, Sarah	42 (1839-45)	40

Name	Volume	Page
Hutchinson, Thomas	20 (1783-86)	318
Hutchinson, Thomas	23 (1786-93)	757
Hutchinson, Thomas, Junr.	24 (1786-93)	826
Hutchinson, William	4 (1736-40)	177
Hutchinson, William	8 (1757-60)	34
Hutson, Richard	26 (1793-1800)	433
Hutson, Timothy	48 (1856-62)	157
Hutson, William	9 (1760-67)	117
Hutson, William	51 (1862-68)	836
Hutton, James	36 (1818-26)	1010
Huxford, Harlock	35 (1818-26)	738
Huxley, William	2 (1727-29)	48
Hyams, Caroline	48 (1856-62)	202
Hyams, Moses D.	51 (1862-68)	842
Hyams, Soloman	41 (1834-39)	635
Hyrne, Burrell M.	13 (1767-71)	880
✳ Hyrne, Henry	9 (1760-67)	432
Hyrne, Henry	21 (1783-86)	660
Hyrne, Mary	26 (1793-1800)	335
Hyrne, Peter Girardeau	24 (1786-93)	1014

I

Name	Volume	Page
Icarden, Louis Marie	39 (1826-34)	1236
Imer, David Lewis	19 (1780-83)	158
Imer, Frederick	13 (1767-71)	1034
Inabnet, John	15 (1771-74)	602
Inglesby, Mary E.	46 (1851-56)	165
Inglesby, William	40 (1834-39)	308
Inglesby, William H.	51 (1862-68)	731
Inglis, Alexander	24 (1786-93)	852
Inglis, Alexander	32 (1807-18)	830
Inglis, Martha Sophia	43 (1839-45)	633
Inglis, Thomas	40 (1834-39)	288
Ingraham, Louisa	45 (1845-51)	585

Name	Volume	Page
Innes, John	44 (1845-51)	14
Innes, Nathaniel	7 (1752-56)	445
Ioens, Rebekah [Joens]	22 (1786-93)	223
I'on, Jacob Bond	26 (1793-1800)	523
I'on, Jacob Bond	48 (1856-62)	496
Irby, Edmund	9 (1760-67)	310
Ireland, Elizabeth	3 (1732-37)	46
Irvin, John	14 (1771-74)	181
Irvine, M.	37 (1826-34)	300
Irvine, Mary	37 (1826-34)	377
Irvine, Moses	44 (1845-51)	383
Irving, George	31 (1807-18)	60
Irving, James	30 (1800-07)	1083
Irving, John Beaufin	32 (1807-18)	767
Irwin, Ann	4 (1736-40)	196
Isaac, Solomon [Isaacs]	8 (1757-60)	14
Isaacs, Abraham M.	32 (1807-18)	845
Isaacs, Samuel	29 (1800-07)	698
Isaacs see also Isaac		
Isack, Abraham	1 (1687-1710)	54
Isnard, Claudius	5 (1740-47)	121
Ives, Mary A.	44 (1845-51)	307
Izard, Alice	39 (1826-34)	1025
Izard, Charles	5 (1740-47)	319
Izard, Charlotte	28 (1800-07)	184
Izard, Claudia S.	47 (1851-56)	671
Izard, Eliza Lucas	45 (1845-51)	874
Izard, Elizabeth	36 (1818-26)	1193
Izard, Esther	34 (1818-26)	159
Izard, George	39 (1826-34)	1121
Izard, John	7 (1752-56)	174
Izard, John (Substitution of Trustee)	19 (1780-83)	42
Izard, Joseph	5 (1740-47)	422
Izard, Julianna	51 (1862-68)	869

Name	volume	Page
Izard, Magdalen Elizabeth ⌜Magdalane⌝	5 (1740-47)	606
Izard, Ralph	1 (1722-24)	73
Izard, Ralph	5 (1740-47)	225
Izard, Ralph	9 (1760-67)	64
Izard, Ralph	29 (1800-07)	656
Izard, Thomas	7 (1752-56)	172
*Izard, Walter	6 (1747-52)	410
Izard, Walter	22 (1786-93)	310

J

Name	volume	Page
Jacks, Ann	45 (1845-51)	712
Jacks, James	35 (1818-26)	782
Jackson, Abraham	22 (1786-93)	67
Jackson, George Sen[r]	49 (1856-62)	878
Jackson, Henry	4 (1736-40)	174
Jackson, Henry	11 (1767-71)	86
Jackson, Capt. John	2 (1724-25)	29
Jackson, John	6 (1747-52)	61
Jackson, John	33 (1807-18)	1331
Jackson, Joseph	21 (1783-86)	559
Jackson, Mary Ann	48 (1856-62)	14
Jackson, Rebecca	42 (1839-45)	222
Jackson, Reginald	6 (1747-52)	458
Jackson, Richard	2 (1727-29)	43
Jackson, Samuel	48 (1856-62)	294
Jackson, Samuell	1 (1692-93)	13
Jackson, Sarah ⌜Hewett, Hewitt⌝	46 (1851-56)	277
Jackson, Tilman M.	49 (1856-62)	759
Jackson, William	8 (1757-60)	487
Jackson, William	33 (1807-18)	1397
Jackson, William	37 (1826-34)	7
Jacobs, Hyman	41 (1834-39)	819
Jacobs, Jacob	26 (1793-1800)	640
Jacobs, Moses	42 (1839-45)	366

Name	volume	Page
Jacobson, Christopher	30 (1800-07)	1031
Jacoby, George	41 (1834-39)	801
Jager, Hans ₍Haris₎	47 (1851-56)	582
Jager, Haris see Jager, Hans		
James, Elizabeth	31 (1807-18)	367
James, Howel	15 (1771-74)	463
James, James	13 (1767-71)	769
James, John	18 (1776-84)	77
James, Mildred	40 (1834-39)	112
James, Shearwood	10 (1760-67)	542
James, William	6 (1747-52)	479
James, William	15 (1771-74)	470
Jameson, William	10 (1760-67)	793
Jamieson, James	14 (1771-74)	333
Jandon, Elias	6 (1747-52)	491
Janneret, Abraham	5 (1740-47)	329
Janvir, Lewis	6 (1747-52)	66
Jarman, John	34 (1818-26)	248
Jarvis, Rebecco	9 (1760-67)	329
Jaudon, Elijah see Jaudon, Elizah		
Jaudon, Elisha	16 (1774-79)	338
Jaudon, Elizabeth	5 (1740-47)	310
Jaudon, Elizah ₍Elijah₎	35 (1818-26)	595
Jaudon, James	31 (1807-18)	292
Jaudon, John	31 (1807-18)	99
Jaudon, Paul	16 (1774-79)	46
Javain, Peter	43 (1839-45)	591
Jay, William	16 (1774-79)	34
Jeanerett see Jeannerett		
Jeanes, Michael	8 (1757-60)	486
Jeanneret, Henry Jacob	10 (1760-67)	661
Jeanneret, John	16 (1774-79)	268
Jeannerett, Elizabeth ₍Jeanerett₎	43 (1839-45)	897
Jeannerett, Henry Fredrick	17 (1774-79)	657

Name	volume	Page
Jeannerett, John Jennings	35 (1818-26)	809
Jeannerett, Mary	24 (1786-93)	1104
Jeffereys see Jefferyes		
Jefferyes, David [Jeffereys]	11 (1767-71)	148
Jeffords, Ann S.	45 (1845-51)	537
Jeffords, Charles M.	44 (1845-51)	9
Jeffords, Daniel, Senr.	27 (1793-1800)	702
Jeffords, Daniel, Junior	30 (1800-07)	942
Jeffords, John	6 (1747-52)	601
Jeffords, John	20 (1783-86)	50
Jefse, Sarah	31 (1807-18)	128
Jefsup, Hannah	24 (1786-93)	1058
*Jehne, August	9 (1760-67)	398
Jehne, Elizabeth	10 (1760-67)	806
Jenings, Mary Margaret	34 (1818-26)	352
Jenings, Raymond	21 (1783-86)	815
Jenins, James	8 (1757-60)	208
Jenkins, Benjamin	19 (1780-83)	337
Jenkins, Benjamin	37 (1826-34)	194
Jenkins, Catherine C.	50 (1862-68)	343
Jenkins, Christopher	16 (1774-79)	17
Jenkins, Christopher	25 (1793-1800)	130
Jenkins, Christopher	38 (1826-34)	780
Jenkins, Daniel (Sr.)	28 (1800-07)	109
Jenkins, Eliza	34 (1818-26)	237
Jenkins, Henrietta Theus	45 (1845-51)	534
Jenkins, John T.	37 (1826-34)	140
Jenkins, Joseph	13 (1767-71)	937
Jenkins, Martha	42 (1839-45)	434
Jenkins, Micah	38 (1826-34)	693
* Jenkins, Richard	14 (1771-74)	337
Jenkins, Richard	36 (1818-26)	925
Jenkins, Robert S.	41 (1834-39)	618
Jenkins, Sarah	16 (1774-79)	103

Name	volume	Page
Jenkins, Susanna	35 (1818-26)	532
Jenkins, William	8 (1757-60)	547
Jenkins, William	13 (1767-71)	906
Jenkins, William S.	32 (1807-18)	824
Jennens, Edward	10 (1760-67)	603
Jennings, Barbara	18 (1776-84)	136
Jennings, Daniel	25 (1793-1800)	86
Jennings, Daniel (Codicil)	25 (1793-1800)	142
Jennings, Elizabeth	32 (1807-18)	490
Jennings, John	18 (1776-84)	257
Jennings, Samuel	6 (1747-52)	427
Jennys, Thomas [Jenys]	5 (1740-47)	440
Jenys, Henrietta	8 (1757-60)	304
Jenys, Paul	4 (1736-40)	178
*Jenys, Paul	6 (1747-52)	623
Jenys see also Jennys		
Jerdon, Abram [Abraham]	8 (1757-60)	303
Jerman, Edward	25 (1793-1800)	76
Jerman, Rebecca A.	45 (1845-51)	841
Jerman, Sarah	36 (1818-26)	1017
Jerman, Thomas Satur	32 (1807-18)	538
Jermon, Edward D.	48 (1856-62)	15
Jernigan, Henry	11 (1767-71)	82
Jervey, James	43 (1839-45)	856
Jervey, James	46 (1851-56)	288
Jervey, P.M.H.	45 (1845-51)	816
Jervey, Thomas H.	44 (1845-51)	30
Jesup, Zadock R.	47 (1851-56)	875
Jevins, Edward	7 (1752-56)	156
Jex, Thomas	3 (1732-37)	320
Jinks, John	9 (1760-67)	243
Jinks, Thomas	6 (1747-52)	239
Joell, Thomas	23 (1786-93)	687
Joens, Rebekah [Ioens]	22 (1786-93)	223

Name	volume	Page
Johnston, Alexander	41 (1834-39)	811
Johnston, Ann	46 (1851-56)	109
Johnston, Charles	29 (1800-07)	614
Johnston, Charlotte	50 (1862-68)	171
Johnston, Dinah	32 (1807-18)	528
Johnston, Edward	37 (1826-34)	152
Johnston, Elizabeth	43 (1839-45)	501
Johnston, James	25 (1793-1800)	196
Johnston, James	42 (1839-45)	119
Johnston, Jane [Johston]	18 (1776-84)	102
Johnston, Jane	31 (1807-18)	72
Johnston, John	4 (1736-40)	202
Johnston, John	5 (1740-47)	322
Johnston, John	23 (1786-93)	606
Johnston, John	38 (1826-34)	731
Johnston, John Wm.	33 (1807-18)	1222
Johnston, Lucinda	45 (1845-51)	806
Johnston, Mary B.	33 (1807-18)	1427
Johnston, Patrick [Johnson]	22 (1786-93)	259
Johnston, Robert	24 (1786-93)	1017
Johnston, Robert	26 (1793-1800)	354
Johnston, Sarah	16 (1774-79)	117
Johnston, William	22 (1786-93)	53
Johnston, William	42 (1839-45)	166
Johston see Johnston		
Johnstone, William	28 (1800-07)	39
*Jolley, Joseph	9 (1760-67)	423
Jones, Abraham	48 (1856-62)	29
Jones, Ann [Anne]	12 (1767-71)	367
Jones, Barnard	40 (1834-39)	363
Jones, Benjamin	8 (1757-60)	452
Jones, Charles	2 (1726-27)	23
Jones, Charles	7 (1752-56)	352
Jones, Christeann C.	46 (1851-56)	309

Name	volume	Page
Jones, Edmund	23 (1786-93)	655
Jones, Elizabeth	48 (1856-62)	55
Jones, Evan	27 (1793-1800)	751
Jones, Evans [Evan]	15 (1771-74)	616
Jones, Francis [Frances, Ffrancis]	1 (1692-93)	17
Jones, Francis	28 (1800-07)	236
Jones, George	23 (1786-93)	661
Jones, Henry	32 (1807-18)	593
Jones, Henry S.	36 (1818-26)	1240
Jones, Isaac	44 (1845-51)	322
Jones, Jefse	23 (1786-93)	548
Jones, Jehu	39 (1826-34)	1172
Jones, John	2 (1729-31)	34
Jones, John	7 (1752-56)	546
Jones, John	9 (1760-67)	356
Jones, John	11 (1767-71)	145
Jones, John	16 (1774-79)	199
Jones, John	40 (1834-39)	394
Jones, John C.	38 (1826-34)	681
Jones, Joseph	33 (1807-18)	1144
Jones, Lewis	5 (1740-47)	367
Jones, Margaret	40 (1834-39)	34
Jones, Mary	40 (1834-39)	278
Jones, Mary	45 (1845-51)	464
Jones, Mary Elizabeth	44 (1845-51)	375
Jones, Mary S.	39 (1826-34)	1017
Jones, Phillip	2 (1727-29)	83
Jones, Phillip [Philip]	9 (1760-67)	282
Jones, Prissilla	6 (1747-52)	621
Jones, Rachel [Rachael]	8 (1757-60)	554
Jones, Rachel [Rachael]	44 (1845-51)	379
Jones, Samuel [Samuell]	2 (1726-27)	45
Jones, Samuel	20 (1783-86)	74
Jones, Samuel	31 (1807-18)	189

Name	Volume	Page
Jones, Samuel B.	33 (1807-18)	975
Jones, Sarah	45 (1845-51)	809
Jones, Sarah B.	50 (1862-68)	337
Jones, Susanna	10 (1760-67)	531
Jones, Thomas	6 (1747-52)	312
Jones, Thomas	9 (1760-67)	93
Jones, Thomas, Sr.	15 (1771-74)	634
Jones, Thomas	18 (1776-84)	263
Jones, Thomas	37 (1826-34)	129
Jones, Thomas L.	39 (1826-34)	904
Jones, William	23 (1786-93)	547
Jones, William	24 (1786-93)	1134
Jones, William	43 (1839-45)	841
Jones, Wiswal	43 (1839-45)	484
Joor, Catharine	21 (1783-86)	658
Joor, Catherine	15 (1771-74)	583
Joor, Cornelia (M)	47 (1851-56)	455
Joor, John	14 (1771-74)	331
Joor, John	24 (1786-93)	804
Joor, Joseph	20 (1783-86)	174
Joor, William	11 (1767-71)	185
Joram, Hannah	3 (1732-37)	86
Jordan, James	14 (1771-74)	220
Jordan, Robert	20 (1783-86)	69
Jordan, William	24 (1786-93)	980
Jordon, Daniel	8 (1757-60)	419
Joseph, Israel	29 (1800-07)	673
Josias, Justine	49 (1856-62)	962
Joulee, Ann	44 (1845-51)	404
Joulee, John	10 (1760-67)	505
Joy, Abraham	28 (1800-07)	340
Joy, Richard	21 (1783-86)	749
Joy, William	15 (1771-74)	461
Joye, Daniel G.	45 (1845-51)	869

Name	volume	Page
Joyeux, Jean Charles	28 (1800-07)	76
Joyner, Rebekah	40 (1834-39)	158
Joyner, Winifred	24 (1786-93)	892
Judge, Charles	49 (1856-62)	996
Jugnot, Charles	48 (1856-62)	158
Jumper, Margaret [Margret]	16 (1774-79)	252
June, Cornel	40 (1834-39)	374
June, John	5 (1740-47)	162
June, John, Sr.	13 (1767-71)	738
June, Josias [Jofias]	2 (1724-25)	87
June, Peter	12 (1767-71)	376
June, Solomon	11 (1767-71)	75
June, Stanley	11 (1767-71)	70
Jurdine, Leonard	14 (1771-74)	242
Just, George	46 (1851-56)	299
Just, Mary Ann [Anne]	46 (1851-56)	136
Justine, (A free black)	32 (1807-18)	831

K

Name	volume	Page
Kaiser, John Jacob	31 (1807-18)	108
Kaiser, Mary C.	33 (1807-18)	990
Kalteisen, Elizabeth	27 (1793-1800)	714
Kalteisen, Michael	31 (1807-18)	18
Kanady, Bryan [Kannady]	6 (1747-52)	334
Kannady see Kanady		
Karwon, Crafton	6 (1747-52)	131
Karwon, Thomas	34 (1818-26)	323
Kavanagh, Hugh	15 (1771-74)	424
Kay, Ann	45 (1845-51)	914
Kean, James	8 (1757-60)	151
Keane, Martin	4 (1736-40)	243
Kearns, Michael [M c Kearns]	32 (1807-18)	596

Name	volume	Page
Keating, Edward	5 (1740-47)	186
Keating, Elizabeth	31 (1807-18)	197
Keating, Maurice	6 (1747-52)	288
Keating, William	31 (1807-18)	47
Keckeley, Conrade	23 (1786-93)	464
Keckeley, George [Keckely]	38 (1826-34)	616
Keckely see Keckeley		
Keeley, Mary G.	50 (1862-68)	212
Keeling, Elizabeth	1 (1692-93)	52
Keeling, George	1 (1692-93)	50
Keen, Thomas	29 (1800-07)	621
Keis, Henry	18 (1776-84)	278
Keith, Alexander	15 (1771-74)	349
Keith, Isaac S., Rev. (Substitution of Trustee)	33 (1807-18)	1234
Keith, Isaac Stockton	32 (1807-18)	758
Keith, Isaac Stockton, Rev. (Substitution of Trustee)	33 (1807-18)	1166
Keith, James	24 (1786-93)	1094
Keith, Jane	45 (1845-51)	479
Keith, Mathew Irvine	48 (1856-62)	111
Keith, William	17 (1774-79)	642
Kellea, Thomas	18 (1776-84)	5
Keller, John Michael	21 (1783-86)	555
Keller, John William [Keller, William]	48 (1856-62)	433
Keller, William see Keller, John William		
Kelley, James	8 (1757-60)	498
Kelley, Mary [Kely]	7 (1752-56)	368
Kelley see also Kelly		
Kelly, Edward [Kelley]	17 (1774-79)	663
Kelly, James	4 (1736-40)	211
Kelly, John	10 (1760-67)	825
Kelly, Mary	42 (1839-45)	81

Name	Volume	Page
Kelly, Patrick C.	32 (1807-18)	944
Kelly, Thomas	46 (1851-56)	60
Kelly, Timothy	21 (1783-86)	514
Kelly, William	17 (1774-79)	785
Kelsall, John	14 (1771-74)	271
Kelsy, Mary	23 (1786-93)	395
Kely see Kelley		
Kelton, Otis H.	49 (1856-62)	768
Kempton, Henrietta	30 (1800-07)	1072
Kennedy, Andrew	28 (1800-07)	345
Kennedy, Dennis	48 (1856-62)	5
Kennedy, Edward	45 (1845-51)	525
Kennedy, James	31 (1807-18)	393
Kennedy, James	37 (1826-34)	100
Kennedy, John	28 (1800-07)	107
Kennedy, Margaret	10 (1760-67)	585
Kennedy, Mathew [Matthew]	20 (1783-86)	343
Kennedy, Matthew [Mathew]	22 (1786-93)	9
Kennedy, Peter	35 (1818-26)	704
Kennedy, William	7 (1752-56)	253
Kennedy, William	41 (1834-39)	840
Kennerly, Thomas	13 (1767-71)	1059
Kenzie see Mc Kenzie		
Keown, Lidia [Lydia]	36 (1818-26)	998
Kerklin, Edward [Kirklin]	13 (1767-71)	740
Kern see Kerns		
Kerns, (J.) Daniel [Kern]	32 (1807-18)	904
Kerr, Alexander	16 (1774-79)	213
Kerr, James	5 (1740-47)	337
Kerr, John	13 (1767-71)	1025
Kershaw, Ann E.	49 (1856-62)	537
Kershaw, Charles	40 (1834-39)	280
Kershaw, Charlotte	37 (1826-34)	196

Name	Volume	Page
Kershaw, Ely	19 (1780-83)	77
Kershaw, Ely	20 (1783-86)	52
Kershaw, Frances R.	42 (1839-45)	248
Kershaw, William	36 (1818-26)	1221
Key, Ann Carlisle	49 (1856-62)	676
Keyes see Keys		
Keys, Hugh [Keyes]	46 (1851-56)	198
Kid, David	3 (1732-37)	110
Kiddell, Arthur [Arther]	47 (1851-56)	853
Kiddell, Benjamin	27 (1793-1800)	676
Kiddell, Rachel	44 (1845-51)	10
Kidgell, Nicholas	2 (1726-27)	13
Killin, James	28 (1800-07)	258
Killingsworth, William (Senr)	9 (1760-67)	288
Killpatrick, David	1 (1721-22)	36
Kilpatrick, Alexander	4 (1736-40)	96
Kilpatrick, Samuel	22 (1786-93)	150
Kimberley, Thomas	4 (1736-40)	24
Kimener, John Martin	14 (1771-74)	161
Kimmell, Mary Agnes	24 (1786-93)	1069
Kimmick, Michael	8 (1757-60)	293
King, Charles	5 (1740-47)	316
✳ King, Dinah	9 (1760-67)	411
King, Elizabeth	39 (1826-34)	876
King, George	2 (1729-31)	32
King, George	33 (1807-18)	1198
King, Hartwell	19 (1780-83)	259
King, Henry Campbell	49 (1856-62)	988
King, Isaac	26 (1793-1800)	586
King, James	27 (1793-1800)	696
King, Janet [alias Neilson]	16 (1774-79)	365
✳ King, Jasper	6 (1747-52)	437
King, Jeremiah, Junior	24 (1786-93)	1107

Name	Volume	Page
King, John	2 (1722-26)	9
King, John	3 (1732-37)	79
King, Dr. John	42 (1839-45)	193
King, John	46 (1851-56)	334
King, John W.	46 (1851-56)	81
King, Lucius M.	39 (1826-34)	916
King, Mary	12 (1767-71)	544
King, Mary	20 (1783-84)	100
King, Mary	42 (1839-45)	323
King, Mitchell	49 (1856-62)	1056
King, Richard	22 (1786-93)	307
King, Samuel	6 (1747-52)	205
King, William	14 (1771-74)	122
King, William	14 (1771-74)	317
King, William S.	46 (1851-56)	80
Kingman, Eliah	40 (1834-39)	420
Kinloch, Francis (Esq rs)	11 (1767-71)	227
Kinloch, George	51 (1862-68)	694
Kinloch, Henry W.	49 (1856-62)	1055
Kinloch, Richmond	46. (1851-56)	46
Kirchner, John	18 (1776-84)	5
Kirk, Eleanor M.	38 (1826-34)	717
Kirk, Francis	6 (1747-52)	348
Kirk, Gideon	27 (1793-1800)	690
Kirk, Henry	39 (1826-34)	1030
Kirkland, John	15 (1771-74)	582
Kirkland, Joseph	33 (1807-18)	1335
Kirkland, Marianne	41 (1834-39)	766
Kirkland, William L.	38 (1826-34)	489
Kirklin see Kerklin		
Kirkpatrick, Andrew	43 (1839-45)	913
Kirkpatrick, John	51 (1862-68)	583
Kitchen, Charles	14 (1771-74)	85

Name	Volume	Page
Klesiek, August	47 (1851-56)	479
Kling, Sebastian	16 (1774-79)	369
Klint, Nils Frederick	43 (1839-45)	498
Knap, John	21 (1783-86)	602
Knepley, Solomon	48 (1856-62)	91
Knight, Jas. D.	46 (1851-56)	1
Knight, John	18 (1776-84)	46
* Knight, Thomas	15 (1771-74)	465
Knight, Thomas	38 (1826-34)	733
Knott, Isabel ⌐Isabell⌐	8 (1757-60)	18
Knox, Andrew	17 (1774-79)	688
Knox, Robert	25 (1793-1800)	101
Knox, Walter	41 (1834-39)	777
Kobb, Henry ⌐Kolb⌐	8 (1757-60)	529
Kockler, Jacob	41 (1834-39)	584
Kohne, Eliza	46 (1851-56)	63
Kohne, Frederick	45 (1845-51)	694
Kolb see Kobb		
Koller, Christian	10 (1760-67)	790
Kolp, Philip	17 (1774-79)	746
Konigmacher, Adam	35 (1818-26)	773
Kortman, Caroline	49 (1856-62)	845
Krebbs, Mathias	17 (1774-79)	577
Kreitner, Barbara	30 (1800-07)	1056
Kreps, Ann	32 (1807-18)	558
Krum, Caroline	50 (1862-68)	200
Kugley, John	35 (1818-26)	586
Kulp, Casper	13 (1767-71)	756
Kunhardt, William	50 (1862-68)	268
Kunzler, Conrad	12 (1767-71)	676
Kynaston, Samuel	7 (1752-56)	305
Kysell, Conrad	15 (1771-74)	366

Name	Volume	Page

L

LaBafs see LeBass

Name	Volume	Page
LaBan, Gabriel	6 (1747-52)	278
Labaufsay, Mary C. C.	40 (1834-39)	441
Labaufsay, Peter	36 (1818-26)	1014
Laborde, Francis	42 (1839-45)	228
LaBruce, Catherine	51 (1862-63)	515
Lachicotte, Jules	49 (1856-62)	777
Lacoste, Elinora F.	45 (1845-51)	793
Lacroix, Catherine	39 (1826-34)	894
Ladson, Abraham [Abram]	23 (1786-93)	668
Ladson, Benjamin	8 (1757-60)	176
Ladson, Charles B.	39 (1826-34)	1064
Ladson, Elizabeth	24 (1786-93)	1000
Ladson, Francis	13 (1767-71)	715
Ladson, Francis	13 (1767-71)	867
Ladson, Isaac	16 (1774-79)	180
Ladson, Jacob	6 (1747-52)	342
Ladson, Jacob	12 (1767-71)	571
Ladson, Captain James	13 (1767-71)	917
Ladson, James	32 (1807-18)	553
Ladson, James H.	51 (1862-68)	816
Ladson, Jane	33 (1807-18)	1256
Ladson, Josephine A.	49 (1856-62)	637
Ladson, Judith	34 (1818-26)	361
Ladson, Margaret	14 (1771-74)	78
Ladson, Martha	6 (1747-52)	552
Ladson, Mary	19 (1780-83)	202
Ladson, Rachel	23 (1786-93)	714
Ladson, Robert	13 (1767-71)	702
Ladson, Robert	22 (1786-93)	364
Ladson, Sarah	15 (1771-74)	590
Ladson, Sarah	26 (1793-1800)	547

Name	Volume	Page
Ladson, Thomas	3 (1731-33)	1
Ladson, Thomas	17 (1774-79)	808
Ladson, Thomas	21 (1783-86)	706
Lafar, David B.	48 (1856-62)	239
Lafar, Joseph D.	34 (1818-26)	71
Laffille, Nicholas	22 (1786-93)	205
L'Affitte, Marianne Ve Peyraube	32 (1807-18)	687
Laffitte, Peter	9 (1760-67)	315
Lafforgue, Marie (E)	40 (1834-39)	32
Lafon, John ₍Jean₎	43 (1839-45)	695
Lafon, Marie Louise	45 (1845-51)	475
Lafont, Elizabeth	39 (1826-34)	973
Lahiffe, John Mills	30 (1800-07)	1138
Lahiffe, Maurice	25 (1793-1800)	201
Laing, Samuel	10 (1760-67)	630
Laird, John	9 (1760-67)	148
Laird, Patrick	9 (1760-67)	189
Lalane, George M.	50 (1862-68)	246
Lamar, Jeremiah	14 (1771-74)	316
Lamar, Thomas	18 (1776-84)	214
Lamb, David	35 (1818-26)	708
Lamb, Isaac	41 (1834-39)	758
Lamb, James	47 (1851-56)	584
Lamb, James	47 (1851-56)	824
Lamb, James (executor's bond)	48 (1856-62)	255
Lamb, Thomas	34 (1818-26)	230
Lambert, Henry	32 (1807-18)	878
Lamboll, Beck Timothy	47 (1851-56)	794
✳ Lamboll, Thomas	18 (1776-84)	120
Lambright, Belteshazzar	6 (1747-52)	502
Lambton, Richard	17 (1774-79)	571
Lamon, Francis	23 (1786-93)	424
Lamond, Robert	9 (1760-67)	349
✳ Lampard, Richard	6 (1747-52)	460

166

Name	Volume	Page
Lampe, John	26 (1793-1800)	475
Lamsae, Susannah ⌐Lansae⌐	6 (1747-52)	170
Lance, Anna Maria	45 (1845-51)	915
Lance, Lambert	15 (1771-74)	613
Lance, Lambert	29 (1800-07)	643
Lanchester, Thomas	30 (1800-07)	1131
Landall, Robert	15 (1771-74)	492
Landen, Thomas	4 (1736-40)	129
Lander, Francis	9 (1760-67)	164
Landreth, David M.	46 (1851-56)	2
Lane, John	32 (1807-18)	890
Lane, Margaret	28 (1800-07)	175
Lane, Robert	32 (1807-18)	668
Lane, William	24 (1786-93)	973
Lane, William	33 (1807-18)	1111
Lang, Robert	11 (1767-71)	100
Langdon, Thomas	19 (1780-83)	313
Lange, Jacob H.	39 (1826-34)	977
Langford, Ann	37 (1826-34)	69
Langley, Jane T.	48 (1856-62)	498
Langrish, John	18 (1776-84)	187
Langstaff, Benjamin	32 (1807-18)	518
Langstaff, John	27 (1793-1800)	766
Lanneau, Basile	47 (1851-56)	868
Lanneau, Bazile	39 (1826-34)	1216
Lansae see Lamsae		
Lansdon, William	31 (1807-18)	93
Lapier, Amy	41 (1834-39)	492
Lapierre, Gilbert Bernard James	32 (1807-18)	841
Lapp, John George	17 (1774-79)	551
Lardant, James	5 (1740-47)	51
Larence, George	41 (1834-39)	687
Laroach, James ⌐Laroch⌐	20 (1783-86)	29
Laroch, James	1 (1720-21)	62

Name	Volume	Page
LaRoch, James	25 (1793-1800)	26
Laroch, John	9 (1760-67)	188
Laroch, Mary	8 (1757-60)	414
Laroch see also Laroach		
LaRoche, James	32 (1807-18)	797
LaRoche, John ₍Laroches₎	2 (1724-25)	4
Laroche, John	22 (1786-93)	341
Laroche, Mary	43 (1839-45)	532
LaRoche, Richard J.	44 (1845-51)	25
La Roche, Thomas	5 (1740-47)	168
Laroches see La Roche		
Larronde, Emile	41 (1834-39)	813
Larry, Robert	34 (1818-26)	180
Lasley, Martha	19 (1780-83)	128
Lasley, Martha	21 (1783-86)	440
Latham, Joseph	30 (1800-07)	1022
Latham, Richard	21 (1783-86)	513
Latour, Charlotte	7 (1752-56)	521
Latta, Alexander	24 (1786-93)	1079
Latta, James	**42 (1839-45)**	**129**
Laugharne, Arthur	**1 (1711-18)**	**70**
Laurans, Peter	37 (1826-34)	34
Laurence, Shubael	42 (1839-45)	428
Laurens, Caroline Olivia	38 (1826-34)	493
Laurens, Caroline Olivia (Memorandum)	38 (1826-34)	515
Laurens, Eliza	43 (1839-45)	514
Laurens, Frederick	37 (1826-34)	236
Laurens, Henry	24 (1786-93)	1152
Laurens, Henry (Substitution of trustee)	28 (1800-07)	170
Laurens, Henry	35 (1818-26)	508
Laurens, James	21 (1783-86)	863
Laurens, John	5 (1740-47)	665
Laurens, John B.	37 (1826-34)	328

168

Name	Volume	Page
Laurens, Keating S.	46 (1851-56)	290
Laurens, Margaret Harleston	48 (1856-62)	271
Laurens, Peter	5 (1740-47)	678
Laurens see also Laurense		
Laurense, Augustus [Laurens]	8 (1757-60)	112
Lavien, Peter	19 (1780-83)	193
✱ Lavington, Samuel	9 (1760-67)	420
Law, John	14 (1771-74)	33
Lawrance, James	11 (1767-71)	252
Lawrence, Elizabeth	36 (1818-26)	949
Lawrence, Ettsel	26 (1793-1800)	483
Lawrence, James [Lawrens]	3 (1732-37)	142
Lawrence, Peter	5 (1740-47)	13
Lawrence, Sarah	31 (1807-18)	147
Lawrence, Sarah Clarke	49 (1856-62)	1025
Lawrence, Synthea W.	50 (1862-68)	246
Lawrence, William	17 (1774-79)	775
Lawrens see Lawrence		
Laws, Robert Senior	35 (1818-26)	449
Lawson, Francis (S)	31 (1807-18)	214
Lawson, James	1 (1711-18)	82
Lawton, Charles	41 (1834-39)	889
Lawton, Joseph	47 (1851-56)	598
Lawton, Josiah	13 (1767-71)	869
Lawton, Roger B.	48 (1856-62)	88
Lawton, William	13 (1767-71)	860
Lawton, William	36 (1818-26)	1033
Lawton, Winborn	49 (1856-62)	823
Lazarus, Adeline	50 (1862-68)	406
Lazarus, Emma	50 (1862-68)	365
Lazarus, Joshua	49 (1856-62)	852
Lazarus, Marks	40 (1834-39)	359
Lazarus, Michael	49 (1856-62)	1070

Name	Volume	Page
Lazarus, Rachel	44 (1845-51)	261
Lea, Joseph ⌐Jofeph⌐	3 (1731-33)	51
Lea, William	25 (1793-1800)	114
Leacroft, Ruth	3 (1731-33)	60
Leader, Mary	49 (1856-62)	894
Leaton, John	17 (1774-79)	794
Leaton, Richard	8 (1757-60)	326
Leavey, John ⌐Leavy⌐	5 (1740-47)	433
Leavitt, Joshua	31 (1807-18)	282
Leavy see Leavey		
Leaycroft, Stephen	4 (1736-40)	98
Le Bass, James ⌐La Bafs⌐	4 (1736-40)	78
Lebby, Catharina Ann A.	32 (1807-18)	501
Lebby, Nathaniel	28 (1800-07)	272
Lebender, Barnerd	25 (1793-1800)	18
Leber, Samuel	16 (1774-79)	30
LeBrafseur see Le Brasseur		
LeBrasseur, Francis ⌐LeBrafseur⌐	3 (1732-37)	341
Le Caron, Charles	41 (1834-39)	951
Lechais, A.	32 (1807-18)	731
Lechais, Francoise	49 (1856-62)	605
Lechais, Gouvignon Ve	36 (1818-26)	1228
Lechais, Marie Josephine	34 (1818-26)	66
Le Chevalier, Oliver	35 (1818-26)	770
Le Chevallier, Peter	1 (1711-18)	48
Le Cog, George	23 (1786-93)	476
Leduc, Laurent	32 (1807-18)	602
Lee, Caty	30 (1800-07)	890
Lee, Dorothea	36 (1818-26)	1007
Lee, Eliza	47 (1851-56)	621
Lee, Elizabeth L. ⌐S.⌐	46 (1851-56)	250
Lee, Henrietta C.	45 (1845-51)	768
Lee, Jane	27 (1793-1800)	660
Lee, Kezia	46 (1851-56)	379

170

Name	Volume	Page
Lee, Mary	21 (1783-86)	494
Lee, Mary	35 (1818-26)	561
Lee, Mary E.	45 (1845-51)	814
Lee, Philip	1 (1694-1704)	1
Lee, Thomas	12 (1767-71)	596
Lee, Thomas	42 (1839-45)	38
Lee, William T.	48 (1856-62)	421
Leech, John	23 (1786-93)	649
Leeson, Joseph	20 (1783-86)	324
Lefesne, Francis	12 (1767-71)	368
Lefaene, Daniel	19 (1780-83)	326
Lefser see Lesser		
Lefsesne, Ann	37 (1826-34)	109
Legare, Abigail	48 (1856-62)	465
Legaré, Alice	32 (1807-18)	600
Legare, Ann	26 (1793-1800)	418
Legare, Ann	48 (1856-62)	169
Legare, Charles	49 (1856-62)	884
Legare, Daniel	24 (1786-93)	846
Legare, Daniel, Jr.	24 (1786-93)	877
Legare, Doctor Daniel	47 (1851-56)	537
Legare, Elizabeth	32 (1807-18)	547
Legare, Frances	28 (1800-07)	61
Legare, Hugh S.	43 (1839-45)	658
Legare, Isaac	28 (1800-07)	291
Legare, James	38 (1826-34)	682
Legare, James Christopher Wilkinson	45 (1845-51)	800
Legare, John	28 (1800-07)	341
Legare, John	30 (1800-07)	1100
Legare, John	48 (1856-62)	25
Legare, John Bewick, Senr. [Berwick]	45 (1845-51)	677
Legare, Joseph	30 (1800-07)	998
Legare, Joseph Daniel	33 (1807-18)	1221
Legare, Mary	25 (1793-1800)	60

Name	Volume	Page
Legare, Mary	41 (1834-39)	519
Legare, Mary	49 (1856-62)	847
Legaré, Mary Swinton	43 (1839-45)	580
Legare, Nathan	20 (1783-86)	14
Legaré, Samuel	26 (1793-1800)	518
Legare, Sarah	37 (1826-34)	364
Legare, Sarah Peronneau	39 (1826-34)	883
Legare, Solomon	9 (1760-67)	10
Legare, Solomon	16 (1774-79)	257
Legare, Susan B.	40 (1834-39)	385
Legare, Thomas	28 (1800-07)	97
Legare, Thomas, Senr	43 (1839-45)	469
Legare, Thomas	47 (1851-56)	648
Legay, Rebecca Sawyer	37 (1826-34)	229
Legé, Jean Marie	41 (1834-39)	860
Le Gendre, Daniel	1 (1687-1710)	32
Leger, Elizabeth Mary	35 (1818-26)	735
Leger, Peter [Pierre	1 (1722-24)	60
Leger, Peter	9 (1760-67)	210
Legg, James	30 (1800-07)	807
Legg, Mary	32 (1807-18)	637
Legge, Ann	38 (1826-34)	422
Legge, Edward	22 (1786-93)	89
Legge, Edward	29 (1800-07)	612
Legge, Mary	25 (1793-1800)	127
Legrand, Isaac	19 (1780-83)	58
Lehoux, Charles Jean Baptiste	22 (1786-93)	324
Lehre, Ann	43 (1839-45)	645
Lehre, Mary	30 (1800-07)	930
Lehre, William	27 (1793-1800)	914
Leigh, Peter	8 (1757-60)	384
Leitch, Andrew	24 (1786-93)	907
Leitch, Duncan	37 (1826-34)	411

Name	Volume	Page
Lesesne, Isaac	14 (1771-74)	257
Lesesne, Isaac	24 (1786-93)	1173
Lesesne, James	6 (1747-52)	615
Lesesne, John	24 (1786-93)	1033
Lesesne, Mary	24 (1786-93)	1020
Lesesne, Mary	37 (1826-34)	128
Lesesne, Peter	41 (1834-39)	616
Lesesne see also Lesene		
Le Siegneur see LeSeigneur		
Leslie, John	29 (1800-07)	622
Lespinar, Joseph	35 (1818-26)	677
Lesser, Harris [Lefser]	46 (1851-56)	191
Levie, Alexander [Livie]	7 (1752-56)	483
Levy, Elias	47 (1851-56)	743
Levy, Jane	50 (1862-68)	415
Levy, Lyon	40 (1834-39)	179
Levy, Marks	46 (1851-56)	199
Levy, Moses C.	41 (1834-39)	909
Levy, Sarah	35 (1818-26)	759
Levy, Sarah C.	41 (1834-39)	683
Lewis, Adam	5 (1740-47)	458
Lewis, Charles	3 (1731-33)	67
Lewis, Charles	12 (1767-71)	634
Lewis, Daniel	15 (1771-74)	661
Lewis, Elias	6 (1747-52)	291
Lewis, Gabriel	27 (1793-1800)	825
Lewis, George	10 (1760-67)	457
Lewis, Henry	9 (1760-67)	27
Lewis, Isaac	46 (1851-56)	12
Lewis, Jenkin	8 (1757-60)	150
Lewis, John	7 (1752-56)	105
Lewis, John	12 (1767-71)	438
Lewis, John	41 (1834-39)	893
Lewis, Martha	14 (1771-74)	225

Name	Volume	Page
Lewis, Mary	7 (1752-56)	400
Lewis, Mary	13 (1767-71)	758
Lewis, Maurice	4 (1736-40)	203
Lewis, Sarah	3 (1732-37)	111
Lewis, Sarah Amelia	45 (1845-51)	554
Lewis, Sedgwick	16 (1774-79)	299
Lewis, Thomas	15 (1771-74)	527
Lewis, Thomas, Senr.	25 (1793-1800)	116
Lewis, Tissee [Tisse]	48 (1856-62)	175
Lewis, William	19 (1780-83)	71
Lewis, William	20 (1783-86)	243
Lewis, William	27 (1793-1800)	833
Liber, Elizabeth	28 (1800-07)	343
Liddele, James [Liddelle]	9 (1760-67)	131
Liddelle see Liddele		
Lide, John	10 (1760-67)	466
Lidell, John	16 (1774-79)	346
*Liebehentz, Henry	24 (1786-93)	1159
Lieubraye see Lieubrey		
Lieubrey, Peter [Lieubraye]	5 (1740-47)	236
Lievingston, Ann	3 (1732-37)	43
Lights, Barnard [Leitz]	25 (1793-1800)	260
Lightwood, Edward	12 (1767-71)	622
Lightwood, Edward	27 (1793-1800)	689
Lightwood, Ed. C.	31 (1807-18)	250
Lightwood, Elizabeth	31 (1807-18)	418
Lightwood, Elizabeth	37 (1826-34)	67
Likly, Sarah [alias Linckly]	1 (1720-21)	25
Limehouse, Robert	45 (1845-51)	908
Linckly see Likly		
Lincoln, Benjamin	36 (1818-26)	1031
Lincoln, Horatio	33 (1807-18)	1361
Lind, Thomas	14 (1771-74)	113
Linder, Lewis [Ludwig]	8 (1757-60)	251

Name	Volume	Page
Lindour, George Henry	22 (1786-93)	192
Lindries, John Casper	41 (1834-39)	707
Lindsay, Henry	5 (1740-47)	193
Lindsay, James L.	49 (1856-62)	992
Lindsay, Robert	29 (1800-07)	500
Lindsay, William	14 (1771-74)	228
Lindsay, William	22 (1786-93)	39
*Lindsey, Patrick ⌐Lindsy⌐	6 (1747-52)	15
Lindstedt, C. H.	49 (1856-62)	925
Lindsy see Lindsey		
Linerieux, Enoch	17 (1774-79)	810
Ling, Robert	39 (1826-34)	1047
Ling, Samuel	49 (1856-62)	558
Lingard, James	13 (1767-71)	928
Lingard, Mary	32 (1807-18)	560
Lining, Charles	32 (1807-18)	695
Lining, Edward Blake	45 (1845-51)	557
Lining, John	33 (1807-18)	1091
Lining, Mary	38 (1826-34)	587
Lining, Polly	41 (1834-39)	503
Lining, Richard H.	44 (1845-51)	67
Lining, Sarah	23 (1786-93)	403
Lining, Sarah Hill	33 (1807-18)	1090
Lining, Thomas	21 (1783-86)	827
Linn, David	16 (1774-79)	277
Linn, James	17 (1774-79)	605
Linson, Elizabeth	46 (1851-56)	343
Linsser, John L.	41 (1834-39)	948
Linsser, Mary Margaret	50 (1862-68)	135
Linter, John	4 (1736-40)	234
Linter, Richard	6 (1747-52)	121
Linthwaite, William	4 (1736-40)	117
Linton, John	16 (1774-79)	152
Linus, Ann	13 (1767-71)	783

176

Name	Volume	Page
Linus, James	6 (1747-52)	617
Liston, Elizabeth	26 (1793-1800)	482
Liston, Martha	19 (1780-83)	118
*Litten, William	9 (1760-67)	402
Little, Elizabeth	24 (1786-93)	798
Little, Robert	21 (1783-86)	682
Little, Robert	43 (1839-45)	565
Little, William	7 (1752-56)	81
Littlejohn, Ann	26 (1793-1800)	558
Littlejohn, Duncan	29 (1800-07)	732
Livie see Levie		
Livingston, Abraham	20 (1783-86)	272
Livingston, Eleanor	28 (1800-07)	177
Livingston, Elizabeth	21 (1783-86)	455
Livingston, George, Jr.	11 (1767-71)	197
Livingston, George	12 (1767-71)	468
Livingston, George	22 (1786-93)	175
Livingston, Henry	2 (1726-27)	40
Livingston, Henry	4 (1736-40)	162
Livingston, Henry, Jr.	10 (1760-67)	617
Livingston, Henry	24 (1786-93)	796
Livingston, Jane	48 (1856-62)	317
Livingston, Joseph H.	31 (1807-18)	465
Livingston, William	1 (1722-24)	54
Livingston, William Smelie	14 (1771-74)	305
Liviston, John	15 (1771-74)	638
Lloyd, Caleb	11 (1767-71)	155
Lloyd, John	8 (1757-60)	280
Lloyd, John [Loyd]	13 (1767-71)	932
Lloyd, John	31 (1807-18)	45
Lloyd, Martha	13 (1767-71)	978
Lloyd, Mary	10 (1760-67)	445
Lloyd, Mary	41 (1834-39)	847
Lloyd, Mary	42 (1839-45)	36

Name	Volume	Page
Lloyd, Thomas	5 (1740-47)	145
Lloyd, William	9 (1760-67)	166
Lloyd, William	47 (1851-56)	850
Lloyd, William	49 (1856-62)	985
Loadholes, Martin	17 (1774-79)	743
Lobken, Roger [Lovken]	7 (1752-56)	95
Lochon, John	25 (1793-1800)	283
Lochon, Vivien	15 (1771-74)	364
Lockart, John	37 (1826-34)	271
Locke, George B.	48 (1856-62)	155
Lockey, George	31 (1807-18)	347
Lockhart, John	17 (1774-79)	672
Locklier, Stephen	40 (1834-39)	42
Lockwood, Caroline D. L.	49 (1856-62)	1014
Lockwood, Joshua, Jr.	41 (1834-39)	562
Lockwood, Joshua W.	49 (1856-62)	744
Lockwood, Susan	35 (1818-26)	573
Lofton, Samuel	43 (1839-45)	918
Logan, George	1 (1720-21)	73
Logan, George	15 (1771-74)	598
Logan, George	25 (1793-1800)	81
Logan, George	41 (1834-39)	837
Logan, George John	41 (1834-39)	874
Logan, Honoria E. M.	50 (1862-68)	19
Logan, John	9 (1760-67)	71
Logan, John	21 (1783-86)	785
Logan, Joseph	24 (1786-93)	1054
Logan, Joseph	36 (1818-26)	1012
Logan, Patrick	2 (1726-27)	17
Logan, Thomas	38 (1826-34)	677
Lombard, E.	38 (1826-34)	735
Long, Felix	21 (1783-86)	461
Long, Mary Sarah	36 (1818-26)	994
Long, Mathew	18 (1776-84)	188

Name	Volume	Page
Loocock, Aaron	25 (1793-1800)	161
Loocock, Mary	29 (1800-07)	537
Lopsus, Jackson	32 (1807-18)	886
Lopez, David	32 (1807-18)	521
Lord, Andrew	19 (1780-83)	151
Lord, Andrew	21 (1783-86)	647
Lord, Archibald B.	44 (1845-51)	68
Lord, Catherine A.	39 (1826-34)	834
Lord, George	23 (1786-93)	526
Lord, James	10 (1760-67)	513
Lord, Margaret	35 (1818-26)	706
Lord, William	23 (1786-93)	608
Lorent, George I.	36 (1818-26)	969
Lorimore, James ₍Lowremore₎	9 (1760-67)	383
Lorman, John	18 (1776-84)	100
Lormier, James	7 (1752-56)	51
Loryea, Isaac	47 (1851-56)	600
Lothrop, Sarah	35 (1818-26)	814
Lothrop, Sarah (substitution of trustee)	41 (1834-39)	590
Loughton, William	2 (1727-29)	26
Love, Duncan	29 (1800-07)	722
Love, James	8 (1757-60)	479
Loveday, John	29 (1800-07)	685
Loveday, Sarah	32 (1807-18)	526
Lovegreen, Andrew A.	51 (1862-68)	879
Lovegreen, Sarah	51 (1862-68)	833
Lovelass, Thomas	6 (1747-52)	31
Lovelefs see Loveless		
Loveless, John ₍Lovelefs₎	12 (1767-71)	520
Lovell, Hannah Frances	44 (1845-51)	387
Loveridge, Lewis	2 (1726-27)	68
Lovett, Samuel	28 (1800-07)	265

Name	Volume	Page
Lovibond, Henry	2 (1727-29)	37
Lovken see Lobken		
Lowe, William	15 (1771-74)	347
Lowle, Samuel	8 (1757-60)	365
Lowndes, Catharine	46 (1851-56)	357
Lowndes, Charles	9 (1760-67)	376
Lowndes, Edward	28 (1800-07)	242
Lowndes, Edward R.	46 (1851-56)	265
Lowndes, Elizabeth Brewton	48 (1856-62)	122
Lowndes, James	41 (1834-39)	875
Lowndes, Mary	29 (1800-07)	679
Lowndes, Rawlins	28 (1800-07)	26
Lowndes, Thomas	43 (1839-45)	720
Lowndes, William	36 (1818-26)	910
Lowremore see Lorimore		
Lowrey, Henry Michael	45 (1845-51)	813
Lowrey, John Fort	49 (1856-62)	751
Lowring, Henry	4 (1736-40)	305
Loyd see Lloyd		
Loyde, John	2 (1727-29)	86
Loyer, Adrien	6 (1747-52)	326
L'Pezant see Pezant		
Lucas, James	5 (1740-47)	132
Lucas, John Hume	46 (1851-56)	306
Lucas, Jonathan	40 (1834-39)	461
Lucas, Jonathan	44 (1845-51)	334
Lucas, Thomas	12 (1767-71)	577
Lucas, Thomas Bennett	48 (1856-62)	534
Lucas, William N.	46 (1851-56)	196
Luckie, Elenor	31 (1807-18)	2
Ludlam, Richard	2 (1727-29)	49
Luers, Frederick	45 (1845-51)	590
Luick, John Wolffgang	19 (1780-83)	81
Lusher, Sarah (M)	44 (1845-51)	80

Name	Volume	Page
Lushington, Richard	23 (1786-93)	673
Lusk, Hannah	4 (1736-40)	299
Luther, Ann	15 (1771-74)	667
Lyall, David	30 (1800-07)	766
Lykes, George	18 (1776-84)	185
Lynah, Elizabeth	42 (1839-45)	281
Lynah, James	31 (1807-18)	271
Lynass, Michael	45 (1845-51)	584
Lynch, Esther	36 (1818-26)	1242
* Lynch, James Geter	30 (1862-68)	156
Lynch, Thomas	18 (1776-84)	231
* Lynch, Thomas	20 (1783-86)	152
Lynch, Thomas	46 (1851-56)	190
Lynes, Elizabeth	46 (1851-56)	298
Lynes, John	25 (1793-1800)	56
Lynes, Samuel	43 (1839-45)	879
Lynn, Valentine [Lynne]	19 (1780-83)	227
Lynne see Lynn		
Lyon, John	19 (1780-83)	169
Lyon, John	28 (1800-07)	140
Lyon, Mordecai	34 (1818-26)	16
Lyon, Philip	2 (1724-25)	21
Lyons, Robert	27 (1793-1800)	904

M

Mabire see Mabrie		
Mabrie, Jean [Mabire]	27 (1793-1800)	875
Macadam, James	41 (1834-39)	736
McAlister, John	4 (1736-40)	249
McAlister, Mary	25 (1793-1800)	280
McAlpin, Henry	46 (1851-56)	348
McAlpin, Mary	42 (1839-45)	183
McAlpine, Colin	14 (1771-74)	193

Name	Volume	Page
McAnally, Elizabeth	49 (1856-62)	780
Macartan, Francis	12 (1767-71)	555
Macarty, John	32 (1807-18)	611
Macaulay, George	37 (1826-34)	20
Macaulay, George	44 (1845-51)	167
Macauley, Alexander	9 (1760-67)	21
Macbeth, Catherine	43 (1839-45)	876
Macbeth, James	35 (1818-26)	514
Macbeth, Louisa	46 (1851-56)	192
McBride, Alexander	32 (1807-18)	718
McBride, Ellinor	43 (1839-45)	858
McBride, James	29 (1800-07)	479
McBride, James	31 (1807-18)	135
McBride, John	10 (1760-67)	871
McBride, John	11 (1767-71)	74
McCalester, Archibald	24 (1786-93)	1051
McCall, Amelia H.	44 (1845-51)	249
McCall, Ann	36 (1818-26)	1024
McCall, Ann Dart	48 (1856-62)	75
McCall, Charlotte Margaret	27 (1793-1800)	769
McCall, Hext	24 (1786-93)	1055
McCall, John	21 (1783-86)	690
McCall, John	25 (1793-1800)	245
McCall, John	28 (1800-07)	96
McCall, John Ward	35 (1818-26)	728
McCall, Joseph P.	51 (1862-68)	798
McCalla, Sarah	41 (1834-39)	732
McCalla, Thos H.	32 (1807-18)	669
McCalla, William	8 (1757-60)	213
McCamon, John	27 (1793-1800)	829
McCan, Edward	31 (1807-18)	222
McCants, Ann	42 (1839-45)	8
McCants, Eliza	43 (1839-45)	531
McCants, Hugh R.	44 (1845-51)	401

Name	Volume	Page
McCants, James	14 (1771-74)	190
McCants, Nathaniel	33 (1807-18)	1092
McCants, Thomas N.	43 (1839-45)	845
McCants, William	48 (1856-62)	378
McCartney, Samuel	45 (1845-51)	578
McCartney, Samuel	45 (1845-51)	580
McCellend see McClelland		
McClallan, David ⌐McClellan⌐	4 (1736-40)	198
McClelan see Mc Clellan		
McCleland see McClellend		
McClellan, Ann Robinah	29 (1800-07)	690
McClellan, Archibald ⌐McClelan⌐	18 (1776-84)	118
McClellan, Archibald	44 (1845-51)	111
McClellan, Esther	29 (1800-07)	481
McClellan, William	19 (1780-83)	301
McClellan see also McClallan		
Mc Clelland, Mary	38 (1826-34)	420
McClellend, James ⌐McCellend, Mc Cleland⌐	9 (1760-67)	169
McClendon, Mary	14 (1771-74)	29
McCluer, James (0)	13 (1767-71)	1054
McClure, Cochran	34 (1818-26)	279
McClure, Wm.	32 (1807-18)	720
McCollogh see McCollough		
McCollough, John	9 (1760-67)	109
McCollough, John ⌐McCollogh⌐	21 (1783-86)	459
McCollum, John	7 (1752-56)	465
McConnell, Hugh	15 (1771-74)	479
McCord, Charles	15 (1771-74)	649
McCord, John	14 (1771-74)	185
McCorkell, Samuel	28 (1800-07)	321
McCormack, John	6 (1747-52)	457
✳ McCormack, Mary	9 (1760-67)	421
Maccormack, William	17 (1774-79)	796

Duplic

Name	Volume	Page
Mc Cormick, Peter	47 (1851-56)	460
✱ Mc Cormick, William	6 (1747-52)	377
McCoul, George	19 (1780-83)	260
McCown, James	6 (1747-52)	484
McCoye, John	12 (1767-71)	595
McCrady, Jane	43 (1839-45)	880
McCrady, John	29 (1800-07)	476
McCrea, John see McCrea, Joseph		
McCrea, Joseph [John]	9 (1760-67)	356
McCredie, David	32 (1807-18)	500
McCree, Jannett	7 (1752-56)	307
McCree, John	10 (1760-67)	685
McCuller see McCullers		
McCullers, John	51 (1862-68)	774
McCullers, Matthew [McCuller]	33 (1807-18)	1245
McCulloch, Elizabeth	18 (1776-84)	205
McCulloch, William	21 (1783-86)	736
McCulloch see also McCullock		
McCullock, Thomas B. [McCulloch]	36 (1818-26)	995
McCullough, William	16 (1774-79)	267
McCully, Robert Ferguson	36 (1818-26)	876
MackDaniel, Daniel	2 (1729-31)	13
McDaniel, Daniel	18 (1776-84)	308
McDermot, Patrick	33 (1807-18)	1307
McDonald, Christopher	42 (1839-45)	252
McDonald, Daniel	7 (1752-56)	509
McDonald, John	13 (1767-71)	942
Macdonald, John	23 (1786-93)	447
McDonald, Ranald	13 (1767-71)	848
McDonald, Sarah	41 (1834-39)	788
McDonald, Susanna	39 (1826-34)	840
McDonall, David	2 (G1729-31)	28
McDonnald, William	27 (1793-1800)	781

Name	Volume	Page
McDonnell, Patrick	27 (1793-1800)	942
McDougall, John	19 (1780-83)	367
McDougall, John	33 (1807-18)	1236
McDow, William	42 (1839-45)	46
McDowall, Andrew	51 (1862-68)	596
McDowall see also McDowell		
McDowel, Elizabeth	9 (1760-67)	176
McDowell, Alexander	10 (1760-67)	787
McDowell, Alexander	27 (1793-1800)	940
McDowell, Alexander [McDowall]	31 (1807-18)	246
McDowell, Esebella [Isebella]	12 (1767-71)	346
McDowell, Hugh	9 (1760-67)	19
McDowell, John	35 (1818-26)	430
McDowell, Mary	39 (1826-34)	887
McElhenney, James	42 (1839-45)	329
McElhenney, Susanna	40 (1834-39)	369
McElhenny, Thomas	18 (1776-84)	43
McElleran, Charles	47 (1851-56)	456
McElleran, Ellen	48 (1856-62)	289
McFaddien see McFaddin		
McFaddin, John [McFaddien]	18 (1776-84)	150
McFarlan, John	30 (1800-07)	778
McFarlan, Mary	36 (1818-26)	1131
McFarland, Catharine [McFarlane]	42 (1839-45)	133
McFarland, Daniel [Mcffarland]	3 (1732-37)	94
McFarlane, John	25 (1793-1800)	175
McFarlane, Peter	26 (1793-1811)	595
McFarlane see also McFarland		
Mc Feeters, Mary Ann	51 (1862-68)	738
Mc ffarland see McFarland		
McFrew, Alexander	18 (1776-84)	235
McGanley, Samuel	48 (1856-62)	22
McGaw, James	7 (1752-56)	416
*McGhie, Patrick	6 (1747-52)	454

Name	Volume	Page
McGill, Hugh	7 (1752-56)	112
McGill, James ₍Wright₎	26 (1793-1800)	367
McGill, Samuel	34 (1818-26)	216
Mc Gilleverey see Mc Gillevery		
McGillevery, James ₍Mc Gilleverey₎	3 (1732-37)	205
* Mc Gillivray, Alexander	9 (1760-67)	403
McGillivray, William	5 (1740-47)	18
MacGiloray, Lanthlan	3 (1732-37)	98
McGilvery, John	3 (1732-37)	283
McGilvray, Alexander	8 (1757-60)	3
McGinlay, Mrs. Jerusha	46 (1851-56)	152
McGinley, Samuel	48 (1856-62)	22
McGinn, James	51 (1862-68)	802
McGivern, Hugh	48 (1856-62)	462
McGovern, Anna	47 (1851-56)	718
McGowen, John	10 (1760-67)	600
McGrath, John	37 (1826-34)	316
McGregor, Alexander	7 (1752-56)	314
McGregor, Daniel ₍Mackgregor₎	2 (1724-25)	19
McGregor, Daniel	13 (1767-71)	683
Mc Gregor, Dorothy	26 (1793-1800)	539
MacGregor, Duncan ₍Dunkan₎	4 (1736-40)	9
McGregor, Malcolm ₍McGrigor₎	25 (1793-1800)	75
McGregor, Martha ₍Griger, McGriger₎	6 (1747-52)	372
McGriger see McGregor		
McGrigor, James	27 (1793-1800)	896
McGrigor see also McGregor		
McHugo, Anthony	29 (1800-07)	687
McInnes, Joseph	45 (1845-51)	902
McIntire, Duncan	14 (1771-74)	194
McIntire, George	40 (1834-39)	426
McIntosh, Elizabeth ₍Mackintosh, Eliza₎	31 (1807-18)	229
McIntosh, Esther	34 (1818-26)	411
McIntosh, James	29 (1800-07)	518

Name	Volume	Page
McIntosh, William	50 (1862-68)	297
McIntyre, Mary M.	50 (1862-68)	90
McIver, John	28 (1800-07)	165
McIver, Rodrick	18 (1776-84)	175
McKay, Charles	17 (1774-79)	478
McKay, John	4 (1736-40)	206
Mackay, John	7 (1752-56)	127
McKay, William	17 (1774-79)	759
McKearns, Michael [Kearns]	32 (1807-18)	596
McKee, Abel	49 (1856-62)	623
McKee, Archibald	18 (1776-84)	266
McKee, David	17 (1774-79)	438
McKee, David Gibson	50 (1862-68)	309
McKee, John	14 (1771-74)	22
Mc Kee, John	39 (1826-34)	908
McKelvey, David	31 (1807-18)	375
McKelvey, James Sumter	36 (1818-26)	937
McKelvey, Margaret	18 (1776-84)	321
McKelvey, Margarett	7 (1752-56)	217
McKelvey, Robert	7 (1752-56)	309
McKelvey, Robert	16 (1774-79)	64
Mc Kemmy, Robert	18 (1776-84)	313
McKendrie, Thomas	33 (1807-18)	1330
Mc Kenna, James	48 (1856-62)	320
Mc Kenney, Roger	16 (1774-79)	363
Mc Kenzie, Ann	39 (1826-34)	1209
Mc Kenzie, Archibald	50 (1862-68)	295
MacKensie, Elizabeth	41 (1834-39)	704
McKenzie, Alexander	19 (1780-83)	6
McKenzie, Alexander	25 (1793-1800)	23
MacKenzie, George	12 (1767-71)	546
Mc Kenzie, Henry M.	50 (1862-68)	13
McKenzie, James	37 (1826-34)	293
McKenzie, John	14 (1771-74)	58

Name	Volume	Page
Mackenzie, John	25 (1793-1800)	291
MacKenzie, John	37 (1826-34)	318
Mackenzie, John	49 (1856-62)	826
Mackenzie, Mary Ann C.	49 (1856-62)	581
Mackenzie, Robert	23 (1786-93)	467
Mc Kenzie, Sarah Ann	47 (1851-56)	547
Mc Kenzie, William ₍Kenzie₎	4 (1736-40)	253
Mc Keown, Bernard	51 (1862-68)	662
Mc Kewn, Archibald	38 (1826-34)	620
Mackewn, Mary	9 (1760-67)	191
Mckewn, Robert, Jr.	10 (1760-67)	604
Mc Kewn, Uphey	38 (1826-34)	755
Mackey, Collo. Alexander ₍M^{cc} Ky₎	1 (1722-24)	103
Mackey, Eliza	44 (1845-51)	148
Mackey, Joseph	3 (1732-37)	279
MacKGregor see McGregor		
Mcc kibben, Ar.	2 (1724-25)	58
Mackie, James	23 (1786-93)	717
Mackie, James	30 (1800-07)	937
Mackie, John	23 (1786-93)	120
Mackie, Margaret	48 (1856-62)	295
McKie, Mary	22 (1786-93)	111
Mackie, Sarah	31 (1807-18)	23
Mackinen, Charles William ₍McKinen₎	19 (1780-83)	60
Mackinfufs, George	27 (1793-1800)	742
McKinley, James	17 (1774-79)	631
McKinley, John	14 (1771-74)	132
McKinley, L.	43 (1839-45)	537
McKinnie, Benjamin	8 (1757-60)	404
Mackintos see McIntosh		
Mackintosh, Donald	50 (1862-68)	260
Mackintosh, John	5 (1740-47)	638
Mackintosh, Lachlan	23 (1786-93)	494

Name	Volume	Page
Mackintosh, Miles	2 (1727-29)	77
Mckown, George	19 (1780-83)	315
Mackoy, John	7 (1752-56)	375
Macksey, Henry	21 (1783-86)	732
M^cc Ky see MacKey		
Mc Lan see McLean		
* McLane, Allen	6 (1747-52)	513
McLane, Charles	8 (1757-60)	306
McLane, G. S.	41 (1834-39)	676
McLaren, James	13 (1767-71)	818
McLaren, James	46 (1851-56)	156
McLaughlin, Darby	4 (1736-40)	197
McLaughling, James	9 (1760-67)	3
McLaughling, James	15 (1771-74)	672
McLaughling, William	15 (1771-74)	389
McLean, Charles [Marclane]	2 (1724-25)	107
McLean, Evean	30 (1800-07)	888
McLean, James	41 (1834-39)	645
McLean, Margaret	40 (1834-39)	70
McLean, William [McLan]	47 (1851-56)	679
McLeod, Donald	35 (1818-26)	453
McLeod, John	12 (1767-71)	615
McLeod, John (Memorandum)	26 (1793-1800)	375
McLeod, Josiah M.	46 (1851-56)	195
McLeod, Normand	36 (1818-26)	1051
McLeod, Normand (Substitution of		
Trustee)	36 (1818-26)	1132
McLeod, Thomas	8 (1757-60)	451
McLeod, William F.	50 (1862-68)	374
McMaster, Andrew [Mc Masters]	10 (1760-67)	519
McMaster, Archibald [McMasters]	25 (1793-1800)	13
Mac Master, Jane	45 (1845-51)	765
McMasters see McMaster		
McMechen, William	3 (1732-37)	70

Name	Volume	Page
McMeecken, William	18 (1776-84)	328
McMullin, Nathaniel	10 (1760-67)	599
McMurdy, Robert	8 (1757-60)	287
McMurtry, John	1 (1720-21)	51
McNabney, James	3 (1731-33)	3
McNairn, Joseph [McNarin]	25 (1793-1800)	186
Macnamara, Dennis	33 (1807-18)	1275
McNarin see McNairn		
McNeal, Eve Catharine	33 (1807-18)	1176
MacNeal, Niel	36 (1818-26)	852
* McNealy, James	9 (1760-67)	418
McNeill, Archibald	16 (1774-79)	157
McNeill, Daniel	39 (1826-34)	1158
McNeill, Henrietta	47 (1851-56)	697
McNeill, Neill	45 (1845-51)	833
McNesh, John	6 (1747-52)	46
McNichol see McNichols		
McNichols, George	7 (1752-56)	142
McNichols, John [McNichol]	13 (1767-71)	1042
McNight, Thomas	18 (1776-84)	148
McNight, William	10 (1760-67)	507
McNorton, Alexander	32 (1807-18)	903
Mc Owen, Patrick	48 (1856-62)	314
McPherson, Catharine [Catherine]	49 (1856-62)	1003
McPherson, Elizabeth	50 (1862-68)	93
McPherson, Isaac	22 (1786-93)	180
McPherson, James, Jr.	9 (1760-67)	259
McPherson, James	14 (1771-74)	25
McPherson, James Elliott [MacPherson]	40 (1834-39)	20
McPherson, John	5 (1740-47)	654
McPherson, John	9 (1760-67)	354
McPherson, John	30 (1800-07)	1051
McPherson, Joshua	16 (1774-79)	176

Name	Volume	Page
McPherson, Sarah	22 (1786-93)	340
McPherson, Susan	40·(1834-39)	248
McPherson, Susan, Mrs. (Substitution of Trustee)	40 (1834-39)	432
McPherson, Susan, Mrs. (Substitution of Trustee)	41 (1834-39)	710
McPherson, Susannah	32 (1807-18)	642
McQueen, Duncan	4 (1736-40)	14
McQueen, John	9 (1760-67)	339
Mc Swiney, Eugene	49 (1856-62)	1068
McSwiney, Patrick	51 (1862-68)	709
Macteer, John ⌜McTeer⌝	7 (1752-56)	144
McTeer, William	11 (1767-71)	310
McTimmany, Barney	37 (1826-34)	294
McTureous, Edwin W.	46 (1851-56)	254
McVicar, Archibald	36 (1818-26)	924
McVicar, Neil	37 (1826-34)	49
McWhann, William	31 (1807-18)	304
McWhirter, Hance	15 (1771-74)	517
McWhite, Joshua ⌜Joshuah⌝	43 (1839-45)	736
McWhite, Stephen	39 (1826-34)	925
McWilliam, Archibald	48 (1856-62)	432
Mader, John Henry	49 (1856-62)	717
Maffet, William	24 (1786-93)	1063
Mafsey see Massey		
Mafsie, Peter	42 (1839-45)	225
Magee, John	47 (1851-56)	787
Maggarrock, Hugh ⌜Maggarrok⌝	10 (1760-67)	658
Maggarrok see Maggarrock		
Maggot, William	2 (1726-27)	71
Magnefs, Sarah	42 (1839-45)	195
Maguire, Jane (A)	44 (1845-51)	235
Maguire, Michiel	50 (1862-68)	326
Magwood, Charles A.	48 (1856-62)	462

Name	Volume	Page
Magwood, James H.	48 (1856-62)	129
Magwood, Simon	40 (1834-39)	475
Maham, Hezekiah	23 (1786-93)	557
Mahoney, Florence	5 (1740-47)	14
Maillard, Ann	43 (1839-45)	597
Maille,	30 (1800-07)	779
Maine, Basil	27 (1793-1800)	876
Maine, Margaret Warner	31 (1801-18)	446
Maine, William	17 (1774-79)	545
Mair, James	35 (1818-26)	791
Mair, Patrick	30 (1800-07)	825
Mair, Thomas	40 (1834-39)	78
Makey, Roger	18 (1776-84)	206
Makky, John	31 (1807-18)	114
Makky, John Jos.	39 (1826-34)	1010
Malcom, Thomas	37 (1826-34)	63
Malcome, Elizabeth	41 (1834-39)	761
Malcomson, James	29 (1800-07)	726
Malcomson, James H. B.	38 (1826-34)	472
Malle see Meall		
Mallet, Daniel	18 (1776-84)	166
Mallet, Gideon	13 (1767-71)	971
Malone, Richard	4 (1736-40)	123
Man, John	48 (1856-62)	232
Man, Spencer	29 (1800-07)	619
Manigault, Ann H.	47 (1851-56)	677
Manigault, Anne ⌐Ann⌐	19 (1780-83)	304
Manigault, Charlotte	34 (1818-26)	236
Manigault, Charlotte	47 (1851-56)	554
Manigault, Gabriel	19 (1780-83)	196
Manigault, Gabriel	21 (1783-86)	518
Manigault, Gabriel	31 (1807-18)	283
Manigault, Joseph	43 (1839-45)	624

Name	Volume	Page
Manigault, Peter	2G(1729-31)	36
Manigault, Peter	16 (1774-79)	26
Manley, James	10 (1760-67)	539
Manning, Jethro	11 (1767-71)	56
Manson, John	27 (1793-1800)	931
Manson, Mary	48 (1856-62)	237
Marcks, Susannah	23 (1786-93)	549
Marclane see McLean		
Marion, Benjamin	3 (1732-37)	170
Marion, Benjamin	17 (1774-79)	782
Marion, Benjamin	20 (1783-86)	160
Marion, Esther	13 (1767-71)	905
Marion, Esther	35 (1818-26)	600
Marion, Frances [Francis]	25 (1793-1800)	270
Marion, Francis	39 (1826-34)	1140
Marion, Gabriel	18 (1776-84)	276
Marion, Gabriel	21 (1783-86)	445
Marion, Harriet	47 (1851-56)	778
Marion, James	12 (1767-71)	491
Marion, Job St. Julien	27 (1793-1800)	943
Marion, Maria	49 (1856-62)	1046
Marion, Mary	28 (1800-07)	230
Marion, Mary Esther	33 (1807-18)	1017
Marion, Paul	4 (1736-40)	55
Marion, Paul	24 (1786-93)	854
Marion, Peter	18 (1776-84)	273
Marion, Robert	32 (1807-18)	497
Marion, Theodore S.	37 (1826-34)	226
Marjenhoff, E. Henning	50 (1862-68)	285
Markley, Abraham	36 (1818-26)	1126
Markley, Jacob	8 (1757-60)	76
Marks, George	21 (1783-86)	712
Marks, Joseph	42 (1839-45)	168
Marlen, Edward	32 (1807-18)	823

Name	Volume	Page
Marley, John	15 (1771-74)	431
Marlow, Hannah	33 (1807-18)	1312
Marmiller see Miller		
Maronsy, Jullian	11 (1767-71)	158
Marquis, Elizabeth	28 (1800-07)	11
Marr, Andrew	19 (1780-83)	79
Marr, Andrew	20 (1783-86)	121
Marr, Ann	36 (1818-26)	1149
Marr, William	2 (1727-29)	6
Marr, William	2 (1727-29)	21
Marsh, James	46 (1851-56)	219
Marshall, Dorothy	38 (1826-34)	615
Marshall, Eleanor	33 (1807-18)	1057
Marshall, George	11 (1767-71)	69
Marshall, Isabel	11 (1767-71)	6
Marshall, James	20 (1783-86)	280
Marshall, Jane	44 (1845-51)	31
Marshall, John	34 (1818-26)	331
Marshall, John T.	49 (1856-62)	680
Marshall, Mary	36 (1818-26)	838
Marshall, Patrick	9 (1760-67)	178
Marshall, William	30 (1800-07)	892
Marten, Christian	37 (1826-34)	269
Martin, Abram	16 (1774-79)	194
Martin, Andrew	18 (1776-84)	112
Martin, Barak	7 (1752-56)	34
Martin, Charlotte	46 (1851-56)	9
Martin, Isaac	6 (1747-52)	158
Martin, Jacob	8 (1757-60)	556
Martin, Jacob	46 (1851-56)	281
Martin, James	6 (1747-52)	17
Martin, James	48 (1856-62)	1
Martin, John	3 (1732-37)	5
Martin, John	16 (1774-79)	195

Name	Volume	Page
Martin, Dr. John Baptiste	37 (1826-34)	220
Martin, John Christian	27 (1793-1800)	910
Martin, John Nicholas [Nichles]	27 (1793-1800)	728
Martin, John P.	39 (1826-34)	1085
Martin, Laughlin	21 (1783-86)	601
Martin, Margaret	29 (1800-07)	575
Martin, Mary J.	50 (1862-68)	263
Martin, Moses	3 (1732-37)	84
Martin, Moses [Mofes]	5 (1740-47)	521
Martin, Oliver	33 (1807-18)	1283
Martin, Patrick	1 (1722-24)	58
Martin, Patrick	27 (1793-1800)	764
Martin, Rebecca	42 (1839-45)	137
Martin, Richard	34 (1818-26)	138
Martin, Robert	46 (1851-56)	223
Martin, Sally Maria	49 (1856-62)	705
Martin, Samuel	24 (1786-93)	630
Martin, Samuel	42 (1839-45)	582
Martin, Samuel T.	48 (1856-62)	444
Martin, Thomas	13 (1767-71)	853
Martin, William	32 (1807-18)	946
Martin, William	49 (1856-62)	904
Martin, William M.	51 (1862-68)	611
Martindale, James C.	36 (1818-26)	918
Martineau, Louis	33 (1807-18)	1322
Mashon, Henry	8 (1757-60)	353
Masker, Elizabeth	43 (1839-45)	646
Mason, Richard	8 (1757-60)	148
Mason, Richard	21 (1783-86)	466
Mason, Susanna	29 (1800-07)	491
Mason, William	28 (1800-07)	171
Massey, Phillip [Mafsey]	4 (1736-40)	182
Massias, Abraham A.	44 (1845-51)	353
Mathewes, Anthony	12 (1767-71)	540

Name	Volume	Page
Mathewes, James	5 (1740-47)	443
Mathewes, James	10 (1760-67)	864
Mathewes, John	6 (1747-52)	480
Mathewes, John Raven	20 (1783-86)	222
Mathewes, John Raven	51 (1862-68)	642
Mathewes, Maria	50 (1862-68)	30
Mathewes, Mary	44 (1845-51)	44
Mathewes, Sarah	8 (1757-60)	493
Mathewes, William ₍Mathews₎	10 (1760-67)	859
Mathewes, William	12 (1767-71)	453
Mathewes, William	44 (1845-51)	368
Mathewes see also Mathews, Matthewes		
Mathews, Anthony	3 (1732-37)	214
Mathews, Edith	26 (1793-1800)	343
Mathews, Edmund ₍Matthews₎	21 (1783-86)	447
Mathews, Elizabeth	39 (1826-34)	1231
Mathews, Elizabeth D.	49 (1856-62)	653
Mathews, George ₍Mathewes₎	12 (1767-71)	579
Mathews, George	32 (1807-18)	947
Mathews, George	40 (1834-39)	238
Mathews, Isaac ₍Matthews₎	45 (1845-51)	713
Mathews, James	43 (1839-45)	816
Mathews, John	8 (1757-60)	424
✳ Mathews, John	18 (1776-84)	86 (dup.
✳ Mathews, John	18 (1776-84)	143 (dup.
Mathews, John	25 (1793-1800)	47
Mathews, John	28 (1800-07)	368
Mathews, John Ward	38 (1826-34)	813
Mathews, Joseph	36 (1818-26)	903
Mathews, Lois ₍Mathewes₎	7 (1752-56)	54
Mathews, Martha	50 (1862-68)	58
Mathews, Mary G.	43 (1839-45)	896
Mathews, Peter Basnett ₍Mathewes₎	28 (1800-07)	56

Name	Volume	Page
May, John	46 (1851-56)	339
May, John	48 (1856-62)	502
May, Margaret	49 (1856-62)	565
May, Martha	15 (1771-74)	362
Maybanck, Susanna ⌊Maybank⌋	2 (1724-25)	16
Maybank, David	1 (1722-24)	67
Maybank, David	11 (1767-71)	25
Maybank, David	31 (1807-18)	49
Maybank, Joseph	5 (1740-47)	177
Maybank, Joseph	20 (1783-86)	18
Maybank, Joseph	43 (1839-45)	768
Maybank, Peter Bonneau	28 (1800-07)	145
Maybank see also Maybanck		
Maynard, John	32 (1807-18)	886
Mayrant, John	11 (1767-71)	44
Mazyck, Alexander	21 (1783-86)	823
Mazyck, Alexander C.	37 (1826-34)	392
Mazyck, Benjamin	28 (1800-07)	79
Mazyck, Benjamin	35 (1818-26)	639
Mazyck, Daniel	32 (1807-18)	666
Mazyck, Elizabeth C. (Substitution of Trustee)	39 (1826-34)	1083
Mazyck, Elizabeth Charlotte	35 (1818-26)	466
Mazyck, Isaac	3 (1732-37)	321
Mazyck, Isaac	14 (1771-74)	1
Mazyck, Isaac	21 (1783-86)	450
Mazyck, Mary	38 (1826-34)	612
Mazyck, Mary	43 (1839-45)	907
Mazyck, Paul	6 (1747-52)	208
Mazyck, Paul	40 (1834-39)	242
Mazyck, Paul Delisle	37 (1826-34)	391
Mazyck, Paul Ravenel	35 (1818-26)	472
Mazyck, Peter	14 (1771-74)	285
Mazyck, Richard	28 (1800-07)	10

Name	Volume	Page
Mazyck, Robert Wilson	46 (1851-56)	264
Mazyck, Stephen	13 (1767-71)	759
Mazyck, Stephen, Junior	31 (1807-18)	150
Mazyck, Stephen	31 (1807-18)	338
Mazyck, Stephen	39 (1806-34)	1088
Mazyck, Susanna	23 (1786-93)	604
Mazyck, William	16 (1774-79)	376
Mazyck, William	43 (1839-45)	922
Mazyck, William	50 (1862-68)	89
Meacher, Ann	44 (1845-51)	142
Mead, William	48 (1856-62)	288
Meade, Joseph [Jofeph]	3 (1731-33)	54
Meall, William Hope [Malle]	7 (1752-56)	161
Mealy, John	47 (1851-56)	796
Means, James	14 (1771-74)	135
Meeker, Samuel	50 (1862-68)	354
Mefshow see Messhow		
Mefswarp, E. W.	33 (1807-18)	1155
Megget, James	5 (1740-47)	528
Meggett, William	21 (1783-86)	763
Meggett, William Crofskeys	38 (1826-34)	670
Mehrtens, C. F.	48 (1856-62)	365
Mehrtens, Jurgen	47 (1851-56)	466
Meifsner, A. E.	47 (1851-56)	815
Mell, James	21 (1783-86)	438
Mell, John	3 (1732-37)	328
Mell, Thomas	8 (1757-60)	406
Mell, Thomas	25 (1793-1800)	241
Mellard, Elisha	41 (1834-39)	528
Mellechamp, Thomas	16 (1774-79)	39
Mellet, Peter, Sr.	10 (1760-67)	310
Melven, Thomas	13 (1767-71)	954
Mendenhall, Elizabeth B. R.	44 (1845-51)	443

Name	Volume	Page
Merceir see Mercier		
Mercer, Richard	20 (1783-86)	236
Merchant, Chana	39 (1826-34)	921
Mercier, John	33 (1807-18)	1025
Mercier, Margaret ⌐Merceir⌐	36 (1818-26)	1003
Mercier, Peter	7 (1752-56)	279
Meree, William	42 (1839-45)	232
Meree see also Merree		
Merree, Thomas H. ⌐Meree⌐	47 (1851-56)	767
Merritt, Margaret ⌐Margeret⌐	8 (1757-60)	245
Mertens, Frederick	47 (1851-56)	499
Messhow, Abraham ⌐Mefshow⌐	3 (1732-37)	200
Metberg, Frederick	36 (1818-26)	1044
Methringham, Elizabeth	13 (1767-71)	909
Metivier, Francis	51 (1862-68)	577
Metivier, Marguerite Pigne	32 (1807-18)	662
Metzger, Henry	17 (1774-79)	723
Meurset, Peter	19 (1780-83)	66
Meurset, Peter	20 (1783-86)	175
Mewhenney, William	24 (1786-93)	890
Mey, Ann	44 (1845-51)	294
Mey, Charles S.	38 (1826-34)	624
Mey, Florian Charles	38 (1826-34)	538
Meyer, C.	42 (1839-45)	291
Meyer, C. William	48 (1856-62)	299
Meyer, Emil I.	48 (1856-62)	177
Meyer, Jacob	46 (1851-56)	160
Meyer, John	50 (1862-68)	137
Meyer, Philip	21 (1783-86)	756
Meyers, Mary	27 (1793-1800)	935
Meyler, Elizabeth	31 (1807-18)	55
Meyrant, Susannah	3 (1732-37)	316
Michal, Vallentan	13 (1767-71)	840

Name	Volume	Page
Michau, Abraham	10 (1760-67)	873
Michau, Abraham	18 (1776-84)	222
Michau, Manafseh	30 (1800-07)	823
Michel, Adrienne L.	48 (1856-62)	374
Michel, Frederick	36 (1818-26)	1188
Michel, John	47 (1851-56)	487
Michel, M. V. de	44 (1845-51)	221
Michel, Mary Louise	36 (1818-26)	1254
Michell, Francis	44 (1845-51)	57
Michie, Kenneth	6 (1747-52)	228
Michie, William	14 (1771-74)	105
Michie see also Mickie		
Mickele see Mickell		
Mickell, Ephiram ₍Mickele; Ephraim₎	2 (1727-29)	82
Mickie, James ₍Michie₎	8 (1757-60)	538
Middleton, Arthur	4 (1736-40)	306
Middleton, Arthur	41 (1834-39)	575
✱Middleton, Elizabeth	21 (1783-86)	538
Middleton, Henry	20 (1783-86)	416
Middleton, Henry	44 (1845-51)	52
Middleton, John	37 (1826-34)	60
Middleton, John Izard	45 (1845-51)	599
Middleton, Mary	29 (1800-07)	513
Middleton, Mary	32 (1807-18)	869
Middleton, Richard	6 (1747-52)	415
Middleton, Sarah	10 (1760-67)	740
Middleton, Sarah	27 (1793-1800)	681
Middleton, Thomas	5 (1740-47)	639
Middleton, Thomas	10 (1760-67)	888
Mifsroon see Missroon		
Mikel see Mikell		
Mikell, Ephraim ₍Mikel₎	5 (1740-47)	174
Mikell, Ephraim ₍Ephrain₎	31 (1807-18)	287
Mikell, Ephraim	41 (1834-39)	717

Name	Volume	Page
Mikell, John	10 (1760-67)	649.
Mikell, John	34 (1818-26)	88
Mikell, Margaret Ann	43 (1839-45)	769
Mikell, Mary	38 (1826-34)	796
Mikell, Providence	44 (1845-51)	99
Mikell, William Joseph	30 (1800-07)	1105
Miles, Allen	19 (1780-83)	30
Miles, Edward	10 (1760-67)	732
Miles, Elizabeth	22 (1786-93)	108
Miles, James	16 (1774-79)	36
Miles, Jeremiah	4 (1736-40)	289
Miles, Jeremiah ₍Jarh.₎	8 (1757-60)	198
Miles, Jeremiah	19 (1780-83)	136
Miles, Jeremiah	24 (1786-93)	1002
Miles, John, Sr.	15 (1771-74)	533
Miles, John Allen	50 (1862-68)	322
Miles, Joseph	13 (1767-71)	986
Miles, Josiah	23 (1786-93)	777
Miles, Lewis	26 (1793-1800)	563
Miles, Mary	10 (1760-67)	625
Miles, Moses	14 (1771-74)	13
Miles, Silas	10 (1760-67)	851
Miles, Smith	49 (1856-62)	758
Miles, Thomas (Senr.)	7 (1752-56)	480
Miles, Thomas, Jr.	8 (1757-60)	68
Miles, Thomas	8 (1757-60)	113
Miles, William	7 (1752-56)	3
Miles, William, Junr.	8 (1757-60)	366
Miles, William	10 (1760-67)	499
Miles, William	16 (1774-79)	151
Miles, William	30 (1800-07)	1087
Milhous, John	25 (1793-1800)	298
Milhous, John	26 (1793-1800)	549

Name	Volume	Page
Milhous, Samuel	18 (1776-84)	137
Milhouse, Robert	7 (1752-56)	386
Milhouse, Robert	14 (1771-74)	126
Mill, Charles	14 (1771-74)	147
Millar, Philip [Phillip]	31 (1807-18)	13
Millar, Thomas	18 (1776-84)	116
Miller, Andrew	21 (1783-86)	485
Miller, Catharine	43 (1839-45)	740
Miller, Conrad	25 (1793-1800)	266
Miller, Eliza	34 (1818-26)	335
Miller, Elizabeth [Marmiller]	9 (1760-67)	292
Miller, Elizabeth	39 (1826-34)	1061
Miller, Elizabeth M.	44 (1845-51)	173
Miller, Jacob	14 (1771-74)	209
Miller, Jacob	45 (1845-51)	798
Miller, James	35 (1818-26)	499
Miller, John	6 (1747-52)	589
Miller, John	28 (1800-07)	327
Miller, John Theodore	31 (1807-18)	467
Miller, Martha S.	33 (1807-18)	1261
Miller, Martin	22 (1786-93)	299
Miller, Mary	30 (1800-07)	927
Miller, Mary	40 (1834-39)	165
Miller, Mathew	42 (1839-45)	197
Miller, Renee	27 (1793-1800)	692
Miller, Robert	10 (1760-67)	597
Miller, Rose Ann	47 (1851-56)	720
Miller, Samuel	8 (1757-60)	237
Miller, Samuel	24 (1786-93)	971
Miller, Samuel	25 (1793-1800)	178
Miller, Samuel	25 (1793-1800)	302
Miller, Samuel Stent	49 (1856-62)	909
Miller, Stephen	18 (1776-84)	159
Miller, William	28 (1800-07)	298

Name	Volume	Page
Miller, Zebulon	33 (1807-18)	1020
Miller see also Mounier		
Milles, Hugh ₍Mills₎	1 (1722-24)	84
Milligan, Jane	49 (1856-62)	762
Milligan, John	28 (1800-07)	227
Milligan, Joseph	31 (1807-18)	252
Milligan, Margaret	49 (1856-62)	929
Milligan, William	31 (1807-18)	406
Milligan, William	43 (1839-45)	648
Milliken, William	47 (1851-56)	439
Mills, Andrew	49 (1856-62)	786
Mills, George	16 (1774-79)	335
Mills, John	2 (1727-29)	74
Mills, Mary Ann	31 (1807-18)	103
Mills, Thomas	38 (1826-34)	729
Mills, William	28 (1800-07)	280
Mills see also Milles		
Millwood, George	32 (1807-18)	882
Milne, Andrew	48 (1856-62)	190
Milne, John	26 (1793-1800)	413
Milne, Martha	39 (1826-34)	1080
Milner, Daniel	26 (1793-1800)	608
Milner, Elizabeth	22 (1786-93)	80
Milner, Joh	9 (1760-67)	338
Milner, John	6 (1747-52)	200
Milner, John	23 (1786-93)	768
Milner, Joseph	3 (1732-37)	3
Milner, Mary	22 (1786-93)	313
Milner, Solomon	8 (1757-60)	126
Milner, Solomon	23 (1786-93)	472
Milwood, Elizabeth	37 (1826-34)	210
Mims, Thomas	48 (1856-62)	323
Minis, Abigail	25 (1793-1800)	296
Minnich, John Adam	21 (1783-86)	569

Name	Volume	Page
Minnick, John	26 (1793-1800)	448
Minott, Josaphat	9 (1760-67)	401
Minott, Susan C.	44 (1845-51)	113
Minting see Mintzing		
Mintzeng see Lintzing		
Mintzing, Anna Maria ⌐Minting; Maris⌐	28 (1800-07)	219
Mintzing, Jacob F.	42 (1839-45)	395
Mintzing, Philip ⌐Mintzeng⌐	19 (1780-83)	247
Minus, Jacob	24 (1786-93)	992
Miot, Alexander	14 (1771-74)	304
Miot, Frances	37 (1826-34)	97
Miot, John	31 (1807-18)	231
Miot see also Miott		
Miott, John ⌐Miot⌐	24 (1786-93)	949
Mirey, John Baptist	25 (1793-1800)	66
Miscampable, James ⌐Miscampble⌐	17 (1774-79)	674
Miscampble see Miscampable		
Mishaw, Francis	44 (1845-51)	451
Misman, John Ludwick	18 (1776-84)	7
Missroon, John S.	51 (1862-68)	524
Missroon, Margaret ⌐Mifsroon⌐	47 (1851-56)	506
Missroon, Margaret ⌐Mifsroon⌐	47 (1851-56)	530
Missroon, William Henry	48 (1856-62)	194
Mitcell see Mitchel		
Mitchel, John Roe ⌐Mitcell⌐	16 (1774-79)	231
Mitchel see also Mitchell		
Mitchell, Alexander R.	51 (1862-68)	578
Mitchell, Amelia D. V.	48 (1856-62)	269
Mitchell, Andrew	26 (1793-1800)	449
Mitchell, Ann	34 (1818-26)	191
Mitchell, Ann ⌐Mitchel⌐	49 (1856-62)	752
Mitchell, Ann E.	38 (1826-34)	592
Mitchell, Catherine	5 (1740-47)	609

Name	Volume	205 Page
Mitchell, Charles	25 (1793-1800)	36
Mitchell, Charlotte	50 (1862-68)	165
Mitchell, Daniel	5 (1740-47)	563
Mitchell, Edward, M. D.	47 (1851-56)	694
Mitchell, Elizabeth	42 (1839-45)	171
Mitchell, Elizabeth	42 (1839-45)	310
Mitchell, Ephraim	24 (1786-93)	1144
Mitchell, George	4 (1736-40)	12
Mitchell, George	6 (1747-52)	245
Mitchell, Ishmael	42 (1839-45)	426
Mitchell, James	12 (1767-71)	450
Mitchell, James	22 (1786-93)	151
Mitchell, James	39 (1826-34)	837
Mitchell, James D.	42 (1839-45)	352
Mitchell, James S.	43 (1839-45)	502
Mitchell, John	5 (1740-47)	48
Mitchell, John ₁Mitchel₁	19 (1780-83)	269
Mitchell, John	21 (1783-86)	443
Mitchell, John	24 (1786-93)	939
Mitchell, John	27 (1793-1800)	975
Mitchell, Joseph	5 (1740-47)	482
Mitchell, Margaret	41 (1834-39)	744
Mitchell, Meriam	18 (1776-84)	306
Mitchell, Moses	17 (1774-79)	446
Mitchell, Nannette	37 (1826-34)	413
Mitchell, Sarah	9 (1760-67)	220
Mitchell, Sarah	34 (1818-26)	169
Mitchell, Sarah E.	48 (1856-62)	67
Mitchell, Thomas	11 (1767-71)	271
Mitchell, Thomas Clarke	49 (1856-62)	871
Mitchell, W. B. R.	46 (1851-56)	213
Mitchell, William	26 (1793-1800)	650
Mitchell, William N.	37 (1826-34)	1
Mitchell, William Osborne	28 (1800-07)	275

Name	Volume	Page
Moer, Thomas	40 (1834-39)	139
Moer, William	30 (1800-07)	1095
Moer, William	35 (1818-26)	715
Moffet, Solomon	11 (1767-71)	222
Moffett, Andrew	45 (1845-51)	579
Moifson, John	38 (1826-34)	797
Moise, Abram, Junr.	46 (1851-56)	235
Moise, Isaac	48 (1856-62)	187
Moles, Margaret	40 (1834-39)	293
Molina, Moses	21 (1783-86)	774
Mompoey, Honore	49 (1856-62)	606
Monahon, Daniel	9 (1760-67)	297
Monatt, John	22 (1786-93)	141
Monck, Thomas	6 (1747-52)	26
Monclair, Amy	6 (1747-52)	595
Monclar, Peter	18 (1776-84)	50
Moncrief, Eleanor [Moncrieff]	20 (1783-86)	13
Moncrieff see Moncrief		
Moncrieffe, John	35 (1818-26)	503
Mondaze, Julia	45 (1845-51)	748
Monefeldt, Marie H.	49 (1856-62)	610
Monger, Gerrard, Capt.	2 (1729-31)	27
Mongin, David	13 (1767-71)	1000
Mongomery, Alexander	11 (1767-71)	1
Monk, James	30 (1800-07)	1080
Monk, John	22 (1786-93)	238
Monk, Joseph	2 (1724-25)	31
Monk, Thomas	10 (1760-67)	449
Monnar, Lewis	39 (1826-34)	1009
Monpoey, Honore	49 (1856-62)	606
Montesquieu, Francoise	44 (1845-51)	409
Montgomerie, Thomas	26 (1793-1800)	511
Montgomery, George	8 (1757-60)	260
Montgomery, Henry	12 (1767-71)	408

Name	Volume	Page
Montgomery, Henry	18 (1776-84)	233
Montgomery, Henry	33 (1807-18)	1313
* Montgomery, Samuel [Mountgomery]	6 (1747-52)	485
Montgomery, Sarah	17 (1774-79)	569
Mood, Peter	35 (1818-26)	583
Moodie, Benjamin	36 (1818-26)	868
Moodie, Rosa Adeline	51 (1862-68)	609
Moody, Catherine [Cathrine]	13 (1767-71)	852
Moody, Thomas	1 (1720-21)	71
Mooll, Bernard	22 (1786-93)	302
Mooney, Ann	42 (1839-45)	376
Moorall, John [Morrall]	13 (1767-71)	990
Moore, Ann	34 (1818-26)	75
Moore, Ann	34 (1818-26)	178
Moore, Elizabeth	24 (1786-93)	843
Moore, Elizabeth A(nn)	43 (1839-45)	623
Moore, Esther	31 (1807-18)	97
Moore, Frances (Senr.)	47 (1851-56)	729
Moore, Francis	14 (1771-74)	60
Moore, Francis	51 (1862-68)	666
Moore, Francis [Frances] (Order)	51 (1862-68)	680
Moore, Henry	3 (1731-33)	48
Moore, James	1 (1722-24)	82
Moore, James (Senr.)	14 (1771-74)	312
Moore, James	44 (1845-51)	395
Moore, Jehu	5 (1740-47)	469
Moore, John	3 (1732-37)	235
* Moore, John	6 (1747-52)	439
Moore, John	13 (1767-71)	920
Moore, John	22 (1786-93)	296
Moore, John	25 (1793-1800)	289
Moore, John	28 (1800-07)	301
Moore, John Elias	32 (1807-18)	540
Moore, Maria C.	50 (1862-68)	350

Name	Volume	Page
Morley, Susan	41 (1834-39)	936
Morrall, Daniel	14 (1771-74)	186
Morrall see also Moorall		
Morrel see Morrell		
Morrell, John [Morrel]	8 (1757-60)	417
Moorhead, James	50 (1862-68)	38
Morrifs, John	2(G1729-31)	30
Morris, Ann	44 (1845-51)	362
Morris, Anna E.	39 (1826-34)	853
Morris, Christopher Gadsden	44 (1845-51)	321
Morris, George	24 (1786-93)	1040
Morris, John Corbin [Corbyn]	19 (1780-83)	344
Morris, Lewis	36 (1818-26)	1079
Morris, Mary	38 (1826-34)	658
Morris, Mary Jones	50 (1862-68)	300
Morris, Thomas	38 (1826-34)	540
Morris, Thomas	48 (1856-62)	149
Morrison, John	28 (1800-07)	376
Morrison, John	35 (1818-26)	485
Morrison, John	38 (1826-34)	583
Morrison, Richard T., Sr.	49 (1856-62)	707
Morrison, Robert	12 (1767-71)	442
Morrison, Simon [Morison]	42 (1839-45)	26
Morrow, Robert	18 (1776-84)	229
Morse, John	31 (1807-18)	48
Morson, James	3 (1731-33)	62
Mortimer, Edward	37 (1826-34)	276
Mortimer, John	3 (1732-37)	115
Mortimur, Richard	8 (1757-60)	169
Morton, E.	35 (1818-26)	435
Morton, John	6 (1747-52)	580
Morton, Joseph	1 (1721-22)	1
Morton, Joseph	31 (1807-18)	223
Moses, Abraham [Abrahaham]	26 (1793-1800)	476

Name	Volume	Page
Moses, Deborah	45 (1845-51)	581
Moses, Elizabeth	8 (1757-60)	43
Moses, Isaiah	33 (1807-18)	1436
Moses, Lyon	35 (1818-26)	635
Moses, Mary	31 (1807-18)	391
Moses, Philip	27 (1793-1800)	848
Moses, Reuben	45 (1845-51)	682
Mothershead, Christopher	17 (1774-79)	795
Mott, Charles	14 (1771-74)	295
Motta, Jacob De La, M. D.	43 (1839-45)	834
Motte, Dorilla	50 (1862-68)	280
Motte, Isaac (Junior)	23 (1786-93)	675
Motte, Isaac	25 (1793-1800)	293
Motte, Jacob	13 (1767-71)	797
Motte, John Abraham	1 (1711-18)	6
Motte, Mary	42 (1839-45)	455
Motte, Rebecca	33 (1807-18)	1005
Mottet, Edward	51 (1862-68)	623
Mouatt, Mary	42 (1839-45)	181
Moulin, Pierre	37 (1826-34)	337
Moultrie, Alexander	47 (1851-56)	844
Moultrie, Hannah	30 (1800-07)	914
Moultrie, John	14 (1771-74)	142
Moultrie, Thomás	19 (1780-83)	198
Moultrie, William Ainslie	31 (1807-18)	459
Moultrie, William Lennox	50 (1862-68)	335
Mouncey, John ⌊Mouncy⌋	9 (1760-67)	316
Mouncy see Mouncey		
Mounier, Estienne ⌊Miller⌋	6 (1747-52)	266
Mountgomery see Montgomery		
Mountgummery, William	13 (1767-71)	968
Mountjoy, Thomas	2 (1729-31)	26
Mouroumet, John ⌊Maurouinet⌋	10 (1760-67)	633

Name	Volume	Page
Mouzon, Charles	47 (1851-56)	862
Mouzon, Henry	6 (1747-52)	292
* Mouzon, Henry (Junr.)	18 (1776-84)	242
Mouzon, Lewis (Junr.)	6 (1747-52)	112
Mouzon, Lewis	7 (1752-56)	420
Mouzon, Lewis	16 (1774-79)	75
Mouzon, Peter	22 (1786-93)	170
Mowbray, Arthur	5 (1740-47)	547
Mowbray, Lelias [Lellias]	10 (1760-67)	645
Mowbray, Thomas	11 (1767-71)	118
Mowry, Edward S.	50 (1862-68)	201
Mowry, Smith, Jr.	49 (1856-62)	817
Moxly, Mary	40 (1834-39)	434
Muckenfufs, Andrew	20 (1783-86)	301
Muckenfufs, Michael	31 (1807-18)	144
Muckenfuss, Catharine	45 (1845-51)	637
Muckenfuss, Henry	48 (1856-62)	136
Mufso see Musso		
Muggridge, Matthew	41 (1834-39)	501
Muirhead, James	28 (1800-07)	91
Muller, Johannah Magdalene	27 (1793-1800)	918
Mulligan, Frances	36 (1818-26)	922
* Mulligan, Joseph	18 (1776-84)	250
Mullings, John	45 (1845-51)	643
Mullins, George	16 (1774-79)	127
Mullins, Mary, Mrs.	2 (1729-31)	46
Mullins, Sarah	31 (1807-18)	20
Munch, Philip H.	33 (1807-18)	1001
Muncreef, Mary	31 (1807-18)	241
Muncreef, Richard	23 (1786-93)	517
Munds, James T	38 (1826-34)	740
Munro, Lucretia	27 (1793-1800)	900
Munro, Margaret	44 (1845-51)	212

Name	Volume	Page
Murden, Eliza	44 (1845-51)	154
Murdoch, Archibold	27 (1793-1800)	801
Murfee, Malachi	18 (1776-84)	329
Murphet, Catharine	12 (1767-71)	448
Murphey, Hugh	10 (1760-67)	763
Murphey, Thomas	22 (1786-93)	330
Murphy, Elizabeth	46 (1851-56)	437
Murphy, James	9 (1760-67)	308
Murphy, James	47 (1851-56)	805
Murphy, John	6 (1747-52)	457
Murphy, John ⌐John E.⌐	49 (1856-62)	754
Murphy, John E. see Murphy, John		
Murphy, Peter	37 (1826-34)	295
Murphy, Thomas	7 (1752-56)	235
Murray, Alexander	5 (1740-47)	608
Murray, Alexander	15 (1771-74)	393
Murray, Alexander	25 (1793-1800)	199
Murray, David	17 (1774-79)	425
Murray, George W.	41 (1834-39)	591
Murray, John	15 (1771-74)	674
Murray, John Michael	38 (1826-34)	548
Murray, Joseph	7 (1752-56)	162
Murray, Joseph James	34 (1818-26)	44
Murray, Peter	3 (1732-37)	66
Murray, Wm. C.	47 (1851-56)	801
Murrell, (Arthur) Priscillah	17 (1774-79)	553
Murrell, Francis	3 (1732-37)	33
Murrell, John	26 (1793-1800)	521
Murrell, Martha	41 (1834-39)	559
Murrell, Paul	22 (1786-93)	309
Murrell, Priscillah see Murrell (Arthur) Priscillah		
Murrell, Thomas	29 (1800-07)	516
Murrell see also Murrill		

Name	Volume	Page
Murriell, Robert	9 (1760-67)	216
Murril, Jonathan	5 (1740-47)	526
Murrill, Francis [Murrell]	7 (1752-56)	263
Murrill, Robert [Murrell]	23 (1786-93)	510
Murrill, Susannah	15 (1771-74)	467
Musso, Antonio [Mufso]	47 (1851-56)	447
Myddelton, William	9 (1760-67)	275
Myers, Charles	17 (1774-79)	687
Myers, David	42 (1839-45)	342
Myers, John	27 (1793-1800)	695
Myers, Joseph	22 (1786-93)	191
Myers, Sarah D.	50 (1862-68)	209
Myers, Tobias	27 (1793-1800)	871
Mylne, James	30 (1800-07)	816

N

Name	Volume	Page
Nagel, Hans	17 (1774-79)	543
* Nail, Daniel	15 (1771-74)	342
Nairne, Elizabeth	1 (1721-22)	40
Napier, Rebekah	50 (1862-68)	426
Napier, Rebekah (Substitution of Trustee)	51 (1862-68)	599
Napier, Thomas	49 (1856-62)	740
Napier, William	3 (1731-33)	69
Nasar, Philip	30 (1800-07)	991
Nash, Ann	2 (1724-25)	18
Nash, Levi	36 (1818-26)	1035
Nash, William	3 (1732-37)	309
Nash, William	45 (1845-51)	739
Nathan, Solomon	38 (1826-34)	545
Nathans, Nathan	47 (1851-56)	543
Nayler, Harriett G. L.	51 (1862-68)	754
Neale, Andrew	17 (1774-79)	522
Neale, William	25 (1793-1800)	112

Name	Volume	Page
Neckar, Martha	22 (1786-93)	107
Neeley, William	14 (1771-74)	255
Neilson, Ann	14 (1771-74)	322
Neilson, James Stockton	33 (1807-18)	1314
Neilson, Jared [Nelson]	7 (1752-56)	401
* Neilson, Jared	15 (1771-74)	351
Neilson, Mathew [Matthew]	14 (1771-74)	47
Neilson, Matthew	5 (1740-47)	299
Neilson, William	8 (1757-60)	79
Neilson, William	14 (1771-74)	166
Neilson see also King		
Neiufuille, John	6 (1747-52)	264
Nell, Jefse	36 (1818-26)	844
Nelson, Francis	31 (1807-18)	10
Nelson, George	5 (1740-47)	160
Nelson, George	37 (1826-34)	107
Nelson, Susannah	33 (1807-18)	995
Nelson see also Neilson		
Neufville, Ann	33 (1807-18)	1351
Neufville, Benjamin S.	47 (1851-56)	712
Neufville, Edward	45 (1845-51)	846
Neufville, Eunice	43 (1839-45)	506
Neufville, John	29 (1800-07)	717
Nevens, Edward	37 (1826-34)	286
Nevill, John	36 (1818-26)	1073
Newell, Thomas	3 (1732-37)	327
Newman, Charles see Newman, Edward		
Newman, Deliverance	8 (1757-60)	318
Newman, Edward [Charles]	9 (1760-67)	168
Newman, Reuben	28 (1800-07)	353
Newman, Samuel	13 (1767-71)	911
Newman, Samuel W.	46 (1851-56)	327
Newnham, Nathaniel	19 (1780-83)	402
Newton, Abraham	23 (1786-93)	635

Name	Volume	Page
Newton, John ⌐Nwton⌐	5 (1740-47)	536
Newton, Mary	39 (1826-34)	1037
Newton, Mary (Substitution of Trustee)	39 (1826-34)	1082
Newton, Mary (Substitution of Trustee)	41 (1834-39)	708
Newton, Mary (Substitution of Trustee)	41 (1834-39)	709
Newton, Mary (Substitution of Trustee)	42 (1839-45)	309
Newton, Mary (Substitution of Trustee)	45 (1845-51)	541
Newton, Richard	1 (1692-93)	16
Newton, William	30 (1800-07)	776
Newton, William	31 (1807-18)	235
Newton, William	50 (1862-68)	63
Neyle, Elizabeth	30 (1800-07)	1091
Neyle, Gilbert	24 (1786-93)	899
Neyle, Gilbert Neville	40 (1834-39)	336
Neyle, Molly	39 (1826-34)	912
Neyle, Philip A.	44 (1845-51)	117
Neyle, Sampson	19 (1780-83)	321
Nicholas, Stephen ⌐Nichols⌐	5 (1740-47)	317
Nicholes, Henry	21 (1783-86)	717
Nicholes, Henry	33 (1807-18)	1221
Nicholes, Isaac	8 (1757-60)	330
Nicholes, Isaac	23 (1786-93)	776
Nicholes, James	26 (1793-1800)	552
Nicholls, Samuel	7 (1752-56)	351
Nichols, Elizabeth	7 (1752-56)	385
Nichols, Henry	2 (1729-31)	48
Nichols, Thomas, Jr.	11 (1767-71)	34
Nichols see also Nicholas		
Nicholson, Frances	16 (1774-79)	12
Nicholson, James	41 (1834-39)	572
Nicholson, John	2 (1729-31)	62

Name	Volume	Page
Nicholson, Joseph	21 (1783-86)	557
Nightingale, Thomas	12 (1767-71)	641
Nisbet, Alexander	16 (1774-79)	78
Nisbett, Abigail	34 (1818-26)	176
Nisbett, Alexander	7 (1752-56)	119
Nisbett, Alexander	32 (1807-18)	652
Nisbett, James	32 (1807-18)	700
✳ Nisbett, William	20 (1783-86)	233
Nisbitt, Unity	38 (1826-34)	776
Niurt, Jacob	27 (1793-1800)	909
Nivison, John	29 (1800-07)	453
Nix, Edward	17 (1774-79)	564
Noah, Nicholas	12 (1767-71)	613
Noble, Catherine Le see Noble La Catherine		
Noble, La Catherine ₍Catherine Le₎	2 (1722-26)	26
Noble, Mary	43 (1839-45)	797
Nohrden, Carsten ₍Carstin₎	49 (1856-62)	876
Noisette, Philip Stanislas	40 (1834-39)	203
Noll, Conrad	26 (1793-1800)	377
Nopie, Martha E.	42 (1839-45)	461
Norman, Barak	13 (1767-71)	949
Norman, George	14 (1771-74)	249
Norman, Henry	49 (1856-62)	622
Norman, John	13 (1767-71)	855
Norman, Joseph	5 (1740-47)	647
Norman, Joseph	10 (1760-67)	567
Norman, Mary	6 (1747-52)	224
Norman, William	2 (1726-27)	60
Normand, Philip	7 (1752-56)	575
Norris, Agnes	39 (1826-34)	1195
Norris, James	41 (1834-39)	924
Norris, Mary	34 (1818-26)	246
Norris, Penelopa	25 (1793-1800)	159

Name	Volume	Page
Norris, Robert	30 (1800-07)	904
Norroy, de Mary Magdalen Cannelle (Ve.) [Mary Magdalen Cannelle (Ve.) de]	37 (1826-34)	98
Norroy see also De Norry		
North, Edward	5 (1740-47)	179
North, Edward	27 (1793-1800)	737
North, Edward	50 (1862-68)	92
North, John	10 (1760-67)	855
Northon see Norton		
Northrop, Mrs. C. M.	47 (1851-56)	555
Norton, Jonathan [Northon]	16 (1774-79)	172
Norwood, Zecheriah	43 (1839-45)	664
Nowell, Edward Brown [Broun]	28 (1800-07)	210
Nowell, Elizabeth	36 (1818-26)	953
Nowell, John	45 (1845-51)	469
Nowell, John F.	36 (1818-26)	1018
Nowell, Margaret	41 (1834-39)	721
Nuffer, Herman	17 (1774-79)	454
Nwton see Newton		
Nyart, Catherine	28 (1800-07)	201
Nygh, Peter	7 (1752-56)	576

O

Name	Volume	Page
Oates, Edward H.	47 (1851-56)	452
Oates, George	46 (1851-56)	423
Oates, Henry T.	47 (1851-56)	777
Oates, John	36 (1818-26)	1110
Oatham, Thomas	8 (1757-60)	385
Oats, Edward	19 (1780-83)	156
Oats, Mary	40 (1834-39)	24
O'Connor, Thomas	32 (1807-18)	771
Odam, Abraham	13 (1767-71)	1032
O'Daniel, Jane E.	48 (1856-62)	104
O'Driscoll, Dennis	33 (1807-18)	1317

Name	Volume	Page
O'Driscoll, Eliza	46 (1851-56)	140
O'Driscoll, Harriett C.	48 (1856-62)	35
Odum, Jane	49 (1856-62)	739
Oetzen, Johann Christian Frederick	45 (1845-51)	607
Ofborn see Osborn		
Ogier, John Martin	38 (1826-34)	599
Ogier, Thomas	39 (1826-34)	1210
Ogilvie, Charles	23 (1786-93)	772
Ogle, Dorothy	1 (1722-24)	16
Ogle, Robert	19 (1780-83)	215
O'Hara, Henry	39 (1826-34)	1219
O'Hear, James	32 (1807-18)	677
O'Hear, James W.	50 (1862-68)	419
O'Hear, Joseph F.	49 (1856-62)	647
O'Hear, Sarah	42 (1839-45)	336
Oland, Deidrick [Diedrick]	46 (1851-56)	335
Oldfeild, Thomas	8 (1757-60)	312
Oldham, Benet	12 (1767-71)	432
Oliphant, Eliza J. [I.]	45 (1845-51)	805
Oliver, George	5 (1740-47)	-231
*Oliver, Isaac	20 (1783-86)	274
Oliver, Jane	24 (1786-93)	1060
Oliver, John	31 (1807-18)	416
Oliver, Margaret [Olivier]	10 (1760-67)	601
Oliver, Stephen	37 (1826-34)	53
Oliver, Thomas	5 (1740-47)	326
Oliver, see also Olliver		
Olivera, Jacob	6 (1747-52)	635
Olivier see Oliver		
Olliver, (Mr.) Mark [Oliver]	2 (1729-31)	53
O'Neal, Charles	13 (1767-71)	729
O'Neal, Frederick	11 (1767-71)	281
O'Neale, Charles	39 (1826-34)	1131
O'Neale, Elizabeth [O'Neall]	46 (1851-56)	164

Name	Volume	Page
O'Neall see O'Neale		
O'Neill, Edmund	45 (1845-51)	461
O'Neill, John	43 (1839-45)	630
O'Neill, Patrick	51 (1862-68)	465
Onsilt, John	24 (1786-93)	1031
Opnnen, Emanuel	28 (1800-07)	339
Oppenheim, Hertz Wolff	46 (1851-56)	284
O'Reilly, Caroline B.	37 (1826-34)	267
O'Reilly, James	34 (1818-26)	408
Organ, Solomon	17 (1774-79)	792
Orr, Robert	5 (1740-47)	629
Orvin, Henry W. J.	48 (1856-62)	522
Osborn, Catharine	42 (1839-45)	189
Osborn, Thomas	31 (1807-18)	191
Osborn, William [Ofborn]	9 (1760-67)	221
Osborne, Henry	30 (1800-07)	846
Osgood, Josiah	4 (1736-40)	30
Osgood, Thomas (Senr.)	2 (1727-29)	63
O'Sullivan, James	46 (1851-56)	244
Oswald, Margaret	20 (1783-86)	76
Oswald, William	21 (1783-86)	633
Ott, John	14 (1771-74)	168
Ott, Martin	16 (1774-79)	210
Otten, Cord	49 (1856-62)	566
Otterson, John	4 (1736-40)	6
Otto, John	29 (1800-07)	410
Ottolengui, Abraham	45 (1845-51)	796
Otzell, Johannes	32 (1807-18)	701
Ouldfield, John	7 (1752-56)	53
Ousley, James	8 (1757-60)	66
Outerbridge, White	31 (1807-18)	345
Overy, Isaiah	5 (1740-47)	530
Owen, Daniel D.	51 (1862-68)	871
Owen, David, Jr.	49 (1856-62)	798

Name	Volume	Page
Owen, Elizabeth	21 (1783-86)	547
Owen, John	6 (1747-52)	381
Owen, John	6 (1747-52)	646
Owen, John	33 (1807-18)	1010
Owen, Mary	6 (1747-52)	217
Owen, Thomas	4 (1736-40)	34
Owens, Alexander	49 (1856-62)	1008
Owens, James	10 (1760-67)	777
Owheeler, Michael [Owheller]	35 (1818-26)	547
Owheller see Owheeler		
Owins, Thomas	26 (1793-1800)	334
Oxendine see Oxindine		
Oxindine, John [Oxendine]	26 (1793-1800)	581

P

Name	Volume	Page
Pachelbell, Charles Theodore	6 (1747-52)	402
Packer, James	36 (1818-26)	1054
Packrow, Sophia	27 (1793-1800)	712
Page, George	5 (1740-47)	211
Page, John	5 (1740-47)	404
Page, Sarah	14 (1771-74)	261
Page, Thomas	19 (1780-83)	154
Page, Thomas	20 (1783-86)	40
Page, William	15 (1771-74)	515
Page, William	44 (1845-51)	153
Pagett, Frances	5 (1740-47)	592
Pagett, Francis	2 (1729-31)	80
Pagett, John	6 (1747-52)	38
Pagett, Thomas	26 (1793-1800)	406
Paine, Thomas	37 (1826-34)	373
Paine, Thomas	49 (1856-62)	559
Painter, Peter	1 (1716-21)	1
Paisley, Robert	9 (1760-67)	50
Paisley, Robert A.	38 (1826-34)	773

Name	Volume	Page
Pallmer see Palmer		
Palmer, Ann	13 (1767-71)	998
Palmer, Elizabeth [Pectmer]	5 (1740-47)	388
Palmer, Elizabeth	8 (1757-60)	395
Palmer, Esther	39 (1826-34)	1019
Palmer, Evans	7 (1752-56)	57(Dup.p.68)
Palmer, Evans	7 (1752-56)	68(Dup.p.57)
Palmer, Francis [Pallmer]	3 (1732-37)	181
Palmer, Francis Gendron	50 (1862-68)	21
Palmer, Harriott	42 (1839-45)	437
Palmer, Henry	14 (1771-74)	61
Palmer, Job	43 (1839-45)	829
Palmer, John	5 (1740-47)	358
Palmer, John	16 (1774-79)	198
Palmer, John	33 (1807-18)	1186
Palmer, John S. Jr.	50 (1862-68)	287
Palmer, Joseph	21 (1783-86)	703
Palmer, Joseph	42 (1839-45)	344
Palmer, Maham	46 (1851-56)	232
Palmer, Marianne G.	47 (1851-56)	741
Palmer, Mary Ann	34 (1818-26)	389
Palmer, Robert	2 (1726-27)	51
Palmer, Samuel J.	46 (1851-56)	337
Palmer, Thomas	6 (1747-52)	236
Palmer, Thomas	6 (1747-52)	327
Palmer, Thomas	32 (1807-18)	515
Palmer, Thomas	35 (1818-26)	757
Palmer, W. J.	49 (1856-62)	1054
Pamor, John	21 (1783-86)	580
Pamor, Jonathan	2 (1729-31)	92
Pamor, Marianne	21 (1783-86)	805
Panknin, Charles H.	49 (1856-62)	734
Panting, Thomas	14 (1771-74)	81
Pappenheimer, Ezias S.	36 (1818-26)	1046
Paris,John Alexander	7 (1752-56)	1

Name	Volume	Page
Park, Catharine	48 (1856-62)	200
Parker, Aldredge ⌈Aldridge⌉	41 (1834-39)	557
Parker, Ann	31 (1807-18)	260
Parker, Anna M.	50 (1862-68)	108
Parker, Arthur M.	51 (1862-68)	848
Parker, Benjamin	36 (1818-26)	1118
Parker, Charles	48 (1856-62)	533
Parker, Elizabeth	43 (1839-45)	915
* Parker, George	18 (1776-84)	252
Parker, George	32 (1807-18)	839
Parker, Harriott	28 (1800-07)	302
Parker, Isaac	36 (1818-26)	955
Parker, John	28 (1800-07)	256
Parker, John	30 (1800-07)	947
Parker, John	32 (1807-18)	765
Parker, John	39 (1826-34)	1109
Parker, John (Codicil)	39 (1826-34)	1125
Parker, John	45 (1845-51)	570
Parker, Joseph	23 (1786-93)	626
Parker, Martha	34 (1818-26)	83
Parker, Mary	37 (1826-34)	137
Parker, Mary	49 (1856-62)	973
Parker, Peter G.	46 (1851-56)	150
Parker, Rachel V.	50 (1862-68)	214
Parker, Samuel	38 (1826-34)	720
Parker, Sarah	31 (1807-18)	256
Parker, Sarah	34 (1818-26)	82
Parker, Sarah P.	44 (1845-51)	183
Parker, Thomas	35 (1818-26)	588
Parker, Thomas	49 (1856-62)	997
Parker, Wellington	40 (1834-39)	54
Parker, William	7 (1752-56)	2
Parker, William	20 (1783-86)	396
Parker, William	30 (1800-07)	908

Name	Volume	Page
Parker, William McKenzie	38 (1826-34)	762
Parker, William McKenzie	49 (1856-62)	763
Parkison, Mary Susannah	46 (1851-56)	346
Parler, Peter	39 (1826-34)	1137
✱ Parmenter, Benjamin	15 (1771-74)	441
Parmenter, John (Senr.)	18 (1776-84)	65
Parmenter, Joseph	25 (1793-1800)	232
Parmenter, Joseph	28 (1800-07)	309
✱ Parmenter, Thomas	6 (1747-52)	434
Parmenter, William	14 (1771-74)	291
Parminter, Phillimon [Phillemon]	4 (1736-46)	86
Parntram, John	16 (1774-79)	189
Parot, William	3 (1732-37)	209
Parris, Alexander	3 (1732-37)	251
Parrock, John	17 (1774-79)	811
Parrot, Hannah	9 (1760-67)	307
Parry, Harriet E.	48 (1856-62)	458
Parsons, Clarinda	46 (1851-56)	153
✱ Parsons, James	18 (1776-84)	344
Parsons, Joseph	36 (1818-26)	858
Parsons, Jane	30 (1800-07)	949
Parsons, Robert	5 (1740-47)	550
Parsons, Susanna	27 (1793-1800)	905
Partridge, Ann	8 (1757-60)	222
Partridge, Nathl., Capt.	1 (1722-24)	33
Pasquereaux, Peter	1 (1721-22)	5
Patchit, William	12 (1767-71)	575
Paterson, John [Patterson]	9 (1760-67)	157
Paterson see also Patterson		
Patient, John	9 (1760-67)	144
Patin, Josephine Grand Jean de fouchy	37 (1826-34)	264
Patiot, Francoise P. J. (née) De Stack	28 (1800-07)	260

Name	Volume	Page
Peak, Elizabeth	35 (1818-26)	755
Peak, John	35 (1818-26)	753
Peak, Oliver D.	34 (1818-26)	376
Peak, Stephen	10 (1760-67)	826
Pearce, Elizabeth	44 (1845-51)	449
Pearce, Frances	24 (1786-93)	1147
Pearce, John [Peirce]	8 (1757-60)	196
✳ Pearce, Offspring	20 (1733-86)	201
Pearis, Robert (Esqr.)	19 (1780-83)	275
Pearson, Enock	18 (1776-84)	180
Pearson, Moses	9 (1760-67)	373
Peart, Joshua	5 (1740-47)	33
Peartree, James	1 (1711-18)	30
Peat, John	17 (1774-79)	788
Pebzer, Anthony	39 (1826-34)	1105
Pecare, Rose	41 (1834-39)	817
Pectmer see Palmer		
Pegler see Peagler		
Peirce, John [Pierce]	10 (1760-67)	551
Peirce see also Pearce		
Pelot, Francis	16 (1774-79)	283
Pelot, John	18 (1776-84)	52
Pelot, Jonas	12 (1767-71)	440
Pendarvis, James	26 (1793-1800)	596
Pendarvis, John	2 (1724-25)	26
Pendarvis, Joseph	1 (1692-93)	37
Pendarvis, Joseph	3 (1732-37)	240
✳ Pendarvis, Thomas, Sr.	20 (1783-86)	183
Pendarvis, William	22 (1786-93)	83
Pendergrafs, Darby	19 (1780-83)	19
Pendleton, Henry	22 (1786-93)	330
Penefather, John	5 (1740-47)	508
Penington, Abraham	7 (1752-56)	528

Name	Volume	Page
Peronneau, Henry	5 (1740-47)	155
Peronneau, Henry	7 (1752-56)	201
Peronneau, Henry	22 (1786-93)	112
Peronneau, Henry W.	48 (1856-62)	440
Peronneau, Henry W. (Substitution of Trustee)	49 (1856-62)	1040
* Peronneau, Mary	15 (1771-74)	340
Peronneau, Mary	44 (1845-51)	225
Peronneau, Mary C.	45 (1845-51)	538
Peronneau, Robert	20 (1783-86)	115
Peronneau, Samuel	12 (1767-71)	439
Peronneau see also Perroneau, Perronneau		
Perott, Benjamin	13 (1767-71)	896
Perret, John, Sr.	18 (1776-84)	284
Perrier, Francoise	48 (1856-62)	452
Perriman, John	5 (1740-47)	520
Perriman, Thomas	1 (1711-18)	22
Perroneau, Mary Ann [Peronneau]	19 (1780-83)	294
Perroneau, Samuel [Peronneau]	7 (1752-56)	431
Perronneau, Alexander, Jr.	15 (1771-74)	636
Perronneau, Arthur [Peronneau]	16 (1774-79)	238
Perronneau, Richard [Peronneau]	24 (1786-93)	916
Perry, Ann	51 (1862-68)	656
Perry Ann Drayton	38 (1826-34)	788
Perry, Benjamin	9 (1760-67)	214
Perry, Benjamin	48 (1856-62)	63
* Perry, Benjamin Lucas	25 (1793-1800)	1
Perry, Edward	7 (1752-56)	369
Perry, Edward	14 (1771-74)	34
Perry, Edward	27 (1793-1800)	882
Perry, Edward, Junior	28 (1800-07)	58
Perry, Francis	11 (1767-71)	13
Perry, Helen	32 (1807-18)	717

Name	Volume	Page
Petsch, Adam	25 (1793-1800)	268
Pettigrew, J. Johnston	50 (1862-68)	130
Pettineau, John [Petineau]	1 (1721-22)	52
Petty, Deborah [Debt]	4 (1736-40)	186
Petty, Henry	6 (1747-52)	89
Peurifoy, Nancy H.	46 (1851-56)	278
Peyn, Jacobus	7 (1752-56)	572
Peyre, David	3 (1732-37)	290
Peyre, Floride	35 (1818-26)	445
Peyre, Francis, Senior	34 (1818-26)	415
Peyre, John	30 (1800-07)	1103
Peyre, Judith	13 (1767-71)	900
Peyre, Mary E.	38 (1826-34)	490
Peyre, Phillip	5 (1740-47)	567
Peyre, Rene	11 (1767-71)	194
Peyre, Rene	15 (1771-74)	642
Peyre, Samuel	8 (1757-60)	203
Peysson, Emelie H.	49 (1856-62)	681
Peyton, Henry	29 (1800-07)	618
Pezant, Bonne Sophie	49 (1856-62)	991
Pezant, John L('Aimable) [L'Pezant]	45 (1845-51)	561
Pezant, John L.	45 (1845-51)	727
Pezant, Louis	50 (1862-68)	142
Pfafhauser see Pofhizer		
Pfeninger, Martin	20 (1783-86)	71
Phelon, Margaret E.	41 (1834-39)	825
Phelps, Thomas	17 (1774-79)	721
Philips, Hugh	22 (1786-93)	374
Philips, John	36 (1818-26)	1028
Philips see also Phillips		
Phillips, Aaron	40 (1834-39)	17
Phillips, Ann	49 (1856-62)	651
Phillips, Bella	49 (1856-62)	1000
Phillips, Dorothra	39 (1826-34)	890

Name	Volume	Page
Phillips, John Christian ₍Philips₎	26 (1793-1800)	371
Phillips, Martha	48 (1856-62)	20
Phillips, Susannah ₍Susanah₎	5 (1740-47)	667
Phillips, Thomas	9 (1760-67)	186
Phillips, Timothy	17 (1774-79)	443
Phillips, William	31 (1807-18)	50
Philp, Mary	21 (1783-86)	672
Philp, Robert	21 (1783-86)	420
Phipps, Anne	23 (1786-93)	569
Phipps, John	5 (1740-47)	582
Phipps, John	28 (1800-07)	232
Phipps, Joseph	12 (1767-71)	565
Phipps, Joseph Steed ₍Steeds₎	27 (1793-1800)	957
Phrisbey, Jonah ₍Frisbie₎	21 (1783-86)	498
Phynney, Josiah	37 (1826-34)	296
Phynney, Josiah D.	49 (1856-62)	1051
Pichard, Charles Jacob ₍Prichard₎	8 (1757-60)	506
Pickering, Ann	26 (1793-1800)	515
Pickering, Joseph	8 (1757-60)	378
Pickering, Martha	31 (1807-18)	384
Pierce see Peirce		
Pierredon, Collins	28 (1800-07)	261
Pight, John	2 (1726-27)	11
Pilkington, Gabriel	11 (1767-71)	103
Pillans, William	11 (1767-71)	178
Pillot, John	35 (1818-26)	570
Pillot, Onerime	37 (1826-34)	40
Pillsbury see Pilsbury		
Pilsbury, Samuel ₍Pillsbury₎	38 (1826-34)	443
Pilsbury, William	28 (1800-07)	183
Pimenta, Leah	11 (1767-71)	301
Pinceel, William	36 (1818-26)	1123
Pinckney, Charles	21 (1783-86)	527
Pinckney, Charles	36 (1818-26)	1048

Name	Volume	Page
Pinckney, Charles Cotesworth	36 (1818-26)	1168
Pinckney, Deborah	22 (1786-93)	377
Pinckney, Eliza	50 (1862-68)	11
Pinckney, Eliza A.	33 (1807-18)	1232
Pinckney, Frances M. see Pinckney, Thomas & Frances (M.)		
Pinckney, Frances Motte	43 (1839-45)	598
Pinckney, Frances Susanna	35 (1818-26)	741
Pinckney, Hannah	37 (1826-34)	242
Pinckney, Harriott	51 (1862-68)	476
Pinckney, Hopson	25 (1793-1800)	123
Pinckney, Jane Mary	46 (1851-56)	95
Pinckney, Lucia	50 (1862-68)	174
Pinckney, Mary	29 (1800-07)	715
Pinckney, Mary	32 (1807-18)	542
Pinckney, Rogers [Roger]	18 (1776-84)	154
Pinckney, Thomas, Junr.	33 (1807-18)	986
Pinckney, Thomas	43 (1839-45)	474
Pinckney, Thomas & Frances (M)	38 (1826-34)	571
Pinney, John	1 (1722-24)	81
Pinny, John	7 (1752-56)	513
Pitcock, John	17 (1774-79)	576
Plaine, Abraham Fleur f De La	1 (1721-22)	24
Platt, John	25 (1793-1800)	82
Platt, John	38 (1826-34)	502
Platts, Jacob	26 (1793-1800)	600
Player, Elizabeth	28 (1800-07)	152
Player, Joseph	17 (1774-79)	641
Player, Roger	1 (1720-21)	10
Player, Thomas (Senr.)	16 (1774-79)	175
Player, Thomas	28 (1800-07)	41
Plifsonau, John Julien	39 (1826-34)	1136
Plifsonau, Marie Claire [Mary]	36 (1818-26)	878
Plowman, John Jacob	12 (1767-71)	626

Name	Volume	Page
Plumet, Antoine	33 (1807-18)	1064
Plunket, Elizabeth	10 (1760-67)	689
Poaug, Charlotte	22 (1786-93)	137
Pofhizer, Conrad ⌐Pfafhauser⌐	25 (1793-1800)	213
Pohl, Joseph	47 (1851-56)	445
Poineignon, Jeanne Coulen	44 (1845-51)	243
Poineignon, John	44 (1845-51)	247
Poineignon, Peter Anthony	36 (1818-26)	854
Poinset see Pointset		
Poinsett, Elisha	14 (1771-74)	17
Poinsett, Elisha	29 (1800-07)	508
Poinsett, Fanny	29 (1800-07)	748
Poinsett, Joel R.	46 (1851-56)	36
Poinsett, Susannah ⌐Susanna⌐	29 (1800-07)	395
Pointset, Joel ⌐Poinset⌐	5 (1740-47)	381
Polony, Jean Louis	30 (1800-07)	875
Polony, Michel Emile	45 (1845-51)	745
Pomer, Michael	6 (1747-52)	401
Pongaudin, James	24 (1786-93)	1098
Pool, Isaac	32 (1807-18)	704
Poole, Joseph	8 (1757-60)	278
Poor, Patrick	6 (1747-52)	227
Pooser, George	20 (1783-86)	278
Poppenheim, Barbara ⌐Barbary⌐	42 (1839-45)	154
Poppenheim, Elizabeth	40 (1834-39)	164
Poppenheim, Lewis	34 (1818-26)	369
Poppenheim, Mary	32 (1807-18)	556
Porcher, Elizabeth	26 (1793-1800)	622
Porcher, Elizabeth Julia	41 (1834-39)	508
Porcher, Elizabeth S.	51 (1862-68)	688
Porcher, H. F.	49 (1856-62)	592
Porcher, Harriett ⌐Hariett⌐	51 (1862-68)	570
Porcher, Isaac	2 (1726-27)	33

Name	Volume	Page
Porcher, Isaac	19 (1780-83)	284
Porcher, Isaac	45 (1845-51)	470
Porcher, J. DuBose	51 (1862-68)	498
Porcher, John P.	41 (1834-39)	930
Porcher, John P.	50 (1862-68)	318
Porcher, Joseph	13 (1767-71)	726
Porcher, Julius T.	50 (1862-68)	219
Porcher, Mariane	22 (1786-93)	105
Porcher, Marianne Gendron	40 (1834-39)	360
Porcher, Marion	32 (1807-18)	572
Porcher, Paul	19 (1780-83)	356
Porcher, Peter	7 (1752-56)	123
Porcher, Peter	19 (1780-83)	233
Porcher, Peter	20 (1783-86)	1
Porcher, Peter, Senr.	26 (1793-1800)	556
Porcher, Peter Ann Elizabeth	37 (1826-34)	122
Porcher, Peter C.	46 (1851-56)	253
Porcher, Philip	28 (1800-07)	50
Porcher, Philip	33 (1807-18)	1400
Porcher, Philip S.	40 (1834-39)	53
Porcher, Rachel	6 (1747-52)	115
Porcher, Samuel	45 (1845-51)	856
Porcher, Thomas	40 (1834-39)	205
Porcher, Thomas	43 (1839-45)	636
Porte, John [Porté]	40 (1834-39)	69
Porter, Fredrick [Frederick]	17 (1774-79)	730
* Porter, John	6 (1747-52)	445
Porter, Joseph Y. (Codicil)	44 (1845-51)	285
Porter, Mary	2 (1724-25)	108
Porter, Matthew	1 (1711-18)	98
Porter, Pricilla	33 (1807-18)	1163
Porter, Sarah	11 (1767-71)	11
Porter, Thomas	7 (1752-56)	405
Porter, William	6 (1747-52)	307

Name	Volume	Page
Porter, William L.	49 (1856-62)	735
Portvan see Portvin		
Portvin, Anthony [Portvan]	2 (1729-31)	114
Post, Reuben	48 (1856-62)	315
Postell, Benjamin	6 (1747-52)	237
Postell, Elijah see Postell, Elizah		
Postell, Elizah [Elijah]	16 (1774-79)	232
Postell, James	15 (1771-74)	541
Postell, James	15 (1771-74)	549
Postell, James, Jr.	21 (1783-86)	771
Postell, John, Junr.	4 (1736-40)	32
Postell, John	5 (1740-47)	479
Postell, John	22 (1786-93)	244
Postell, J(ohn) Glen	42 (1839-45)	272
Postell, Judith	9 (1760-67)	388
Postell, Margaret	7 (1752-56)	27
Postell, Samuel	8 (1757-60)	36
Postell, Sarah	45 (1845-51)	851
Postell, Susannah	28 (1800-07)	66
Postell, Thomas	24 (1786-93)	1042
Postell, William	35 (1818-26)	729
Potter, Humphrey	1 (1722-24)	24
Potter, John	17 (1774-79)	460
Potter, John	45 (1845-51)	659
Pottes, Robert	32 (1807-18)	950
Potts, Thomas	10 (1760-67)	502
Pou, Garvin [Gavin]	16 (1774-79)	354
Poulnot, Nicholas	33 (1807-18)	1208
Poulton, Rachael [Rachel]	41 (1834-39)	854
Pouncey see Pouncy		
Pouncy, Anthony [Pouncey]	11 (1767-71)	33
Powel, Thomas	21 (1783-86)	683
Powel see also Powell		
Powell, Benjamin	31 (1807-18)	171

Name	Volume	Page
Powell, George ₍Powel₎	20 (1783-86)	16
Powell, Dr. John	4 (1736-40)	286
Powell, John	21 (1783-86)	731
Powell, John	23 (1786-93)	546
Powell, Joseph	18 (1776-84)	94
Powell, Martha	39 (1826-34)	863
Powell, Ruth	27 (1793-1800)	936
Power, Edward	34 (1818-26)	141
Power, Nicholas	28 (1800-07)	191
Powers, Richard	7 (1752-56)	540
Powys, John	1 (1692-93)	19
Poyas, Catharine	41 (1834-39)	495
Poyas, Daniel	27 (1793-1800)	971
Poyas, James	27 (1793-1800)	892
Poyas, Jean Louis	7 (1752-56)	503
Poyas, John E.	36 (1818-26)	1038
Poyas, John Ernest	22 (1786-93)	4
Poyas, Providence G A(dams)	49 (1856-62)	820
Poyas, William	50 (1862-68)	75
Pratt, Samuel H.	31 (1807-18)	419
Prauninger, Leonhard	32 (1807-18)	846
Preble, George	31 (1807-18)	366
Preble see also Prible		
Preele, George	13 (1767-71)	709
Prefsly, Catharine	23 (1786-93)	665
Prefsly, Catherine Ann ₍Catharine₎	40 (1834-39)	174
Prefsly, David	21 (1783-86)	567
Prefsly, William	34 (1818-26)	263
Prentice, Cephas ₍Prentifs₎	26 (1793-1800)	637
Prentice, John ₍Province₎	7 (1752-56)	61
Prentifs see Prentice		
Prescot, John	23 (1786-93)	691
Presley, David	6 (1747-52)	132
Pressley, Margaret J.	44 (1845-51)	445

Name	Volume	Page
Pressly, John	6 (1747-52)	406
Preston, Rosanna	48 (1856-62)	197
Pretty see Prittey		
Prible, Mary [Preble]	35 (1818-26)	808
Price, Ann	40 (1834-39)	39
Price, John	31 (1807-18)	9
Price, Joseph	10 (1760-67)	760
Price, Mary	47 (1851-56)	493
Price, Philip Smith	50 (1862-68)	432
Price, Rice	8 (1757-60)	135
Price, Thomas H.	33 (1807-18)	1157
Price, Thomas William	39 (1826-34)	1123
Price, William	6 (1747-52)	329
Price, William	22 (1786-93)	300
Price, William, Junior	34 (1818-26)	5
Price, William	36 (1818-26)	898
Prichard see Richard		
Pricher, Conrod	40 (1834-39)	151
Prigg, John	17 (1774-79)	493
Prigge, Claus	49 (1856-62)	703
Primerose, Catherine [Catharine]	40 (1834-39)	31
Primerose, Robert	36 (1818-26)	867
Prince, Charles	41 (1834-39)	783
Pring, James	34 (1818-26)	227
Pringle, Ann Amelia	44 (1845-51)	32
Pringle, Elizabeth Mary	43 (1839-45)	659
Pringle, James R.	42 (1839-45)	157
Pringle, John Julius	43 (1839-45)	584
Pringle, Robert	17 (1774-79)	646
Pringle, Robert	49 (1856-62)	749
Pringle, Robert A.	38 (1826-34)	516
Prioleau, Ann	30 (1800-07)	958
Prioleau, Catharine [Catherine]	39 (1826-34)	1054
Prioleau, Catharine	45 (1845-51)	568

Name	Volume	Page
Prioleau, Davis	45 (1845-51)	657
Prioleau, Elijah	12 (1767-71)	653
Prioleau, Elisha	5 (1740-47)	566
Prioleau, Jane B.	38 (1862-34)	609
Prioleau, John	32 (1807-18)	508
Prioleau, John Cordes	36 (1818-26)	1144
Prioleau, Mary Magdalen	15 (1771-74)	604
Prioleau, Philip Gendron	43 (1839-45)	774
*Prioleau, Samuel	6 (1747-52)	626
Prioleau, Samuel	24 (1786-93)	977
Prioleau, Samuel	32 (1807-18)	657
Prioleau, Samuel (Substitution of Trustee)	39 (1826-34)	1066
Prioleau, Samuel	42 (1839-45)	92
Prior, Sarah	32 (1807-18)	937
Prior, Seth	27 (1793-1800)	719
Prise, Hopkin	19 (1780-83)	281
Pritchard, George	30 (1800-07)	847
Pritchard, Paul	24 (1786-93)	963
Pritchard, Paul, Senr.	32 (1807-18)	817
Pritchard, William, Junr.	33 (1807-18)	1297
Prittey, Thomas [Pretty]	8 (1757-60)	38
Prize, Richard	1 (1687-1710)	52
Proctor, Hannah	10 (1760-67)	647
Provaux, Elizabeth	33 (1807-18)	1179
Province see Prentice		
Provost, Joseph M.	43 (1839-45)	699
Prudhomme, Anthoine [Prudomen]	1 (1692-93)	56
Prud' homme, Eugenie	43.(1839-45)	757
Prudomen see Prudhomme		
Prue, John	15 (1771-74)	413
Purcell, Ann	40 (1834-39)	471
Purcell, Edward Henry	43 (1839-45)	884
Purcell, Joseph	30 (1800-07)	1074
Purcell, Patrick	29 (1800-07)	702

Name	Volume	Page
Purcell, Richard	5 (1740-47)	252
Purcell, Thomas	3 (1732-37)	81
Purdie, Archibald	22 (1786-93)	61
Purkes, Mary	15 (1771-74)	494
Purvis, Burridge	33 (1807-18)	1239
Pyatt, Elizabeth	29 (1800-07)	567
Pyatt, John	9 (1760-67)	82
Pye, Peter	32 (1807-18)	716
Pyeatt, Peter	33 (1807-18)	1377
Pyne, James	20 (1783-86)	176
Pyper, John	23 (1786-93)	734

Q

Name	Volume	Page
Quarterman, Thomas	3 (1732-37)	277
Quash, Constantia	49 (1856-62)	711
Quash, Constantia	50 (1862-68)	288
Quash, Elizabeth	16 (1774-79)	201
Quash, Elizabeth (P)	43 (1839-45)	703
Quash, Robert	14 (1771-74)	205
Quash, Robert	32 (1807-18)	479
Quelch, Andrew	20 (1783-86)	12
Querard, M. Sophie	49 (1856-62)	906
Quiggins, Mary	36 (1818-26)	1032
Quigly, Esther	29 (1800-07)	383
Quigly, Thomas	29 (1800-07)	765
Quince, Susanna	33 (1807-18)	1117
Quincey, Elizabeth	7 (1752-56)	192
Quinlan, Mary	41 (1834-39)	588
Quinlon, Michael	38 (1826-34)	432
Quinnan, Barberry	47 (1851-56)	575
Quintyne, Richard	1 (1692-93)	48

R

Name	Volume	Page
Rabb, Jacob	49 (1856-62)	849

Name	Volume	Page
Race, Benjamin	7 (1752-56)	299
Radcliffe, Elizabeth	27 (1793-1800)	955
Radcliffe, Lucretia Constance	35 (1818-26)	506
Radcliffe, Thomas	30 (1800-07)	1035
Rae, John	9 (1760-67)	73
Rahall, Patrick	50 (1862-68)	14
Raiford, Philip	9 (1760-67)	155
Raiford, William	9 (1760-67)	208
Railey, Joannah [Reyley, Raily; Joanna]	20 (1783-86)	339
Railey, William	31 (1807-18)	372
Raily see Railey		
Raisford, Philip	6 (1747-52)	82
Rake, Thomas	9 (1760-67)	250
Ralston, Robert	34 (1818-26)	231
Ralston, Robert	41 (1834-39)	901
Ramadge, Frances	34 (1818-26)	365
Ramsay, David	33 (1807-18)	959
Ramsay, David	50 (1862-68)	134
Ramsay, Eleanor Henry Laurens	48 (1856-62)	81
Ramsay, John	3 (1732-37)	102
Ramsay, John A.	45 (1845-51)	891
Ramsay, Joseph Hall	29 (1800-07)	543
Ramsay, Mrs. M. E.	44 (1845-51)	418
Ramsay, Martha H. L.	43 (1839-45)	729
Ramsay, Sarah	9 (1760-67)	317
Ramsay, William	3 (1732-37)	48
Ramsey, James	7 (1752-56)	67
Randal, Robert	14 (1771-74)	327
Randall, William	7 (1752-56)	371
Randell, John Bond	27 (1793-1800)	932
* Rantowle, James	18 (1776-84)	265
Raper, Robert	19 (1780-83)	240
Raper, William	22 (1786-93)	194
Rasch see Rash		

Name	Volume	Page
Rash, Behrend ⌊Rasch⌋	46 (1851-56)	40
✱ Ratcliff, Charles	6 (1747-52)	638
Ratcliffe, Samuel, Sen.ʳ	17 (1774-79)	744
Rattray, Hellen	17 (1774-79)	495
Rattray, John	9 (1760-67)	192
Ravanel, Susan Ann	46 (1851-56)	328
Raven, William	10 (1760-67)	728
Raven see also Ravin		
Ravenel, Abigail	46 (1851-56)	4
Ravenel, Catharine	45 (1845-51)	559
Ravenel, Charlotte J.	37 (1826-34)	201
Ravenel, Damaris Elizabeth	20 (1783-86)	202
Ravenel, Daniel ⌊Ravenele⌋	4 (1736-40)	1
✱ Ravenel, Daniel	16 (1774-79)	240
Ravenel, Daniel	19 (1780-83)	205
Ravenel, Daniel	30 (1800-07)	1142
Ravenel, Daniel James	41 (1834-39)	565
Ravenel, Elizabeth	22 (1786-93)	245
Ravenel, Elizabeth Jane	30 (1800-07)	1066
Ravenel, Francis G. ⌊Frances⌋	49 (1856-62)	1027
Ravénel, Henry	21 (1783-86)	679
Ravenel, Henry	36 (1818-26)	856
Ravenel, Henry	48 (1856-62)	528
Ravenel, Henry	51 (1862-68)	785
Ravenel, James	33 (1807-18)	1336
Ravenel, John	49 (1856-62)	993
Ravenel, Maria	45 (1845-51)	667
Ravenel, Paul ⌊Payl⌋	4 (1736-40)	41
Ravenel, Paul De St. Julien	34 (1818-26)	257
Ravenel, Rene (Junr.)	6 (1747-52)	382
Ravenel, Rene	35 (1818-26)	695
Ravenel, Stephen	34 (1818-26)	91
Ravenel see also Ravenell		
Ravenele see Ravenel		

Name	Volume	Page

Ravenell, Damaris Eliz.
   [Ravenel; Eli] · 19 (1780-83) · 83

Ravin, John [Raven] Ravan · 10 (1760-67) · 576

Ravina, Anne · 40 (1834-39) · 149

Ravina, J. D. · 46 (1851-56) · 176

Ravot, Francis Gabriel [Francois] · 12 (1767-71) · 654

Rawlins, Edward (E) · 1 (1687-1710) · 10

Rawlins, Edward (E) · 1 (1692-93) · 73

Rawlins, Robert · 14 (1771-74) · 155

Raworth, George F. · 40 (1834-39) · 257

Ray, John, Jr. · 9 (1760-67) · 139

Ray, John · 12 (1767-71) · 386

Ray, John · 24 (1786-93) · 934

Ray, Nicholas · 21 (1783-86) · 795

Ray, Peter · 15 (1771-74) · 630

Ray, Thomas, Sen.[r] · 39 (1826-34) · 1107

Ray, William · 43 (1839-45) · 708

Raymond, William H. · 35 (1818-26) · 761

Raynolds, John · 3 (1732-37) · 294

Raynolds, Penelope · 4 (1736-40) · 100

Rea, James · 28 (1800-07) · 141

Read, Catherine · 37 (1826-34) · 382

Read, Jacob · 33 (1807-18) · 1096

Read, John Harleston · 48 (1856-62) · 485

Read, Rebecca · 21 (1783-86) · 816

Read, William · 8 (1757-60) · 257

Read, William · 43 (1839-45) · 863

Reader, Philip · 33 (1807-18) · 1175

Readhimer, Peter · 32 (1807-18) · 621

Reddwood see Redwood

Redfern, Elizabeth · 50 (1862-68) · 105

Redfern, John · 41 (1834-39) · 953

Redman, John · 5 (1740-47) · 658

Redmond, Andrew · 24 (1786-93) · 793

Name	Volume	Page
Redwood, Isaac [Reddwood]	1 (1687-17.10)	20
Reed, Bartholomew	32 (1807-18)	884
Reed, Thomas	5 (1740-47)	387
Reeve, Lewis	16 (1774-79)	275
Reeves, Aeneas S.	35 (1818-26)	772
Reichert, John	19 (1780-83)	125
Reicke, George	46 (1851-56)	11
Reid, Andrew	20 (1783-86)	170
Reid, Eleanor Gale	31 (1807-18)	468
Reid, James	12 (1767-71)	651
Reid, John	25 (1793-1800)	46
Reid, John	30 (1800-07)	979
Reid, John	34 (1818-26)	182
Reid, Martha	19 (1780-83)	122
Reid, Patrick	7 (1752-56)	238
Reid, Robert	9 (1760-67)	441
Reid, Sarah [Ferris]	40 (1834-39)	18
Reighton, Elizabeth	14 (1771-74)	150
Reigne, John	41 (1834-39)	738
Reigné, Louisa	42 (1839-45)	369
Reiley, Barnebe [Barnebey]	6 (1747-52)	19
Reiley, Martha	7 (1752-56)	293
Reilley, Thomas	29 (1800-07)	505
Reilly, Charles	30 (1800-07)	886
Reilly, George	33 (1807-18)	997
Reilly, Honoria	46 (1851-56)	421
Reilly, Mary Ann	49 (1856-62)	939
Reilly, Thomas	49 (1856-62)	983
Reily, Bryan	6 (1747-52)	574
Rembert, Andre	4 (1736-40)	37
Rembert, Andrew	18 (1776-84)	170
Rembert, Andrew, Sr.	18 (1776-84)	173
Rembert, Elisha [Elizha]	37 (1826-34)	244
Rembert, Isaac	41 (1834-39)	770

Name	Volume	Page
Rembert, Madelaine	3 (1732-37)	99
Remington, Jacob	23 (1786-93)	589
Remington, John	17 (1774-79)	441
Remington, John	19 (1780-83)	99
Remington, John	28 (1800-07)	22
Remington, Margaret	23 (1786-93)	743
Remington, William	24 (1786-93)	855
Remley, John	22 (1786-93)	44
Remley, Paul D.	50 (1862-68)	196
Remley, William	44 (1845-51)	170
Renoise see Benoist		
Rentz, Catharina see Rentz, Catterneher		
Rentz, Catterneher Catharina	21 (1783-86)	698
Rentz, Jacob	29 (1800-07)	638
Rentz, John	44 (1845-51)	64
Revell, Hannah	41 (1834-39)	563
Revell, John	27 (1793-1800)	658
Reweld; Thomas ₍Rule₎	9 (1760-67)	137
Reyley see Railey		
Reynolds, Archibald	36 (1818-26)	1172
Reynolds, Benjamin	37 (1826-34)	104
Reynolds, Elenor	17 (1774-79)	475
Reynolds, George Norton	50 (1862-68)	251
Reynolds, Ignatius Aloysius	47 (1851-56)	567
Reynolds, Jacob	24 (1786-93)	982
Reynolds, John	25 (1793-1800)	194
Reynolds, John	27 (1793-1800)	753
✳ Reynolds, Joseph	24 (1786-93)	1163
Reynolds, Mary E.	35 (1818-26)	436
Reynolds, Micheal	2 (1727-29)	40
Reynolds, Richard	8 (1757-60)	301
Reynolds, William (Junr.)	7 (1752-56)	558
Reynolds, William, Senior	22 (1786-93)	348

244

Name	Volume	Page
Reynolds, William	34 (1818-26)	154
Rhett, Edmund	50 (1862-68)	39
Rhett, James Smith {Smith; H.}	47 (1851-56)	580
Rhett, Collo. William	1 (1722-24)	12
Rhett, William	2 (1727-29)	70
Rhod, Etienne	17 (1774-79)	707
Ricard, Francois	38 (1826-34)	821
Ricardo, Joseph	48 (1856-62)	47
Rich, Christopher	27 (1793-1800)	741
Rich, John	22 (1786-93)	118
Richard, Clement	27 (1793-1800)	952
Richard, James	5 (1740-47)	166
Richards, Betsey	44 (1845-51)	172
Richards, Elizabeth	26 (1793-1800)	594
Richards, Mary	38 (1826-34)	716
Richards, Robert	23 (1786-93)	609
Richardson, Adam	1 (1692-93)	27
Richardson, Ann	37 (1826-34)	287
Richardson, Barnard	26 (1793-1800)	540
Richardson, Henry	12 (1767-71)	434
Richardson, John	33 (1807-18)	1391
Richardson, Mary Eliza	44 (1845-51)	423
Richardson, Samuel	23 (1786-93)	461
Richardson, Sarah	39 (1826-34)	1150
Richardson, Thomas	24 (1786-93)	1023-½
Richardson, William	14 (1771-74)	87
Richbourg, Charles	24 (1786-93)	1059
Richbourg see also Richbourgh		
Richbourgh, Samuel {Richbourg}	18 (1776-84)	208
✳ Richebourg, Charles	6 (1747-52)	553
Richebourg, John	5 (1740-47)	240
Richebourg, Rene	5 (1740-47)	303
Ricker, William	33 (1807-18)	1029
Riddlespurger, Christian	23 (1786-93)	729

Name	Volume	Page
Ridgill, William	13 (1767-71)	826
Ridwell, Nevill	2 (1726-27)	1
Riecke, Gerd	49 (1856-62)	687
Rife, Philip	26 (1793-1800)	527
Rigg, Alexander	14 (1771-74)	92
Riggs, Samuel	27 (1793-1800)	691
Riggs, Thomas	7 (1752-56)	176
Righton, Elizabeth	47 (1851-56)	579
Righton, Elizabeth P.	38 (1826-34)	415
Righton, John M.	49 (1856-62)	801
Righton, Joseph	44 (1845-51)	144
Righton, McCully	33 (1807-18)	1151
Righton, Margaret Ann	48 (1856-62)	182
Rightoon, Florence	37 (1826-34)	9
Rikchie, Alex.	31 (1807-18)	125
Riley, John	11 (1767-71)	43
Riley, William	35 (1818-26)	599
Ringer, Frederick	26 (1793-1800)	638
Ringer, Henry	26 (1793-1800)	569
Rinker, Charles F.	50 (1862-68)	253
Rippen, Hannah	11 (1767-71)	174
Rippon, Edward	13 (1767-71)	863
Rippon, Richard	10 (1760-67)	530
Ritchie, Euphan	40 (1834-39)	254
Rivers, Daniel	10 (1760-67)	496
Rivers, Elijah	21 (1783-86)	789
Rivers, Elizabeth	28 (1800-07)	186
Rivers, Elizabeth	39 (1826-34)	355
Rivers, Francis, Senr.	35 (1818-26)	822
Rivers, George	6 (1747-52)	182
Rivers, George	21 (1783-86)	643
Rivers, George	36 (1818-26)	1155
Rivers, George A. C.	42 (1839-45)	164
Rivers, Henry S.	37 (1826-34)	227

Name	Volume	Page
Rivers, Isaac	17 (1774-79)	697
Rivers, John	2 (1724-25)	59
Rivers, John	4 (1736-40)	246
Rivers, John	15 (1771-74)	475
Rivers, John Senior	24 (1786-93)	1084
Rivers, John	48 (1856-62)	138
Rivers, John E. (Substitution of Trustee)	48 (1856-62)	49
Rivers, John Elijah	45 (1845-51)	724
Rivers, Jonah	29 (1800-07)	609
Rivers, Joseph	7 (1752-56)	380
Rivers, Joseph	22 (1786-93)	220
Rivers, Josiah	28 (1800-07)	329
Rivers, Mallory	21 (1783-86)	726
Rivers, Martha	43 (1839-45)	558
Rivers, Martha S.	50 (1862-68)	125
Rivers, Miles	2 (1726-27)	37
Rivers, Nehemiah	13 (1767-71)	791
Rivers, Rawlins	48 (1856-62)	500
Rivers, Robert	15 (1771-74)	645
Rivers, Robert	19 (1780-83)	180
Rivers, Robert	20 (1783-86)	55
Rivers, Robert	24 (1786-93)	850
Rivers, Rose	41 (1834-39)	886
✱ Rivers, Samuel	20 (1783-86)	242
Rivers, Samuel	40 (1834-39)	172
Rivers, Sarah	23 (1786-93)	599
Rivers, Sarah E.	50 (1862-68)	49
Rivers, Susanna [Susannah]	34 (1818-26)	276
Rivers, Susannah	22 (1786-93)	86
Rivers, Thomas	23 (1786-93)	504
Rivers, Thomas	31 (1807-18)	141
Rivers, Thomas	38 (1826-34)	628
Rivers, William	6 (1747-52)	599

Name	Volume	Page
Rivers, William	15 (1771-74)	539
Rivers, William, Senr.	26 (1793-1800)	424
Rivers, William	29 (1800-07)	533
Rivers, William	41 (1834-39)	594
Rivers, William (Substitution of Trustee)	50 (1862-68)	138
Roach, Elizabeth	19 (1780-83)	21
Roach, Elizabeth	20 (1783-86)	166
Roach, James	19 (1780-83)	2
Roach, James	20 (1783-86)	165
Roach, Nash	48 (1856-62)	250
Roach, Richard	1 (1722-24)	10
Road, Catharina	12 (1767-71)	369
Robb, Charles	32 (1807-18)	901
Robb, James	48 (1856-62)	422
Robbinson see Robinson		
Roberson, Ann	8 (1757-60)	115
Robert, David	11 (1767-71)	293
Robert, Peter [Pierre]	2 (1729-31)	94
Roberts, Benjamin	7 (1752-56)	104
Roberts, Benjamin	14 (1771-74)	282
Roberts, Elizabeth	41 (1834-39)	818
Roberts, Enos	40 (1834-39)	291
Roberts, John	2 (1729-31)	58
Roberts, John	8 (1757-60)	435
Roberts, John	28 (1800-07)	195
Roberts, John	30 (1800-07)	839
Roberts, Jonah	17 (1774-79)	581
Roberts, Lynch	32 (1807-18)	626
Roberts, Martha	14 (1771-74)	70
Roberts, Mary	29 (1800-07)	419
Roberts, Owen	21 (1783-86)	646
Roberts, Robert T.	38 (1826-34)	646
Roberts, Thomas	5 (1740-47)	119

Name	Volume	Page
Roberts, Thomas	23 (1786-93)	471
Roberts, William	25 (1793-1800)	247
Robertson, Adam	41 (1834-39)	851
Robertson, Alexander	2 (1724-25)	37
Robertson, David	17 (1774-79)	415
Robertson, Francis	34 (1818-26)	293
Robertson, James	20 (1783-86)	34
Robertson, James	46 (1851-56)	215
Robertson, John	6 (1747-52)	567
Robertson, John	39 (1826-34)	895
Robertson, Mary	51 (1862-68)	453
Robertson, Peter	31 (1807-18)	374
Robertson, Susan Boone	51 (1862-68)	851
Robertson, Susanne Boone ₁Susanna₁	43 (1839-45)	843
Robertson, William	39 (1826-34)	1059
Robertson, William	48 (1856-62)	532
Robinet, Francis C.	31 (1807-18)	427
Robins, Anthony	50 (1862-68)	224
Robinson, Edmond	2 (1727-29)	47
Robinson, Edmund ₁Robbinson₁	2 (1727-29)	95
Robinson, Elizabeth	32 (1807-18)	529
Robinson, James K.	51 (1862-68)	707
Robinson, Jane	7 (1752-56)	329
Robinson, John	1 (1711-18)	76
Robinson, John	7 (1752-56)	500
Robinson, John	13 (1767-71)	821
Robinson, John	14 (1771-74)	90
Robinson, John	28 (1800-07)	149
Robinson, John	45 (1845-51)	509
Robinson, Jonathan	9 (1760-67)	225
Robinson, Joseph	5 (1740-47)	455
Robinson, Septimus	28 (1800-07)	123
Robinson, Simon A.	50 (1862-68)	319

Name	Volume	Page
Robinson, Susan	48 (1856-62)	334
Robinson see also Robison		
Robison, Robert ┌Robinson┐	17 (1774-79)	682
Robison, William	15 (1771-74)	578
Robson, James	27 (1793-1800)	890
Roche, Ebenezer	20 (1783-86)	401
Roche, Edward L.	41 (1834-39)	696
Roche, Franois	11 (1767-71)	259
Roche, Jeremiah	24 (1786-93)	1146
Roche, John	39 (1826-34)	835
Roche, John (Substitution of Trustee)	40 (1834-39)	448
Roche, Patrick	26 (1793-1800)	503
Roches, Grolleau des	37 (1826-34)	209
Rochford, James	5 (1740-47)	217
Rochford, James	9 (1760-67)	235
Rock, John George	7 (1752-56)	313
Roddey, James	33 (1807-18)	1387
Roddom, Joseph	29 (1800-07)	440
Roddy, John Joseph	43 (1839-45)	778
Roddy, Martin	45 (1845-51)	605
Roddy, Mary	48 (1856-62)	31
Rodger, James	9 (1760-67)	224
Rodgers, Charles	34 (1818-26)	317
Rodgers, Ebenezer H.	50 (1862-68)	436
Rodgers, James	12 (1767-71)	534
Rodgers, Samuel W.	48 (1856-62)	4
Rodriguez, (Madame) Mary	34 (1818-26)	172
✳ Rodus, Joseph	15 (1771-74)	408
Rofs see Rose		
Rofs, Charlotte P.	46 (1851-56)	89
Rofs, Eliza C.	47 (1851-56)	856
Rofs, Elizabeth	29 (1800-07)	663
Rofs, Elizabeth Mary	42 (1839-45)	354

Name	Volume	Page
Rofs, George	23 (1786-93)	693
Rofs, Hugh	35 (1818-26)	727
Rofs, Isaac	16 (1774-79)	382
Rofs, James	41 (1834-39)	902
Rofs, Jane	28 (1800-07)	248
Rofs, Kenneth	27 (1793-1800)	668
Rofs, Phantom	27 (1793-1800)	872
Rofs, Thomas	30 (1800-07)	1082
Rofsignol, Anne Viuve	31 (1807-18)	311
Rofsignol, Renne	33 (1807-18)	1339
Roger, Thomas, J.	47 (1751-56)	817
Rogers, Charles	27 (1793-1800)	724
Rogers, Charles	42 (1839-45)	271
Rogers, David	22 (1786-93)	77
Rogers, Jacob (I)	42 (1839-45)	335
Rogers, James	25 (1793-1800)	193
Rogers, Joe	39 (1826-34)	1168
Rogers, Nicholas	8 (1757-60)	503
Rogers, Priscilla E.	44 (1845-51)	47
Rogers, Robert	7 (1752-56)	151
Rogers, Sarah	39 (1826-34)	1144
Rogers, Silas B.	47 (1851-56)	623
Rogers, Revd. Zabdiel	46 (1851-56)	208
Rogerson, John	11 (1767-71)	84
Rogerson, Josiah	10 (1760-67)	467
Rolando, Isabella	40 (1834-39)	315
Rolinson, Daniell	1 (1692-93)	30
Roman, Dupier	26 (1793-1800)	517
Romsey, (Capt.) Benjamin	2 (1727-29)	35
Romsey, Benjamin	7 (1752-56)	72
Rooney, Michael	46 (1851-56)	161
Rooney, Paul	39 (1826-34)	1060
Roper, Barbara C.	47 (1851-56)	716
Roper, Benjamin D. (Substitution of Trustee)	49 (1856-62)	617

Name	Volume	Page
Roper, Benjamin Dart, Sr.	46 (1851-56)	201
Roper, Hannah	37 (1826-34)	329
Roper, Joseph	27 (1793-1800)	869
Roper, Martha R	51 (1862-68)	845
Roper, Micah Jenkins	48 (1856-62)	530
Roper, Robert William	43 (1839-45)	889
Roper, Thomas	38 (1826-34)	555
Roper, William	14 (1771-74)	172
Roper, William	23 (1786-93)	506
Roper, William	38 (1826-34)	483
Roper, William Henry	32 (1807-18)	896
Rose, Alexander	28 (1800-07)	132
Rose, Amelia	50 (1862-68)	70
Rose, Anna Maria	48 (1856-62)	426
Rose, Elizabeth	8 (1757-60)	338
Rose, Elizabeth H.	49 (1856-62)	932
Rose, Francis	19 (1780-83)	340
Rose, Hugh	9 (1760-67)	311
Rose, Hugh	42 (1839-45)	314
Rose, Jeremiah	29 (1800-07)	437
Rose, John [Rofe]	34 (1818-26)	318
Rose, Lewis Antonio	47 (1851-56)	719
Rose, Margaret Louisa	51 (1862-68)	532
Rose, Rebecca	38 (1826-34)	606
Rose, Thomas	7 (1752-56)	515
Rose, Thomas	20 (1783-86)	125
Rose, William	7 (1752-56)	463
Rose, William	7 (1752-56)	477
Rosenbohem, John Henry	43 (1839-45)	911
Ross, Harriet C.	50 (1862-68)	259
Ross, James	47 (1851-56)	872
Roth, Jacob	12 (1767-71)	336
Roth, Peter	8 (1757-60)	468
Rothmahler, Ann	13 (1767-71)	691

Name	Volume	Page
Rottenbery, Charles	32 (1807-18)	822
Roud, Martin	4 (1736-40)	303
Rouk, George	15 (1771-74)	397
Roulain, Abraham	22 (1786-93)	281
Roulain, Ann	19 (1780-83)	105
Roulain, Catharine	43 (1839-45)	702
Roulain, James	27 (1793-1800)	958
Roulain, Robert	33 (1807-18)	1149
Roumillat, Jacques	35 (1818-26)	552
Roumillat, Rose Guenveur	42 (1839-45)	12
Roupell, Elizabeth	34 (1818-26)	93
Roupell, Mary	43 (1839-45)	826
Rousham, James	7 (1752-56)	285
Rout, Eliza	49 (1856-62)	631
Rout, George	28 (1800-07)	356
Rout, William George	42 (1839-45)	257
Roux, Ann	44 (1845-51)	324
Roux, Francis Louis Noah	32 (1807-18)	954
Roux, Lewis	41 (1834-39)	725
Row, Mary	19 (1780-83)	376
Rowand, Charles E.	40 (1834-39)	331
Rowand, Charles E.	41 (1834-39)	872
Rowand, Charles Elliott	40 (1834-39)	269
Rowand, Mary	28 (1800-07)	278
Rowand, Robert	33 (1807-18)	1081
Rowe, James	37 (1826-34)	333
Rowland, Catherine	2 (1726-27)	66
Rowser, Richard	3 (1732-37)	53
Rowser, Sarah	1 (1722-24)	27
Rowser, William	12 (1767-71)	414
Royall, William	19 (1780-83)	167
Royall, William	40 (1834-39)	187
Royall, William (Substitution of Trustee)	41 (1834-39)	624

Name	Volume	Page
Royall, William (Substitution of Trustee)	41 (1834-39)	642
Royer, John	1 (1721-22)	32
Royer, John	7 (1752-56)	130
Ruberry, John	2 (1724-25)	70
Ruberry, Mary	33 (1807-18)	1435
Rudd, Burlingham	40 (1834-39)	396
Rudd, Elias	44 (1845-51)	304
Rudd, Mary	45 (1845-51)	738
Ruddock, Susannah C.	41 (1834-39)	570
Rufs, Abijah ₍Russ₎	4 (1736-40)	268
Rufs, Benjamin	26 (1793-1800)	410
Rufs see also Russ		
Rufsell, Alexander	13 (1767-71)	1021
Rufsell, Benjamin	32 (1807-18)	607
Rufsell, Elizabeth Eleanor	26 (1793-1800)	480
Rufsell, Mary	7 (1752-56)	291
Rufsell, Mary	34 (1818-26)	232
Rufsell, Nathaniel	34 (1818-26)	265
Rufsell, Samuel	8 (1757-60)	93
Rufsell, Sarah	43 (1839-45)	854
Rufsell, Walter	18 (1776-84)	49
Rufsell, William	16 (1774-79)	92
Rufsell, William	22 (1786-93)	257
Rufsell, William	32 (1807-18)	920
Rufsell see also Russell		
Rugeley, Rowland	18 (1776-84)	258
Ruger, John	22 (1786-93)	1
Ruger, Valentine	42 (1839-45)	165
Rule see Reweld		
Rumney, Joseph	27 (1793-1800)	712
Rump see Rumph		
Rumph, Abraham	17 (1774-79)	699 (Dup. P
Rumph, Abraham	17 (1774-79)	713 (Dup. P

Name	Volume	Page
Rumph, David, Sr.	19 (1780-83)	406
Rumph, John	26 (1793-1800)	601
Rumph, Peter ⌐Rump¬	9 (1760-67)	132
Runken, Seade John	49 (1856-62)	982
Rush, Catharine	36 (1818-26)	1210
Rush, Joseph	33 (1807-18)	1376
Rusliut, John ⌐Rusluit¬	18 (1776-84)	237
Rusluit see Rusliut		
Russ, John ⌐Rufs¬	9 (1760-67)	362
Russ, Jonathan ⌐Rufs¬	2 (1727-29)	3
Russ, Jonathan ⌐Rufs¬	9 (1760-67)	363
Russ see also Rufs		
Russel, Richard	50 (1862-68)	425
Russell, Charles	4 (1736-40)	19
Russell, Eliza ⌐Rufsell¬	38 (1826-34)	475
Russell, Jeremiah ⌐Rufsell¬	6 (1747-52)	188
Russell, Mary	51 (1862-68)	805
Russell, Lyra	48 (1856-62)	56
Russell, Sarah	49 (1856-62)	968
Rutherford, Charlotte	22 (1786-93)	129
Rutherford, David	17 (1774-79)	417
Rutherford, Isabella	22 (1786-93)	272
Rutledge, Andrew	7 (1752-56)	399
Rutledge, Andrew	14 (1771-74)	248
Rutledge, Caroline	50 (1862-68)	10
Rutledge, Edward	27 (1793-1800)	947
Rutledge, Francis	43 (1839-45)	649
Rutledge, H.	31 (1807-18)	415
Rutledge, Harriott Pinckney	48 (1856-62)	326
Rutledge, John	7 (1752-56)	395
Rutledge, John	34 (1818-26)	194
Rutledge, Mary	41 (1834-39)	678
Rutledge, Sarah	27 (1793-1800	836
Rutledge, Sarah	47 (1851-56)	605

Name	Volume	Page
Rutledge, William	35 (1818-26)	703
Ryan, Elizabeth	41 (1834-39)	727
Ryan, Ellen M.	49 (1856-62)	957
Ryan, Laurence	42 (1839-45)	393
Ryan, Mary T.	50 (1862-68)	265
Ryan, Peter (Saul)	27 (1793-1800)	684
Ryan, Thomas	51 (1862-68)	692
Ryckbosch, Francis	35 (1818-26)	698

S

Sabb, William	10 (1760-67)	877
Sacheverall, Thomas [Sacheverell]	9 (1760-67)	435
Sacheverall see also Scheverall		
Sacheverell, Thomas	5 (1740-47)	475
Sacheverell see also Sacheverall		
Safford, Isabella	38 (1826-34)	526
Safs, Jacob	40 (1834-39)	391
St. John, Audeon	23 (1786-93)	397
St. John, James	5 (1740-47)	195
St. John, James	24 (1786-93)	1071
St. John, John	7 (1752-56)	444
St. John, Mary	25 (1793-1800)	170
St. John, Melle.	8 (1757-60)	24
St. John, Stephen	25 (1793-1800)	37
St. Julian, Susanna De [St. Julien, De St. Julian]	20 (1783-86)	344
St. Julien, de Pierre [Pierre de]	1 (1720-21)	16
St. Julien, Henry De	12 (1767-71)	476
St. Julien, Pierre de see St. Julien, de Pierre		
St. Julien see also St. Julian		
Saint Mark, Benjamin	33 (1807-18)	1284
St. Martin, Phillippine	23 (1786-93)	477
St. Pierre, L. de	17 (1774-79)	481
Sallen see Sallens		

256

Name	Volume	Page
Sallens, Peter ₍Sallen₎	2 (1727-29)	13
Sallens, Robert	8 (1757-60)	41
Salmond, George	41 (1834-39)	822
Saltar see Salter		
Salter, Joanna C. ₍Saltar₎	50 (1862-68)	79
Salter, Thomas Richard	46 (1851-56)	175
Saltus, Richard	15 (1771-74)	472
Salvador, Joseph	22 (1786-93)	94
Salzer, Christopher	12 (1767-71)	411
Samory, Claude Nicholas	36 (1818-26)	1015
Sams, Joseph	7 (1752-56)	428
Sams, Robert	8 (1757-60)	524
Sams, Robert	8 (1757-60)	531
Sams, Susana	24 (1786-93)	941
Samson, George	51 (1862-68)	740
Samway, James	2 (1726-27)	14
Samways, Henry	1 (1711-18)	46
Samways, Henry	9 (1760-67)	437
Samways, Thomas	20 (1783-86)	120
Sanchez, Joseph M.	39 (1826-34)	1032
Sanders, Ann	22 (1786-93)	50
Sanders, Charles	6 (1747-52)	226
Sanders, Charles	22 (1786-93)	168
Sanders, George	14 (1771-74)	179
Sanders, George R.	51 (1862-68)	772
Sanders, John	2 (1724-25)	46
Sanders, John	5 (1740-47)	171
Sanders, John	10 (1760-67)	479
Sanders, John	24 (1786-93)	870
Sanders, John	32 (1807-18)	552
Sanders, John	48 (1856-62)	211
Sanders, Joseph	10 (1760-67)	554
Sanders, Joshua	6 (1747-52)	519

Name	Volume	Page
Sanders, Lambert	1 (1671-1727)	7
Sanders, Laurence ⌐Lawrence⌐	23 (1786-93)	581
Sanders, Lawrence	6 (1747-52)	486
Sanders, Margaret	21 (1783-86)	696
Sanders, Peter	2 (1729-31)	22
Sanders, Peter	35 (1818-26)	724
Sanders, Robert ⌐Saunders⌐	5 (1740-47)	415
Sanders, Samuel	2 (1727-29)	71
Sanders, Sarah	25 (1793-1800)	214
Sanders, Sarah	27 (1793-1800)	793
Sanders, Septimus	47 (1851-56)	819
Sanders, Susannah	26 (1793-1800)	333
Sanders, Thomas	50 (1862-68)	6
Sanders, William	5 (1740-47)	43
Sanders, William	7 (1752-56)	496
Sanders, William	18 (1776-84)	11
Sanders, William	24 (1786-93)	816
Sanders, William	24 (1786-93)	988
Sanders, William	24 (1786-93)	1011
Sanders, Wilson	3 (1732-37)	254
Sanderson, Alexander	18 (1776-84)	241
Sandiford, James see Sandiford, John		
Sandiford, John ⌐James⌐	6 (1747-52)	248
Sandiford, Ralph	9 (1760-67)	234
Sandwell, Elianor	6 (1747-52)	557
Sandys, William	17 (1774-79)	467 ⎫ Duplicate
Sandys, William	17 (1774-79)	664 ⎭
Sanks, George	14 (1771-74)	199
Sansean, John ⌐Sausean⌐	2 (1729-31)	88
Sansum, John	21 (1783-86)	520
Saragosa, Francis	14 (1771-74)	277
Sarjant see Serjant		
Sarrazin, Catherine	39 (1826-34)	1129
Sarrazin, Mary	38 (1826-34)	534

258

Name	Volume	Page
Sasportas, Abraham	36 (1818-26)	1067
Sass, Edward George	44 (1845-51)	456
Sass, Jacob Keith	50 (1862-68)	338
Satur, Abraham	5 (1740-47)	533
Saunders, Francis	19 (1780-83)	50
Saunders, Jean [Jane]	27 (1793-1800	687
Saunders, Roóger [Roger]	5 (1740-47)	76
Saunders, William	25 (1793-1800)	48
Saunders see also Sanders		
Sausean see Sansean		
Savage, Ann	39 (1826-34)	949
Savage, Benjamin	6 (1747-52)	367
* Savage, Benjamin	6 (1747-52)	430
Savage, Martha	9 (1760-67)	99
Savage, Martha	36 (1818-26)	1100
Savage, Mary Elliott	23 (1786-93)	499
Savage, Richard	23 (1786-93)	583
Savage, Samuel	33 (1807-18)	1052
Savage, Sarah H.	47 (1851-55)	549
Savage, Thomas	22 (1786-93)	24
Saverance see Saverence		
Saverence, Thomas [Saverance]	27 (1793-1800)	784
Saverence see also Seaverance		
Savineau, Jane	10 (1760-67)	509
Savineau, Nathaniel	26 (1793-1800)	325
Sawyer, Andrew	17 (1774-79)	470
Sawyer, Ann (Blake)	26 (1793-1800)	372
Sawyer, Elisha	19 (1780-83)	13
Sawyer, Elisha	21 (1783-86)	545
Saxby, Sarah	6 (1747-52)	41
Saxby, William	6 (1747-52)	42
Saxe, Henry	36 (1818-26)	1179
Sayle, William (Governor)	1 (1671-1727)	1

Name	Volume	Page
Saylor, David	24 (1786-93)	865
Sayr, Ananias	15 (1771-74)	648
Scanlan see Scanland		
Scanland, Mary [Scanlan]	9 (1760-67)	204
Scanlin, Deborh	33 (1807-18)	1024
Scarlett, James	5 (1740-47)	683
Schachte, John [Shachte]	51 (1862-68)	619
Scheib, M.	47 (1851-56)	462
Schem, Adelade	42 (1839-45)	274
Schem, John F.	32 (1807-18)	691
Schencking, Benjamen [Shenckingh]	3 (1732-37)	39
Scheurer, Elizabeth	15 (1771-74)	606
Scheverall, Margaret [Sacheverall; Margarett]	1 (1692-93)	10
Scheverall, Thomas (Elder) [Sacheverall]	1 (1692-93)	8
Schirer, Harriett	51 (1862-68)	853
Schirer, John	37 (1826-34)	221
Schivener, John [Scrivener]	16 (1774-79)	333
Schmidt, Elizabeth	48 (1856-62)	69
Schmidt, John W, Jr.	49 (1856-62)	654
Schmidt, John W.	51 (1862-68)	549
Schmidt, John William	46 (1851-56)	286
Schnell, John Jacob	38 (1826-34)	760
Schneyder, Johannes Casper Hendrik	29 (1800-07)	471
Schnierle, John Michael	43 (1839-45)	764
Scholars, Mary	26 (1793-1800)	545
Schoug, Frederick	41 (1834-39)	816
Schrade, Dorothe	23 (1786-93)	552
Schreiber see Screiber		
Schriefer, Carsten	42 (1839-45)	308
Schroeder, Andrew	50 (1862-68)	26
Schulz, Susan F.	46 (1851-56)	181
Schulz, Wade Hampton	42 (1839-45)	58

Name	Volume	Page
Schutt, Casper Christian	29 (1800-07)	474
Schutt, Godfrey C.	37 (1826-34)	307
Schutt, John Glen	42 (1839-45)	253
Schutt, Lewis H. C.	35 (1818-26)	804
Schwartz, John	34 (1818-26)	160
Schwartzkopff, Jacob Nicholas	14 (1771-74)	302
Schwecke, Lucinda	49 (1856-62)	856
Scot, Janet	14 (1771-74)	273
Scot see also Scott		
Scott, Ann	33 (1807-18)	1280
Scott, Ann	36 (1818-26)	947
Scott, Archibald [Fcott]	8 (1757-60)	295
Scott, Archibald	21 (1783-86)	813
Scott, David	24 (1786-93)	937
Scott, Elizabeth	13 (1767-71)	929
Scott, Euphame	50 (1862-68)	315
Scott, George	12 (1767-71)	537
Scott, James	4 (1736-40)	213
Scott, James	6 (1747-52)	405
Scott, John	6 (1747-52)	651
Scott, John [Scot]	8 (1757-60)	398
Scott, John	13 (1767-71)	1016
Scott, John	22 (1786-93)	240
Scott, John, Junr.	22 (1786-93)	358
Scott, John	31 (1807-18)	22
Scott, John	32 (1807-18)	880
Scott, Jonathan	20 (1783-86)	360
Scott, Joseph	6 (1747-52)	313
Scott, Joseph	8 (1757-60)	442
Scott, Margaret	49 (1856-62)	626
Scott, Mary	45 (1845-51)	492
Scott, Rebecca E.	45 (1845-51)	763
Scott, Samuel	14 (1771-74)	73
Scott, Samuel	17 (1774-79)	432

Name	Volume	Page
Scott, Thomas	11 (1767-71)	136
Scott, William	3 (1732-37)	41
Scott, William	3 (1732-37)	265
Scott, William	10 (1760-67)	650
Scott, William	26 (1793-1800)	525
Scott, William	34 (1818-26)	233
Scott, William	43 (1839-45)	821
Scott, William Edward	31 (1807-18)	86
Scottow, Samuel	25 (1793-1800)	20
Scottow, Susannah	32 (1807-18)	586
Scouler, Thomas	32 (1807-18)	824
Screiber, Mary Ann Hall [Schreiber]	30 (1800-07)	1010
Screven, Elisha	8 (1757-60)	190
Screven, Elisha	9 (1760-67)	14
Screven, James	8 (1757-60)	215
Screven, Joshua	10 (1760-67)	443
Screven, Rebecca	40 (1834-36)	456
Screven, Thomas	29 (1800-07)	649
Screven, Thos.	39 (1826-34)	1153
Screven, William, Sen.	7 (1752-56)	530
Screven see also Scriven		
Scriven, Samuel [Screven]	3 (1731-33)	70
Scrivener see Schivener		
Scull, Edward	5 (1740-47)	328
Scurlock, Catherine	8 (1757-60)	158
Scurlock, Peter	6 (1747-52)	645
Seabrook, Andrew D.	47 (1851-56)	553
Seabrook, Ephraim Mikell	49 (1856-62)	860
Seabrook, Ephriam Mikell, Sen. [Ephraim]	44 (1845-51)	36
Seabrook, Henry	44 (1845-51)	98
*Seabrook, John	6 (1747-52)	373
Seabrook, John	25 (1793-1800)	256
Seabrook, John	30 (1800-07)	1108

Name	Volume	Page
Seabrook, Joseph	39 (1826-34)	975
Seabrook, Margaret	36 (1818-26)	939
Seabrook, Robert	1 (1720-21)	44
Seabrook, Thomas B.	41 (1834-39)	927
Seabrook, William	41 (1834-39)	536
Seabrooke, John	1 (1711-18)	51
Sealy, John	5 (1740-47)	49
Sealy, John	11 (1767-71)	244
Sealy, John	16 (1774-79)	62
Sealy, Joseph	3 (1731-33)	23
Sealy, Joseph	6 (1747-52)	413
Sealy, Joseph	11 (1767-71)	107
Sealy, Mikell	9 (1760-67)	254
Sealy, Samuel	10 (1760-67)	847
Sealy, William	6 (1747-52)	45
Sealy, William	16 (1774-79)	155
Seaman, Dirk	38 (1826-34)	692
Seaman, George	12 (1767-71)	495
Searle, William	51 (1862-68)	585
Sears, Edward	1 (1711-18)	39
Sears, Thomas	46 (1851-56)	426
Seaver, Abraham	38 (1826-34)	702
Seaver, Han.ʰ	39 (1826-34)	833
Seaverance, John ⌈Saverence⌋	1 (1722-24)	65
Seawright, Samuel	11 (1767-71)	128
Secraft, John ⌈Seecraft, Seecroft⌋	8 (1757-60)	201
Seebeck, Dederick	44 (1845-51)	78
Seecraft see Secraft		
Seecroft see Secraft		
Seiler, Daniel	29 (1800-07)	424
Seixas, David C.	48 (1856-62)	167
Selby, George	28 (1800-07)	335
Selin, Peter	42 (1839-45)	265
Seller, Mathias	14 (1771-74)	253

Name	Volume	Page
Semple, James	21 (1783-86)	533
Semple, Rattrey	22 (1786-93)	273
Serjant, Richard [Sarjunt]	8 (1757-60)	77
Serjeant, Margaret L.	34 (1818-26)	204
Serre, Noah	2 (1729-31)	90
Serre, Noah	5 (1740-47)	500
Servant, Jane	7 (1752-56)	50
Sewright, William	8 (1757-60)	582
Seyle, Samuel	47 (1851-56)	797
Seymour, John	16 (1774-79)	370
Seymour, Sarah	36 (1818-26)	1008
Seymour, Stephen	30 (1800-07)	1025
Shachte see Schachte		
Shaffer, Frederick	48 (1856-62)	473
Shannon, Robert	6 (1747-52)	459
Shareman, William	1 (1711-18)	5
Sharp, Alexander	17 (1774-79)	793
Sharp, James	13 (1767-71)	689
Sharp, James	21 (1783-86)	603
Sharples, Ann	14 (1771-74)	141
Sharwood see Shearwood		
Shaw, Alexander	10 (1760-67)	687
Shaw, Daniel	5 (1740-47)	382
Shaw, Launch	9 (1760-67)	146
Shaw, Robert	11 (1767-71)	38
Shaw, William D.	33 (1807-18)	1363
Shea, Francis	45 (1845-51)	634
Shea, Richard	39 (1826-34)	953
Sheapheard, Charles	6 (1747-52)	47
Shearwood, John [Sharwood]	7 (1752-56)	466
Sheout, Mary E.	50 (1862-68)	190
Shed, Jacob D.	32 (1807-18)	884
Sheed, George	27 (1793-1800)	859
Sheehan, Thomas	31 (1807-18)	156

Name	Volume	Page
Sheerin, Francis	38 (1826-34)	768
Shehan, David	5 (1740-47)	558
Sheiller, Jacob	19 (1780-85)	579
Sheively, George [Shiviely]	34 (1818-26)	9
Sheldon, Henry	36 (1818-26)	1114
Shenckingh see Schencking		
Shepard, James [Shepheard]	8 (1757-60)	328
Shepard, Margaret	10 (1760-67)	462
Shepheard, Thomas R.	33 (1807-18)	1124
Shepheard see also Shepard		
Shepherd, James	41 (1834-39)	922
Shepherd, John	22 (1786-93)	372
Sheppard, Daniel	46 (1851-56)	400
*Sheppard, Francis	6 (1747-52)	446
Sheppard, John	22 (1786-93)	379
Sheppard, John	33 (1807-18)	999
Sheppard, Thomas	31 (1807-18)	216
*Sheriff, Henry	6 (1747-52)	525
Sherman, Elizabeth	34 (1818-26)	95
Sherman, George W.	34 (1818-26)	36
Sherriff, William	2 (1724-25)	90
Sherry, Arthur	25 (1793-1800)	308
Shettig, John [Johannes]	5 (1740-47)	6
Shingler, Frederick	36 (1818-26)	1101
Shingler, James S.	48 (1856-62)	435
Shingleton, William	3 (1732-37)	155
Shirer, John	39 (1826-34)	1024
Shirras, Alexander	31 (1807-18)	472
Shirtliff, Elizabeth C	50 (1862-68)	369
Shirtliff, William	32 (1807-18)	634
Shiviely see Sheively		
Shoemaker, Elizabeth	10 (1760-67)	884
Shokes, Francis Gwin	50 (1862-68)	220
Shokes, George	47 (1851-56)	831

Name	Volume	Page
Shokes, John	49 (1856-62)	591
Shoolbred, Henry	23 (1786-93)	750
Shoolbred, James	44 (1845-51)	237
Shoolbred, James (Substitution of Trustee)	44 (1845-51)	288
Shoolbred, John G.	49 (1856-62)	618
Short, William	35 (1818-26)	751
Shreiner, Nicholas	30 (1800-07)	1041
Shrewsbury see Shrowberry		
Shrewsbury, Edward	4 (1736-40)	194
Shrewsbury, Stephen	33 (1807-18)	962
Shrewsbury, Susannah M.	37 (1826-34)	233
Shrowberry, Edward ⌈Shrewsburry, Shrowsburry⌉	25 (1793-1800)	10
Shrowsburry see Shrowberry		
Shrubsole, William	8 (1757-60)	253
Shubrick, Mary	39 (1826-34)	1057
Shubrick, Mary Elliott	32 (1807-18)	820
Shubrick, Richard	16 (1774-79)	327
Shubrick, Thomas	31 (1807-18)	336
Shuler, Daniel	16 (1774-79)	66
Shute, John	5 (1740-47)	75
Shute, John	11 (1767-71)	266
Shute, Rebecca ⌈Rebeccah⌉	6 (1747-52)	133
Shuter, James	7 (1752-56)	259
Shuter, James	7 (1752-56)	260
Shutterling, Maria	28 (1800-07)	263
Shyrer, John	30 (1800-07)	1125
Siegling, John, Jr.	48 (1856-62)	174
Siegling, John	51 (1862-68)	775
Sigston, Robert	6 (1747-52)	555
Sikes, Mary	38 (1826-34)	590
Sikes, Thomas	30 (1800-07)	1140
Silberg, Nicholas	28 (1800-07)	231
Silliman, John Hubbard	39 (1826-34)	922

(handwritten annotation to the right of the Shuter, James entries: }Dupl)

266

Name	Volume	Page
*Simmons, Eben-Ezer ₍Ebenezer₎	9 (1760-67)	391
Simmons, Ebenezer	13 (1767-71)	704
Simmons, Esther	10 (1760-67)	712
Simmons, Francis	32 (1807-18)	776
Simmons, Francis Y.	41 (1834-39)	838
Simmons, George	20 (1783-86)	178
*Simmons, James	18 (1776-84)	129
Simmons, Jane	22 (1786-93)	294
Simmons, John, Jr.	1 (1722-24)	29
Simmons, Sarah Ruth	46 (1851-56)	184
Simmons, Silas	26 (1793-1800)	346
Simmons, Thomas	6 (1747-52)	163
Simmons, Thomas	30 (1800-07)	1080
Simmons, Vincent	13 (1767-71)	956
Simmons, William	7 (1752-56)	323
Simmons see also Simons		
Simms, William	18 (1776-84)	74
Simons, Ann	17 (1774-79)	491
Simons, Anthony	26 (1793-1800)	330
Simons, Benjamin	14 (1771-74)	235
Simons, Benjamin	23 (1786-93)	585
Simons, Benjamin Bonneau	43 (1839-45)	795
Simons, Catharine	34 (1818-26)	391
Simons, Edward	,17 (1774-79)	434
Simons, Edward P.	36 (1818-26)	936
Simons, Eleanor	37 (1826-34)	216
Simons, Eliza	46 (1851-56)	145
Simons, Eliza Lucilla	45 (1845-51)	593
Simons, Francis	2 (1729-31)	115
Simons, Francis	14 (1771-74)	116
Simons, John ₍Simmons₎	5 (1740-47)	1
Simons, John A.	47 (1851-56)	687
Simons, Keating	40 (1834-39)	82
Simons, Keating Lewis	34 (1818-26)	188

Name	Volume	Page
Simons, Maurice	21 (1783-86)	746
Simons, Maurice, Jun.r	40 (1834-39)	377
Simons, Maurice	43 (1839-45)	888
Simons, Mountague	32 (1807-18)	706
Simons, Peter	17 (1774-79)	557
Simons, Peter	31 (1807-18)	5
Simons, Rachel	47 (1851-56)	453
Simons, Sampson	31 (1807-18)	455
Simons, Samuel	8 (1757-60)	376
Simons, Samuel	36 (1818-26)	972
Simons, Thomas Grange	50 (1862-68)	46
Simpson, Archibald	26 (1793-1800)	426
Simpson, Christopher	12 (1767-71)	576
Simpson, James [Simson]	5 (1740-47)	207
Simpson, James	24 (1786-93)	896
Simpson, James	29 (1800-07)	565
Simpson, Lydia M.	47 (1851-56)	620
Simpson, Margaret	31 (1807-18)	201
Simpson, Patrick	24 (1786-93)	967
Simpson, Peter	36 (1818-26)	1157
Simpson, Sarah	19 (1780-83)	5
Simpson, Thomas	10 (1760-67)	455
Simpson, William	17 (1774-79)	635
Simrell, John	2 (1724-25)	88
Simrell see also Symrall		
Sims, Edward L.	41 (1834-39)	639
Simson see Simpson		
Sinclair, Alexander	41 (1834-39)	806
Sinclair, Daniel	28 (1800-07)	180
Sinclair, John	7 (1752-56)	365
Sinclair, Margaret	49 (1856-62)	879
Sinclair, Richard	3 (1732-37)	74
Sinclare, George	2 (1729-31)	20
Sindrey, Daniel	1 (1687-1710)	36

Name	Volume	Page
Sineath, Francis	37 (1826-34)	217
Singellton, Benjamin, Jr.	13 (1767-71)	1029
Singellton, Benjamin	23 (1786-93)	417
Singellton, Elizabeth	11 (1767-71)	163
Singellton, John	19 (1780-83)	346
Singellton, Peter	14 (1771-74)	318
Singellton, Rebecah [Rebcah]	16 (1774-79)	96
Singellton see also Singleton		
Singelton see Singleton		
Singletary, Benjamin, Senr.	31 (1807-18)	39
Singletary, John	24 (1786-93)	862
Singletary, Sarah	27 (1793-1800)	678
Singleton, Benjamin	16 (1774-79)	401
* Singleton, Benjamin [Singellton]	18 (1776-84)	97
* Singleton, Mary Ann	18 (1776-84)	107
Singleton, Richard	3 (1732-37)	258
* Singleton, Richard [Singelton]	9 (1760-67)	412
Singleton, Ripley	27 (1793-1800)	838
Singleton, Samuel [Singellton]	18 (1776-84)	67
* Singleton, Susannah [Singellton; Susanna]	7 (1752-56)	396
Singleton, Thomas	28 (1800-07)	154
Singuefield, Francis	19 (1780-83)	138
Sinkler, Elizabeth	20 (1783-86)	266
Sinkler, James	28 (1800-07)	119
Sinkler, Jane [Jean]	12 (1767-71)	678
Sinkler, Margaret	35 (1818-26)	623
Sinkler, Peter	19 (1780-83)	393
Sinkler, Peter	24 (1786-93)	989
Sinkler, William	46 (1831-56)	292
Sinkler, William H.	47 (1851-56)	812
Sinning, John	9 (1760-67)	28
Sires, Peter J.	51 (1862-68)	686
Skeen, James	48 (1856-62)	27
Skeene, Thomas [Skene]	3 (1757-60)	423

Name	Volume	Page
Skene, Alexander	5 (1740-47)	40
Skene, George	10 (1760-67)	823
Skene see also Skeene; Skine		
Skine, John [Skene]	12 (1767-71)	584
Skinner, David	4 (1736-40)	136
Skipper, Benning	5 (1740-47)	298
Skipper, William	2 (1724-25)	79
Skipton, William	36 (1818-26)	962
Skirving, Bethia	43 (1839-45)	538
Skirving, Charles	22 (1786-93)	153
Skirving, Charlotte	31 (1807-18)	261
Skirving, James	22 (1786-93)	210
Skirving, William M.	51 (1862-68)	752
Skottowe, Thomas	23 (1786-93)	482
Skrine, Margaret G.	43 (1839-45)	929
Slade, Henry	19 (1780-83)	32
Slade, Henry	20 (1783-86)	290
Slann, Andrew	20 (1783-86)	354
Slann, Peter	20 (1783-86)	353
Slater, Edward	4 (1736-40)	167
Slawson, Nathaniel	38 (1826-34)	500
Sleigh, Hugh	16 (1774-79)	352
Sleigh, Mary	18 (1776-84)	326
Sleigh, Samuel	11 (1767-71)	115
Sleigh, Samuel (Junr)	14 (1771-74)	320
Sloan, Allan	42 (1839-45)	96
Sloman, John	4 (1736-40)	28
Slumburger, Mary	22 (1786-93)	82
Sluter, Maria	48 (1856-62)	7
Small, Richard	51 (1862-68)	321
Small, Samuel	3 (1732-37)	297
Smart, Samuel R.	33 (1807-18)	1204
Smelie, John	6 (1747-52)	355
Smelie, John	20 (1783-86)	356

270

Name	Volume	Page
Smelie, John	32 (1807-18)	661
Smelie, Mary	22 (1786-93)	277
Smelie, Sarah M.	45 (1845-51)	871
Smelie, Susanna	7 (1752-56)	45
Smelie, William ₍Smilie₎	7 (1752-56)	301
Smelie, William	28 (1800-07)	68
Smerdon, Elias	32 (1807-18)	689
Smerdon, Henry	33 (1807-18)	1128
Smiley, John ₍Smilie₎	2 (1727-29)	7
Smilie, Susanna	36 (1818-26)	839
Smilie see also Smelie; Smiley		
Smiser, Jacob	20 (1783-86)	334
*Smiser, Paul	21 (1783-86)	830
Smith, Agnes	40 (1834-39)	7
Smith, Alexander	5 (1740-47)	428
Smith, Alice	5 (1740-47)	425
Smith, Allin ₍Allen₎	48 (1856-62)	36
Smith, Amelia Rosina	46 (1851-56)	97
Smith, Ann	38 (1826-34)	703
Smith, Ann	43 (1839-45)	657
Smith, Anne D.	34 (1818-26)	115
Smith, Archar	9 (1760-67)	1
Smith, Archar	12 (1767-71)	521
Smith, Archer ₍Archar₎	30 (1800-07)	802
Smith, Barbary	34 (1818-26)	90
Smith, Benjamin	13 (1767-71)	831
Smith, Benjamin	14 (1771-74)	71
Smith, Benjamin	23 (1786-93)	679
Smith, Benjamin	38 (1826-34)	632
Smith, Benjamin	46 (1851-56)	102
Smith, Charles	4 (1736-40)	183
Smith, Charles	5 (1740-47)	471
Smith, Charles	24 (1786-93)	994
Smith, Charlotte	17 (1774-79)	627

Name	Volume	Page
Smith, Charlotte Georgina	39 (1826-34)	1133
Smith, Christopher	5 (1740-47)	573 ⎫ Duplicates
Smith, Christopher	5 (1740-47)	577 ⎭
Smith, Christopher	32 (1807-18)	796
Smith, Daniel	6 (1747-52)	619
Smith, Daniel	39 (1826-34)	1222
Smith, Edward	7 (1752-56)	492
Smith, Eliphalet	21 (1783-86)	662
Smith, Eliza C.	49 (1856-62)	785
Smith, Elizabeth	6 (1747-52)	511
Smith, Elizabeth	16 (1774-79)	145
Smith, Elizabeth	44 (1845-51)	70
Smith, Elizabeth	50 (1862-68)	205
Smith, Elizabeth A.	46 (1851-56)	372
Smith, Emanuel	5 (1740-47)	331
Smith, Francis	21 (1783-86)	573
Smith, George, Jr.	21 (1783-86)	456
Smith, George	22 (1786-93)	25
Smith, George	22 (1786-93)	359
Smith, George Henry	44 (1845-51)	391
Smith, Henrietta	42 (1839-45)	70
Smith, Henry	19 (1780-83)	222
Smith, Henry	20 (1783-86)	22
Smith, Hester	36 (1818-26)	1105
Smith, Hugh	37 (1826-34)	39
Smith, Jacob	23 (1786-93)	597
Smith, Jacob	47 (1851-56)	601
Smith, James	21 (1783-86)	632
Smith, James	32 (1807-18)	727
Smith, James	41 (1834-39)	682
Smith, James	50 (1862-68)	149
Smith, Jane	33 (1807-18)	1127
Smith, John	2 (1724-25)	48
Smith, John	2 (1729-31)	117
Smith, John	3 (1732-37)	61

Name	Volume	Page
Smith, Paul	24 (1786-93)	851
Smith, Peter	33 (1807-18)	1068
Smith, Peter	35 (1818-26)	538
Smith, Peter, Senior	36 (1818-26)	1060
Smith, Philip	26 (1793-1800)	385
Smith, Polly Ann	36 (1818-26)	1152
Smith, Rebecca	32 (1807-18)	750
Smith, Richard	3 (1732-37)	161
Smith, Richard	48 (1856-62)	147
Smith, Richard Furman	48 (1856-62)	199
Smith, Robert	28 (1800-07)	206
Smith, Robert	32 (1807-18)	919
Smith, Roger	30 (1800-07)	881
Smith, Rosella Blanche	43 (1839-45)	887
Smith, Samuel	7 (1752-56)	146
Smith, Samuel	13 (1767-71)	1057
Smith, Samuel W.	32 (1807-18)	719
Smith, Sarah	9 (1760-67)	345
Smith, Sarah	31 (1807-18)	360
Smith, Sarah	49 (1856-62)	552
Smith, Stephen	15 (1771-74)	437
Smith, Susan P.	44 (1845-51)	42
Smith, Thomas (Memorandum)	1 (1692-93)	33
Smith, Thomas Esqr.	1 (1722-24)	91
Smith, Thomas, Jun[r].	2(G1729-31)	52
Smith, Thomas	4 (1736-40)	143
Smith, Thomas	9 (1760-67)	335
Smith, Thomas	12 (1767-71)	608
Smith, Thomas	23 (1786-93)	519
Smith, Thomas	23 (1786-93)	689
Smith, Thomas (S.O.B.)	35 (1818-26)	554
Smith, Thos., Junr.	38 (1826-34)	802
Smith, Thomas Branford	32 (1807-18)	548
Smith, Thomas Loughton	15 (1771-74)	487

Name	Volume	Page
Snow, George	19 (1780-83)	114
Snow, George	20 (1783-86)	312
Snow, John	6 (1747-52)	591
Snow, Nathaniel	2 (1727-29)	38
Snow, Nathaniel	6 (1747-52)	408
Snow, Susanna [Susannah]	11 (1767-71)	151
Snowden, Ann	40 (1834-39)	258
Snowden, Charles	29 (1800-07)	627
Snowden, Laura Ann	49 (1856-62)	635
Snowdy, Fergus	21 (1783-86)	635
Snyder, Rebecka	23 (1786-93)	644
Sohliiter, Julius Lewis [Ludewig]	20 (1783-86)	317
Solan, Timothy	33 (1807-18)	1115
Sollee, Carolina Neyle	51 (1862-68)	800
Sollee, Harriett	47 (1851-56)	615
Solomon see Solomons		
Solomons, Hart	33 (1807-18)	1348
Solomons, Hyman [Hyam]	28 (1800-07)	147
Solomons, Joseph [Solomon]	31 (1807-18)	166
Solon, Margaret	28 (1800-07)	240
Somerhoeff, John Peter	5 (1740-47)	130
Somervill see Somerville		
Somerville, Sarah [Summerville]	4 (1736-40)	54
Somerville, Tweedie [Somervill]	3 (1732-37)	123
Sommers, George	17 (1774-79)	600
Sommers, Henrietta	19 (1780-83)	18
Sommers, Humphry	22 (1786-93)	353
Sommers, James	24 (1786-93)	1166
Sommers, John	23 (1786-93)	631
Sommers, Rose	42 (1839-45)	214
Sompayrac, Theodore	35 (1818-26)	775
Sorency, Florence	1 (1720-21)	30
Southworth, Rufus	38 (1826-34)	478
Sowre, William	23 (1786-93)	544
Sparkman William	32 (1807-18)	739

Name	Volume	Page
Sparuick, Henry	50 (1862-68)	154
Spear, Laura A.	46 (1851-56)	53
Spears, James	31 (1807-13)	63
Spears, James H.	37 (1826-34)	332
Spears, Jane	50 (1862-68)	262
Spence, Henry	48 (1856-62)	195
Spencer, George	31 (1807-13)	444
Spencer, John	4 (1736-40)	90
Spencer, John	19 (1780-83)	46
Spencer, Joseph, Senr.	2 (1729-31)	1
Spencer, Joseph	5 (1740-47)	585
Spencer, Joseph	12 (1767-71)	656
Spencer, Oliver	6 (1747-52)	356
Spencer, Sebastian	33 (1807-18)	1281
Spencer, William	6 (1747-52)	482
Spencken, Martin	50 (1862-68)	387
Spidel, Abraham	20 (1783-86)	10
Spidel, Eberhart	28 (1800-07)	179
Spicle, John	14 (1771-74)	121
Spidle, John G(eorge)	43 (1839-45)	833
Spines, Ruth	19 (1780-83)	16
Splat see Splatt		
Splatt, Benjamin	9 (1760-67)	274
Splatt, Hannah	21 (1783-86)	819
Splatt, John	6 (1747-52)	218
Splatt, John	7 (1752-56)	29
Splatt, Richard [Splat]	2 (1727-29)	54
Spoad see Spoade		
Spoade, William [Spoad]	10 (1760-67)	880
Spooler, Philip	10 (1760-67)	636
Spooler, Philip	19 (1780-83)	123
Spoon, William	25 (1793-1800)	290
Spry, Henry	13 (1767-71)	1007
Spry, Joseph	11 (1767-71)	36

Name	Volume	Page
Spry, Mary	22 (1786-93)	65
Spry, Royal	13 (1767-71)	947
Spry, Royale [Royal, Royall]	5 (1740-47)	611
Spry, Samuel	9 (1760-67)	325
Squires, Ann	28 (1800-07)	229
Stack, Hannah	6 (1747-52)	281
Stafford, Arthur	21 (1783-86)	517
Stafford, William Junkin	35 (1818-26)	818
Stall, Frederick	48 (1856-62)	228
Stanley, Peter	4 (1736-40)	75 } Duplicates
Stanley, Peter	4 (1736-40)	113
Stanyarn, James [Stanyarne]	1 (1722-24)	63
Stanyarn, Jehu	5 (1740-47)	627
Stanyarne, Ann	37 (1826-34)	51
Stanyarne, Anna	40 (1834-39)	388
Stanyarne, Annah	23 (1786-93)	641
Stanyarne, Archibald	15 (1771-74)	528
Stanyarne, Benjamin	7 (1752-56)	10
Stanyarne, Elizabeth	21 (1783-86)	478
Stanyarne, Frances	23 (1786-93)	747
Stanyarne, James	19 (1780-83)	253
Stanyarne, James	20 (1783-86)	101
Stanyarne, Jane	50 (1862-68)	68
Stanyarne, John (Son of John)	9 (1760-67)	252
Stanyarne, John	15 (1771-74)	369
Stanyarne, John	19 (1780-83)	124
Stanyarne, Joseph	14 (1771-74)	263
Stanyarne, Rivers	7 (1752-56)	261
Stanyarne, Sarah	8 (1757-60)	400
Stanyarne, Susanna	31 (1807-18)	19
Stanyarne, Thomas	2 (1729-31)	99
Stanyarne, William	21 (1783-86)	499
Stanyarne see also Stanyarn		
Staples, Abraham	6 (1747-52)	329

278

Name	Volume	Page
Stapleton, Crawford	38 (1826-34)	748
Stapleton, Mary	40 (1834-39)	334
Star, Anthony	31 (1807-18)	449
Starlin, Marshfield	39 (1826-34)	943
Starling, Mary	10 (1760-67)	565
Starling, Mary	12 (1767-71)	664
Starling, William	24 (1786-93)	789
Starling, Zacharias	22 (1786-93)	204
Starling see also Sterling		
Starr, Edwin P.	47 (1851-56)	757
Starrat, Archibald	11 (1767-71)	240
Starrat, George	9 (1760-67)	87
Statham, Rowland	4 (1736-40)	188
Stattler, John Benedict	22 (1786-93)	183
Steacy, Edward	21 (1783-86)	597
Stead, Benjamin	17 (1774-79)	595
Stead, William	21 (1783-86)	800
Steal, Robert	6 (1747-52)	36
Steedman, Elizabeth	42 (1839-45)	286
Steedman, James	27 (1793-1800)	717
Steedman, Mary	41 (1834-39)	869
Steek, Anthony	9 (1760-67)	330
Steel, James	8 (1757-60)	444
Steel, Peter	30 (1800-07)	941
Steele, Edwin C.	49 (1856-62)	787
Steele, John	42 (1839-45)	423
Steele, Sarah	33 (1807-18)	1194
Steele, William G.	42 (1839-45)	122
Steimet, Barron	44 (1845-51)	385
Stelling, Eibe Fredidrick	49 (1856-62)	808
Stenson, James	21 (1783-86)	483
Stent, Daniel	8 (1757-60)	298
Stent, Esther	22 (1786-93)	381
Stent, John	12 (1767-71)	490

Name	Volume	Page
Stent, John	33 (1807-18)	1137
Stent, John H.	31 (1807-18)	277
Stent, Paul	29 (1800-07)	639
Stent, Samuell	1 (1711-18)	61
Stent, William	19 (1780-83)	277
Stent, William	20 (1783-86)	33
Stephen, William	31 (1807-18)	245
Stephens, Edward	4 (1736-40)	189
Stephens, James [Stevens]	1 (1711-18)	92
Stephens, Robert	21 (1783-86)	453
Stephens, William	23 (1786-93)	603
Stephens see also Stevens		
Stephenson, James	18 (1776-84)	283
Stephenson, William	23 (1786-93)	525
Sterling, John [Starling]	6 (1747-52)	215
Sterling, William	4 (1736-40)	314
Sterne, Miriam	49 (1856-62)	609
Steven see Stevens		
Stevenfon see Stevenson		
Stevens, Abigail	3 (1732-37)	76
Stevens, Benjamin	13 (1767-71)	993
Stevens, Clement H.	50 (1862-68)	278
Stevens, David	9 (1760-67)	334
Stevens, Elizabeth	13 (1767-71)	1050
Stevens, Elizabeth S.	45 (1845-51)	719
Stevens, Henry L.	49 (1856-62)	1029
Stevens, Jacob, Jr.	14 (1771-74)	192
Stevens, Jacob	21 (1783-86)	636
Stevens, Jeannet	6 (1747-52)	605
Stevens, Jervais Henry [Jervis]	38 (1826-34)	433
Stevens, John	1 (1720-21)	4
Stevens, John	5 (1740-47)	134
✱ Stevens, Joseph [Steven]	6 (1747-52)	8
Stevens, Margaret [Margarett]	6 (1747-52)	417

Name	Volume	Page
Stevens, Mary	20 (1783-86)	211
Stevens, Mary	24 (1786-93)	817
Stevens, Mary Smith	49 (1856-62)	683
Stevens, Nicholas	2 (1724-25)	96
Stevens, O'Neal Gough	29 (1800-07)	572
Stevens, Richard	10 (1760-67)	796
Stevens, Robert	1 (1720-21)	37
Stevens, Robert	3 (1732-37)	87
Stevens, Samuel [Stephens; Samuel]	8 (1757-60)	484
Stevens, Samuel F.	45 (1839-45)	838
Stevens, Sarah	14 (1771-74)	144
Stevens, Sarah	50 (1862-68)	284
Stevens, Sarah F.	45 (1845-51)	627
Stevens, Susan M.	49 (1856-62)	746
Stevens, Thomas	7 (1752-56)	178
Stevens, Thomas	32 (1807-18)	568
Stevens, William	15 (1771-74)	508
Stevens see also Stephens		
Stevenson, James	25 (1793-1800)	100
Stevenson, Jane	28 (1800-07)	142
Stevenson, John [Stevenson]	3 (1732-37)	166
Stevenson, John	15 (1771-74)	506
Stevenson, John	22 (1786-93)	385
Stevenson, Peter	18 (1776-84)	193
Stewart, Alexander	11 (1767-71)	94
Stewart, Alexander	29 (1800-07)	469
Stewart, Andrew	22 (1786-93)	134
Stewart, Ann (Anne)	2 (1722-26)	11
Stewart, Charles	1 (1720-21)	14
Stewart, Charles Howard	50 (1862-68)	390
Stewart, Elizabeth	10 (1760-67)	886
Stewart, Hannah	19 (1780-83)	82
Stewart, Isaac	4 (1736-40)	190
Stewart, James [Stuart]	8 (1757-60)	224

Name	Volume	Page
Stewart, James	15 (1771-74)	655
Stewart, Jane	50 (1862-68)	408
Stewart, John	5 (1740-47)	39 0
* Stewart, Mary	6 (1747-52)	5
Stewart, Mary	6 (1747-52)	423
Stewart, Mary	16 (1774-79)	47
Stewart, Patrick	16 (1774-79)	78
Stewart, Rebecca [Rebeckah]	25 (1793-1800)	92
Stewart, Rebecca Budd	34 (1818-26)	131
Stewart, Robert	18 (1776-84)	63
Stewart, Robert Lyle	46 (1851-56)	84
Stewart, Thomas	1 (1722-24)	31
Stewart, Thomas	22 (1786-93)	319
Stewart, Thomas	30 (1800-07)	1046
Stewart, William	38 (1826-34)	565
Stewart see also Stuart		
Stiff, Richard	32 (1807-18)	850
Stiles, Ann	14 (1771-74)	231
Stiles, Benjamin, Junior	30 (1800-07)	770
Stiles, Benjamin	30 (1800-07)	882
Stiles, Jane	35 (1818-26)	810
Stiles, Rebekah	6 (1747-52)	213
Stillman, Susannah [Susanna]	19 (1780-83)	265
Stobo, Archibald	5 (1740-47)	64
Stobo, Elizabeth	23 (1786-93)	711
Stobo, James	19 (1780-83)	95
Stobo, James	20 (1783-86)	109
Stobo, James	25 (1793-1800)	97
Stobo, Jane	21 (1783-86)	475
Stobo, Mary	21 (1783-86)	653
Stobo, Norton W.	34 (1818-26)	239
Stobo, Richard Park	21 (1783-86)	639
Stobo, Samuel	9 (1760-67)	206
Stock, Gabriel	14 (1771-74)	164

Name	Volume	Page
Stock, John	21 (1783-86)	471
Stock, Margaret	40 (1834-39)	398
Stock, Rachel	16 (1774-79)	306
Stock, Thomas	5 (1740-47)	400
Stock, Thomas	10 (1760-67)	829
Stock, Thomas	32 (1807-18)	504
Stocker, Alfred B.	44 (1845-51)	134
Stocks, Jonathan	3 (1732-37)	329
Stokes, Grace	7 (1752-56)	571
Stokes, Joseph	9 (1760-67)	337
Stoll, David	14 (1771-74)	97
Stoll, Mary	14 (1771-74)	280
Stoll, Phebe	23 (1786-93)	561
Stone, Benjamin	13 (1767-71)	878
Stone, Isabella	36 (1818-26)	1129
Stone, Jane	14 (1771-74)	82
Stone, John	9 (1760-67)	67
Stone, Joseph	8 (1757-60)	130
Stone, Love	27 (1793-1800)	718
Stone, Margaret	51 (1862-68)	749
Stone, Peter	20 (1783-86)	32
*Stone, Robert	6 (1747-52)	554
Stone, Ruth	22 (1786-93)	91
Stone, Thomas	4 (1736-40)	165
Stone, Thomas	11 (1767-71)	255
Stone, Thomas (Junior)	25 (1793-1800)	17
Stone, William	20 (1783-86)	346
Stoney, John	41 (1834-39)	834
Story, Elizabeth	6 (1747-52)	467
Story, Ellicott	7 (1752-56)	344
Story, John	3 (1732-37)	293
Story, Lachariah	3 (1732-37)	42
Stott, Nathaniel	14 (1771-74)	329
Stoutamier, J. T.	51 (1862-68)	676

Name	Volume	Page

Stoutebourgh   see Stoutenburgh

Stouteburgh   see Stoutenburgh

Stoutenborough, Priscilla Raven
 ₍Priscilia₎   25 (1793-1800)   58

Stoutenburgh, Luke ₍Stouteburgh₎   5 (1740-47)   191 ⎫ Duplica
Stoutenburgh, Luke ₍Stoutebourgh₎   5 (1740-47)   221 ⎭

Stoutenburgh, Sarah   12 (1767-71)   345

Strain, Adam   9 (1760-67)   283

Strain, David   14 (1771-74)   182

Strane, Margaret   16 (1774-79)   229

Stratford, Hatten   20 (1783-86)   87

Stratford, Hatton   19 (1780-83)   9

Stratton, Gordon   26 (1793-1800)   497

Streater, James   12 (1767-71)   374

Streater, James   19 (1780-83)   100

Street, Henry T.   49 (1856-62)   781

Street, Horatio G.   45 (1845-51)   623

Street, Martha   41 (1834-39)   835

Street, William   4 (1736-40)   29

Strickland, Robert   27 (1793-1800)   815

Stringer, Mary   51 (1862-68)   490

Strobel, Daniel   30 (1800-07)   1068

Strobel, Eliza   45 (1845-51)   905

Strobel, Elizabeth   37 (1826-34)   224

Strobel, Robert Hayne   49 (1856-62)   1026

Strobel, Stephen B.   43 (1839-45)   928

Strobhar, Jacob   11 (1767-71)   176

Strohecker, Agnes T.   47 (1851-56)   503

Strohecker, John   45 (1845-51)   502

Strohecker, Oswald Eve   50 (1862-68)   304

Stroman, Jacob   19 (1780-83)   219

Strother, Charles   15 (1771-74)   611

✴Strother, George   15 (1771-74)   353

Strother, Mary   37 (1826-34)   192

Name	Volume	Page
Strouble, Frederick	10 (1760-67)	473
Stuart, Adam ₍Stewart₎	11 (1767-71)	159
Stuart, Duncan	6 (1747-52)	68
Stuart, George	28 (1800-07)	363
Stuart, Mary Ann	48 (1856-62)	439
Stuart see also Stewart		
Sturgis, Mary	47 (1851-56)	745
Stuve, Adolph	46 (1851-56)	163
Styles, Samuel	5 (1740-47)	396
Such, John	16 (1774-79)	319
Sudre, Peter	31 (1807-18)	269
Sudrie, Jn.	32 (1807-18)	714
Sulivan, John ₍Sulivun₎	26 (1793-1800)	609
Sulivun see Sulivan		
✻ Sullivan, Richard West	24 (1786-93)	1162
Summers, James	7 (1752-56)	242
Summers, John	5 (1740-47)	273
Summers, John	5 (1740-47)	398
Summers, Samuel ₍Samuell₎	3 (1732-37)	18
Summers, Thomas	2 (1729-31)	66
Summhervill, Thomas	16 (1774-79)	356
Summerville see Somerville		
Sumner, David	6 (1747-52)	67
Sumner, Joanna	5 (1740-47)	65
Sumner, Mary	6 (1747-52)	316
Sumner, Samuel	7 (1752-56)	185
Sutcliff see Sutcliffe		
Sutcliffe, Elizabeth ₍Sutcliff₎	41 (1834-39)	870
Sutcliffe, Jane	38 (1826-34)	517
Sutcliffe, John	25 (1793-1800)	513
Sutcliffe, John	27 (1793-1800)	763
Sutcliffe, John Ph.	40 (1834-39)	392
Suter, Maria	48 (1856-62)	7
Sutton, Thomas	25 (1793-1800)	221

Name	Volume	Page
Swadler, Abraham	8 (1757-60)	490
Swadler, George	16 (1774-79)	68
Swadler, Mary	25 (1793-1800)	284
Swain, Luke	28 (1800-07)	217
Swan, Edward	7 (1752-56)	322
Swancin, John	12 (1767-71)	600
Swaney, Hester	39 (1826-34)	1193
Swann, Samuel [Samuell]	3 (1732-37)	109
Sweatman, Mary	48 (1856-62)	457
Sweatman, Stephen A.	50 (1862-68)	226
Sweeny, Bryan	31 (1807-18)	389
Sweeny, Elizabeth M.	49 (1856-62)	959
Sweeny, Patrick	34 (1818-26)	34
Swetman, James	36 (1818-26)	996
Swetn, Lewis	35 (1818-26)	462
*Swindershime, Nicholas	18 (1770-84)	106
Swint, John	19 (1780-83)	148
Swint, John	20 (1783-86)	129
Swinton, Ann Jane Bruce	39 (1826-34)	1074
Swinton, Eliza	44 (1845-51)	316
Swinton, Hannah	43 (1839-45)	603
Swinton, Hugh	31 (1807-18)	200
Swinton, Margaret	28 (1800-07)	194
Swinton, Margaret	41 (1834-39)	623
Swinton, Susannah	35 (1818-26)	718
Swinton, William	5 (1740-47)	110
Swinton, William H.	41 (1834-39)	753
Swintzer, John Rodolph [Switzer]	31 (1807-18)	576
Switzer, Leonard	11 (1767-71)	220
Switzer see also Swintzer		
Sykes, John	5 (1740-47)	123
Sym, Isaac	6 (1747-52)	33
Syme, Andrew	16 (1774-79)	154
Syme, John	30 (1800-07)	864

Name	Volume	Page
Symonds see Symons		
Symons, Henry [Symonds]	1 (1692-93)	47
Symons, John	51 (1862-68)	586
Symrall, John [Simrell]	1 (1720-21)	33

T

Taggart, James	4 (1736-40)	176
Taggart, John	36 (1818-26)	1201
Taggart, William	20 (1783-86)	355
Taglierani, Nicholas	49 (1856-62)	927
Tailfer, Patrick	5 (1740-47)	461
Taillor, John	1 (1720-21)	1
Tait, James	33 (1807-18)	1420
Talbert, James	9 (1760-67)	382
Talbert, James	46 (1851-56)	271
Talbot, Daniel	28 (1800-07)	46
Talley, Caroline L.	34 (1818-26)	43
Talvande, Ann Marson [Marsan]	45 (1845-51)	779
Tamplet, Joseph	19 (1780-83)	378
Tamplet, Mary	23 (1786-93)	694
Tamplet, Peter	5 (1740-47)	183
Tamplet, Peter	25 (1793-1800)	135
Tamplet, Peter	25 (1793-1800)	168
Tamplet, Sarah	45 (1845-51)	617
Tanner, Edward	34 (1818-26)	287
Tardiff, William	40 (1834-39)	241
Tart, Nathan	12 (1767-71)	335
Tart, Nathan	25 (1793-1800)	286
Tate, James	38 (1826-34)	594
Tatnall, Thomas [Tatnell]	5 (1740-47)	546
Tatnell see Tatnall		
Tauvron, Estienne [Stephen]	2 (C1729-31)	14
Taveau, Martha Caroline	44 (1845-51)	229
Tavel, Charles	41 (1834-39)	531

Name	Volume	Page
Tavel, J. F.	38 (1826-34)	519
Taylor, Adam Felstead [Felsted, Adam]	16 (1774-79)	11
Taylor, Bennett	27 (1793-1800)	963
Taylor, Catherine	8 (1757-60)	44
Taylor, Charles Fox	28 (1800-07)	23
Taylor, Eben Ezer	1 (1721-22)	27
Taylor, George	28 (1800-07)	44
Taylor, James	8 (1757-60)	206
Taylor, James	18 (1776-84)	178
Taylor, Jane Baynes	8 (1757-60)	21
Taylor, John	11 (1767-71)	29
Taylor, John	13 (1767-71)	940
Taylor, John	13 (1767-71)	945
Taylor, Joseph	37 (1826-34)	412
Taylor, Josiah	44 (1845-51)	196
Taylor, Michael	13 (1767-71)	699
Taylor, Paul	34 (1818-26)	11
Taylor, Peter	10 (1760-67)	718
Taylor, Robert	49 (1856-62)	804
Taylor, Sabina	3 (1732-37)	207
Taylor, (Reverend Doctor) William	40 (1834-39)	193
Teague, John	1 (1687-1710)	30
Teasdale, Isaac	30 (1800-07)	1136
Teasdale, Mary	37 (1826-34)	207
Tebout, Judith	35 (1818-26)	443
Tefsier, Charles	32 (1807-18)	832
Telfair, Alexander	23 (1786-93)	515
Telfair, John	23 (1786-93)	518
Tennens, Peter	12 (1767-71)	396
Tennent, Ann Martha	49 (1856-62)	554
Tennent, E. S.	51 (1862-68)	759
Tennent, William	3 (1732-37)	96
Tennent, William	17 (1774-79)	704

Name	Volume	Page
Tennent, William	50 (1862-68)	146
Terry, Champnefs	17 (1774-79)	502
Tew, Charles	37 (1826-34)	248
Tew, George	22 (1786-93)	92
Tew, Mary	31 (1807-18)	463
Tharin, Daniel	22 (1780-93)	327
Thayer, Caroline S.	40 (1834-39)	422
Thayer, John W.	33 (1807-18)	1289
Theus, Jeremiah	16 (1774-79)	161
Theus, Rosanna	29 (1800-07)	397
Theus, Simeon	8 (1757-60)	504
Theus, Thomas	30 (1800-07)	1112
Thomas, Adolphe (D)	32 (1807-18)	874
Thomas, Betty	42 (1839-45)	303
Thomas, Cecilia	12 (1767-71)	493
Thomas, Elizabeth	13 (1767-71)	816
Thomas, James	6 (1747-52)	117
Thomas, James	39 (1826-34)	1205
Thomas, John	1 (1687-1710)	49
Thomas, John, Jr.	12 (1767-71)	416
Thomas, John	34 (1818-26)	413
Thomas, John James	31 (1807-18)	101
Thomas, Marianne	9 (1760-67)	285
Thomas, Mary G.	44 (1845-51)	140
Thomas, Mary Lamboll	33 (1807-18)	1263
Thomas, Mary Magdalena Inglis	34 (1818-26)	183
Thomas, Samuel	15 (1771-74)	354
Thomas, Samuel, Jr.	15 (1771-74)	627
Thomas, Samuel	24 (1786-93)	997
Thomas, Samuel	32 (1807-18)	647
Thomas, Sarah	31 (1807-18)	461
Thomas, Sarah	39 (1826-34)	972
Thomas, Walter	23 (1786-93)	619
Thomas, William	23 (1786-93)	643

Name	Volume	289 Page

Name	Volume	Page
Thomfon see Thompson		
Thompson, Anna	44 (1845-51)	361
Thompson, Doctrina ₍Thomfon, Tomson₎	3 (1731-33)	40
Thompson, Frances	47 (1851-56)	558
Thompson, George ₍Thomson₎	26 (1793-1800)	469
Thompson, George	31 (1807-18)	323
Thompson, George, Jun.	37 (1826-34)	48
Thompson, Hannah	50 (1862-68)	115
Thompson, Isaac	11 (1767-71)	325
Thompson, John	23 (1786-93)	460
Thompson, John	23 (1786-93)	748
Thompson, John	42 (1839-45)	32
Thompson, John ₍Thomson₎	44 (1845-51)	133
Thompson, Mary	7 (1752-56)	195
Thompson, Mary ₍Thomson₎	22 (1786-93)	215
Thompson, Mary C. ₍Thomson₎	44 (1845-51)	95
Thompson, Mathew	17 (1774-79)	566
Thompson, Robert	5 (1740-47)	144
Thompson, Robert H.	48 (1856-62)	201
Thompson, Samuel	13 (1767-71)	871
Thompson, William, Jr. ₍Thomson₎	5 (1740-47)	125
Thompson, William	21 (1783-86)	571
Thompson, William	49 (1856-62)	691
Thomson, David	13 (1767-71)	962
Thomson, Eliza Y.	36 (1818-26)	1141
Thomson, Esther	24 (1786-93)	1019
Thomson, George	38 (1826-34)	771
Thomson, Hugh	16 (1774-79)	272
Thomson, Hugh	16 (1774-79)	372
Thomson, James	5 (1740-47)	410
Thomson, James Hamden	25 (1793-1800)	274
Thomson, Jean ₍Thonson₎	6 (1747-52)	110
Thomson, John	5 (1740-47)	143
Thomson, John, Sr.	6 (1747-52)	350

Name	Volume	Page
Thomson, John	11 (1767-71)	113
Thomson, John	13 (1767-71)	1040
Thomson, John	20 (1783-86)	99
Thomson, Mofes	14 (1771-74)	156
Thomson, Moses, Jun.	13 (1767-71)	931
Thomson, William	11 (1767-71)	298
Thomson, William	16 (1774-79)	105
Thomson see also Thompson		
Thonson see Thomson		
Thorne, John G.	35 (1818-26)	419
Thorne, John G. (Petition)	35 (1818-26)	578
Thorne, John G. (Petition)	35 (1818-26)	655
Thorne, John S.	36 (1818-26)	1034
Thorney, William	28 (1800-07)	37
Thornhill, Catharine [Harvey]	39 (1826-34)	864
Thornley, Robert	30 (1800-07)	841
Thornton, Joseph	4 (1736-40)	320
Thornton, Mary	14 (1771-74)	56
Thornton, Samuel	13 (1767-71)	766
Thorpe, Robert	6 (1747-52)	299
Thorpe, Samuel	17 (1774-79)	749
Thradcraft, Sarah	12 (1767-71)	471
Threadcraft, Bethel	32 (1807-18)	861
Thrower, Eden	42 (1839-45)	420
Thurston, Sarah Constance	48 (1856-62)	304
Thweatt, David	40 (1834-39)	413
Thwing, Edward	43 (1839-45)	732
Ticer, William (W.)	12 (1767-71)	394
Tidyman, Hester	42 (1839-45)	275
Tidyman, Hester (Substitution of Trustee)	48 (1856-62)	113
Tidyman, Philip [Tydiman]	19 (1780-83)	7
Tidyman, Philip	20 (1783-86)	138
Tidyman, Philip	45 (1845-51)	715

Name	Volume	Page
Tiencken, John	51 (1862-68)	737
Tietyen, Dederick	49 (1856-62)	700
Tietyen, John H.	47 (1851-56)	465
Tifsot, John James	11 (1767-71)	92
Tilly, Benjamin	17 (1774-79)	633
Tilly, William, Sen[r.]	5 (1740-47)	290
Tilton, Rebecca	50 (1862-68)	100
Timmerly, Ann	18 (1776-84)	104
Timmons, Ann	32 (1807-18)	723
Timmons, George	41 (1834-39)	765
Timmons, Isabella	43 (1839-45)	696
Timmons, Richard	8 (1757-60)	536
Timmons, Thomas	9 (1760-67)	95
Timothy, Ann	24 (1786-93)	1138
Timothy, Ann	42 (1839-45)	204
Timothy, Elizabeth	8 (1757-60)	64
Timothy, Peter	20 (1783-86)	95
Timothy, Robert Smith	28 (1800-07)	314
Timrod, Christiana	21 (1783-86)	515
Timrod, Henry	25 (1793-1800)	220
Tipet, Henry	31 (1807-18)	52
Tobias, Abraham	47 (1851-56)	820
Tobias, Isaac	49 (1856-62)	596
Tobias, Jacob	18 (1776-84)	1
Tobias, Judith	33 (1807-18)	1055
Tobias, Margaret	15 (1771-74)	562
Tobias, Sarah	16 (1774-79)	54
Tobias, Sarah	18 (1776-84)	183
Todd, Henry	29 (1800-07)	429
Todd, Jane	38 (1826-34)	742
Todd, Joseph	25 (1793-1800)	64
Todd, Richard	22 (1786-90)	75
Todd, Rich[d] D.	34 (1818-26)	147

Name	Volume	Page
Todd, Ruth Savage	34 (1818-26)	111
Tollsen, Tories	26 (1793-1800)	360
Tomlinson, Arthur	11 (1767-71)	183
Tomlinson, Josiah	9 (1760-67)	114
Tomkins, John	23 (1786-93)	576
Tomson see Thompson		
Tonge, John	15 (1771-74)	624
Tonge, Susannah [Susanna]	38 (1826-34)	464
Tookerman see Tuckerman		
Toomer, Ann	37 (1826-34)	305
Toomer, Anthony	27 (1793-1800)	758
Toomer, Anthony V.	47 (1851-56)	869
Toomer, David	16 (1774-79)	308
Toomer, John	9 (1760-67)	212
Toomer, Joshua	26 (1793-1800)	444
Toomer, Joshua Washington	42 (1839-45)	174
Torpy, Matthew	47 (1851-56)	492
Torquet, James	6 (1747-52)	127
Torquett, Paul	1 (1711-18)	27
Torrans, John Gordon	28 (1800-07)	328
Torrans see also Torrens		
Torre, Peter	34 (1818-26)	303
Torrens, John [Torrans]	19 (1780-83)	27
Torrens, John [Torrans]	20 (1783-86)	140
Torshell, Samuel	3 (1732-37)	180
Touch, Kathrine [Katharine]	21 (1783-85)	585
Touchstone, Daniel	11 (1767-71)	286
Touchstone, Frederick	41 (1834-39)	821
Toufsiger, James	23 (1786-93)	780
Toufsiger, Margaret	32 (1807-18)	644
Touhy, Maurice	46 (1851-56)	332
Toutain, Peter Nicholas Gervais	30 (1800-07)	944
Tovey, Henry C.	42 (1839-45)	16

Name	Volume	Page
Tovey, Sarah	44 (1845-51)	254
Townesend see Townsend		
Townsend, Abigail	15 (1771-74)	629
Townsend, Andrew	19 (1780-83)	176
Townsend, Ann	24 (1786-93)	1066
Townsend, Daniel [Daniell]	5 (1740-47)	593
Townsend, Daniel	21 (1783-86)	565
Townsend, Daniel	42 (1839-45)	442
Townsend, John	5 (1740-47)	569
Townsend, Joseph	4 (1736-40)	10
Townsend, Nicholas [Townesend]	1 (1692-93)	28
Townsend, Sarah	29 (1800-07)	712
Townsend, Thomas	3 (1732-37)	6
Townsend, William	11 (1767-71)	249
Tradd, Robert	2 (1729-31)	73
Trammell, Daniel	17 (1774-79)	727
Trapier, James Heyward	51 (1862-68)	463
Trapier, Mary Elizabeth	50 (1862-68)	64
Trapier, Paul	2 (1727-29)	33
Trapier, Sarah A.	43 (1839-45)	802
Trapman, John Peter Louis [Trapmann]	47 (1851-56)	607
Trapmann see Trapman		
Travers, Francis	18 (1776-84)	247
Travers, Judith	7 (1752-56)	566
Treadway, Elijah	46 (1851-56)	200
Trescot, Edward	34 (1818-26)	41
Trescot, George	37 (1826-34)	299
Trezevant, Dinah	50 (1862-68)	116
Trezevant, Lewis	31 (1807-18)	74
Trezevant, Theodore	28 (1800-07)	158
Trezvant, Daniel	2 (1726-27)	27
Trifsel, Nathaniel	7 (1752-56)	153
Trink, Paul	28 (1800-07)	199

Name	Volume	Page
Trott, Nickolas [Nikolas]	4 (1736-40)	326
Trott, Sarah	5 (1740-47)	456
Troup, John	25 (1793-1800)	262
Trout, William	49 (1856-62)	790
Trowell, Thomas	6 (1747-52)	79
Truchet, Mare	12 (1767-71)	508
Truelle, Jacque Charles	31 (1807-18)	164
Truesdell, David	47 (1851-56)	723
Trunker, Mary	23 (1786-93)	413
Trusler see Trustler		
Trustler, Edward [Trusler]	9 (1760-67)	141
Tucker, Arthur	11 (1767-71)	327
Tucker, Charles S.	37 (1826-34)	326
Tucker, Henry	29 (1800-07)	443
Tucker, Isaac Waight	32 (1807-18)	798
Tucker, John	13 (1767-71)	892
Tucker, John H.	48 (1856-62)	466
Tucker, Joseph	5 (1740-47)	223
Tucker, Mary	25 (1793-1800)	84
Tucker, Mary	35 (1818-26)	597
Tucker, Thomas	21 (1783-86)	590
Tucker, William	19 (1780-83)	242
Tucker, William	30 (1800-07)	1139
Tuckerman, Katherine [Tookerman; Kathrenie]	2 (1724-25)	98
Tull, Henry	31 (1807-18)	62
Tully, Mary	22 (1786-93)	81
Tumley see Tunley		
Tunley, William [Tumley]	2 (1727-29)	35
Tunno, Adam	39 (1826-34)	1100
Tunno, Adam	39 (1826-34)	1242
Tunno, Sarah C.	47 (1851-56)	728
Tuqiut, Elizabeth	16 (1774-79)	188
Turbevil, John	11 (1767-71)	87

Name	Volume	Page
Turk, John	7 (1752-56)	441
Turly, Samuel	3 (1732-37)	1
Turnbul, Walter	11 (1767-71)	268
Turnbull, Andrew	24 (1786-93)	1009
Turnbull, Anna B.	49 (1856-62)	1028
Turnbull, Joseph	41 (1834-39)	605
Turnbull, Patrick	16 (1774-79)	187
Turnbull, Robert J.	39 (1826-34)	1164
Turnbull, William E. (Nuncupative, Memo.)	41 (1834-39)	716
Turner, Daniel	30 (1800-07)	1057
Turner, Eliza	37 (1826-34)	89
Turner, Jacob	7 (1752-56)	196
Turner, James	11 (1767-71)	59
Turner, Jane	31 (1807-18)	280
✳ Turner, John	18 (1776-84)	212
Turner, Samuel ₍Samuell₎	1 (1720-21)	42
Turner, Samuel	1 (1722-24)	78
Turner, Thomas	31 (1807-18)	296
Turner, William	18 (1776-84)	199
Turner, William McAllester	30 (1800-07)	1047
Turpin, Hugh	17 (1774-79)	798
Turpin, William	40 (1834-39)	224
Tutten, William	2 (1726-27)	64
Tweed, Alexander	29 (1800-07)	427
Tweed, William	19 (1780-83)	261
Tweed, William	23 (1786-93)	719
Tybout, Margaret	12 (1767-71)	553
Tydiman see Tidyman		
Tynte, Edward	1 (1687-1710)	55
Tyrrell, Gracey	50 (1862-68)	371
Tyrrell, Walter	42 (1839-45)	218
Tyson, Abraham	25 (1793-1800)	316

Name	Volume	Page

Name	Volume	Page
Vanderhorst, Arnoldus	10 (1760-67)	620
Vander Horst, Arnoldus	32 (1807-18)	924
Vanderhorst, James	21 (1783-86)	543
Vanderhorst, John	22 (1786-93)	126
Vanderhorst, Joseph	6 (1747-52)	270
Vanderhorst, Joseph	11 (1767-71)	80
Vanderhorst, Joseph	21 (1783-86)	600
Vanderhorst, Mary	42 (1839-45)	87
Vanderhorst, Richard W.	39 (1826-34)	988
Vanderhorst, William	11 (1767-71)	45
Vanderwick, Mary	7 (1752-56)	20
Van Dyne, Jane S.	41 (1834-39)	630
Van Dyne, Sarah J.	51 (1862-68)	835
Van Homrigh, Cornelias ₍Cornelis₎	26 (1793-1800)	451
Van Marjen Hoff, John ₍Van Marjin Hoff₎	24 (1786-93)	920
Van Marjenhoff, John, Sr.	20 (1783-86)	194
Van Marjin Hoff see Van Marjen Hoff		
Van Rhyn, Ann Eleanor	37 (1826-34)	342
Van Rhyn, John M.	42 (1839-45)	75
Van Rhyn, Susan (H)	43 (1839-45)	777
Vanroeven, Maria Elizabeth	38 (1826-34)	674
Van Susteren see Vansusteron		
Vansusteron, John ₍Van Susteren₎	1 (1692-93)	20
Vanvalkinburgh, Martin ₍vanVolkinburgh₎	28 (1800-07)	199
Vanvelsen, Edward	6 (1747-52)	49
Vanvelsen, Edward	6 (1747-52)	52
Van Velsen, Garret	5 (1740-47)	256
Vanvelsen, Thomas G.	39 (1826-34)	1238
van Volkinburgh see Vanvalkinburgh		
Van Winkle, Mary E(lizabeth)	50 (1862-68)	399
Varambout, Francis	11 (1767-71)	170
Vardell, Eliz	30 (1800-07)	833
Vardell, Susan	48 (1856-62)	325

}Duplic

Name	Volume	Page
Vardell, Thomas	14 (1771-74)	118
Varin, Samuel	5 (1740-47)	513
Varine, Jeremiah	2 (G1729-31)	41
Varner, William L.	50 (1862-68)	144
Varni, Nicholas [Nicilis]	45 (1845-51)	466
Varnor, Samuel	18 (1776-84)	10
Vaughan, Jefse	31 (1807-18)	379
Vaughan, John	5 (1740-47)	427
Vaughan, John [Vaughn]	25 (1793-1800)	166
Vaughan, Rowland	3 (1732-37)	310
Vaughn see Vaughan		
Vausc, John T.	48 (1856-62)	65
Vaux, John	17 (1774-79)	638
Vening, R. M. [Venning]	48 (1856-62)	16
Venning, Ann	47 (1851-56)	522
Venning, Elizabeth	50 (1862-68)	163
Venning, Henry Martyn	51 (1862-68)	474
Venning, Jonah M.	50 (1862-68)	359
Venning, Nicholas	40 (1834-39)	259
Venning, Nicholas	47 (1851-56)	710
Venning, Nicholas	50 (1862-68)	368
Venning, Samuel, Senior	35 (1818-26)	535
Venning, Samuel	42 (1839-45)	152
Venning see also Vening		
Verdety, Theodore	1 (1720-21)	27
Verdier, Andrew	10 (1760-67)	761
Veree, Elizabeth	42 (1839-45)	400
Vereen, Jeremiah [Jerimiah]	12 (1767-71)	412
Vergereau, Susanna	17 (1774-79)	680
Verlin, John	23 (1786-93)	554
Verree, George	30 (1800-07)	808
Verree, Rebekah	42 (1839-45)	317
Verret, Fauvette	30 (1800-07)	828

Name	Volume	Page
Vesey, Maria	38 (1826-34)	568
Vessor, William	5 (1740-47)	46
Vialhauer see Fillhauer		
Viart, Jacob	9 (1760-67)	390
Vicaridge, John	4 (1736-40)	323
Vicars, John	30 (1800-07)	983
*Videau, Ann ₎Anne₎	15 (1771-74)	344
Videau, Henry	15 (1771-74)	514
Videau, Peter	20 (1783-86)	118
Vieufse, Benoit	33 (1807-18)	967
Vilaret see Vilvaret		
Villepontaux, Drake	38 (1826-34)	530
Villeponteaux, William D.	35 (1818-26)	448
Villepontoux, Benjamin	46 (1851-56)	245
Villepontoux, Francis	24 (1786-93)	1123
Villepontoux, Judith	27 (1793-1800)	731
Villepontaux, Peter	6 (1747-52)	55
Villepontoux, Susannah	6 (1747-52)	294
Villepontoux, Zachariah	19 (1780-83)	112
Villepontoux, Zachariah	20 (1783-86)	61
Villepontoux, Zacharias ₎Zachariah₎	22 (1786-93)	235
Vilvaret, Mary ₎Vilaret₎	25 (1793-1800)	197
Vincent, Eliza ₎Elizabeth₎	33 (1807-18)	1223
Vincent, Richard	1 (1720-21)	8
Vincent, Thomas	34 (1818-26)	124
Vinson, George	7 (1752-56)	335
Vinson, James	5 (1740-47)	532
Vinson, John	8 (1757-60)	430
Vinyard, John	22 (1786-93)	198
Vinyard, John	46 (1851-56)	10
Vior, Marie Elizabeth Durand de St. Romes	43 (1839-45)	650
Virgent, George	26 (1793-1800)	327
Virgint, Elizabeth ₎Eliza₎	31 (1807-18)	309
Virtue, David	32 (1807-18)	803

Name	Volume	Page
Volger, Bernard	48 (1856-62)	322
Vollers, Hanke	45 (1845-51)	911
Von Soosten, Martin	49 (1856-62)	984
Vos, Andrew	30 (1800-07)	1097
Vouloux, James ₍Jacques₎	6 (1747-52)	92

W

Wachope, John	4 (1736-40)	208
Waddell, Haynes	21 (1783-86)	715
Waddingham, Samuel	18 (1776-84)	56
Wade, Richard	16 (1774-79)	374
Wadsworth, Susannah	30 (1800-07)	805
Wadsworth, Thomas	27 (1793-1800)	884
Wadsworth, William	37 (1826-34)	272
Wagner, Christopher	30 (1800-07)	867
Wagner, George	31 (1807-18)	58
Wagner, John	26 (1793-1800)	579
Waight, Abraham	5 (1740-47)	587
Waight, Abraham	24 (1786-93)	897
Waight, Ann	6 (1747-52)	129
Waight, Isaac	5 (1740-47)	466
Waight, Jacob	1 (1720-21)	77
Waight, Jacob	5 (1740-47)	394
Waight, Jacob	10 (1760-67)	594
Waight, William	19 (1780-83)	263
Wainwright, Ann	35 (1818-26)	690
Wainwright, Samuel	19 (1780-83)	159
Wainwright, Samuel	21 (1783-86)	507
Waite, Ezra	12 (1767-71)	637
Waldburger, Jacob	13 (1767-71)	735
Waldron, George Zabriskie	48 (1856-62)	152
Waldron, Jacob	17 (1774-79)	676
Walker, Alexander	24 (1786-93)	1110
Walker, Ann	32 (1807-18)	673

Name	Volume	Page
Walker, Ann	45 (1845-51)	893
Walker, Benjamin	24 (1786-93)	1013
Walker, Charles	6 (1747-52)	362
Walker, David ₁Davis₁	29 (1800-07)	708
Walker, Elizabeth	23 (1786-93)	641
Walker, Elizabeth	23 (1786-93)	684
Walker, Hannah	33 (1807-18)	1395
Walker, Henery	2 (1724-25)	66
Walker, James	7 (1752-56)	302
Walker, James	50 (1862-68)	412
Walker, Joel	20 (1783-86)	130
Walker, John	42 (1839-45)	62
Walker, John C.	49 (1856-62)	686
Walker, John Falls	42 (1839-45)	305
Walker, Mary Ancrum	36 (1818-26)	889
Walker, Nathaniel	22 (1786-93)	256
Walker, Penelope	20 (1783-86)	316
Walker, Robert	38 (1826-34)	601
Walker, Robert	39 (1826-34)	1185
Walker, Samuel	8 (1757-60)	62
Walker, Thomas	9 (1760-67)	247
Walker, Thomas	41 (1834-39)	775
Walkutt, Ebenezer	1 (1722-24)	37
Wall, John	2 (1729-31)	106
Wall, John	37 (1826-34)	46
Wall, Mary	28 (1800-07)	234
Wall, Richard	42 (1839-45)	378
Wallace, Ann	41 (1834-39)	624
Wallace, James	24 (1786-93)	826
Wallace, Thomas	33 (1807-18)	1167
Wallace, Thomas	49 (1856-62)	930
Wallace, William	5 (1740-47)	16
Waller, Ann	20 (1783-86)	146
Waller, Bayfield	30 (1800-07)	1098

Name	Volume	Page
Waller, Charlotte	40 (1834-39)	37
Wallexelson, Thomas	6 (1747-52)	632
Walling, Thomas	31 (1807-18)	73
Walling, Thomas T.	46 (1851-56)	233
Wallis, Jane	5 (1740-47)	264
Wallis, Margaret	42 (1839-45)	196
Wallis, Thomas	5 (1740-47)	373
Walpole, Horace	49 (1856-62)	639
Walpole, Martha W.	47 (1851-56)	876
Walser, Andrew	9 (1760-67)	172
Walsh, Antoine ₍Atoine₎	26 (1793-1800)	382
Walsh, Edmund	8 (1757-60)	496
Walsh, Michael P.	40 (1834-39)	435
Walter, Elizabeth	48 (1856-62)	183
Walter, Harriet	24 (1786-93)	1135
Walter, Jerry	45 (1845-51)	743
* Walter, John	6 (1747-52)	4
Walter, John, Jr.	19 (1780-83)	274
Walter, John, Senr.	20 (1783-86)	143
Walter, John, Jr.	20 (1783-86)	214
Walter, John Alleyne	22 (1786-93)	142
Walter, Richard	20 (1783-86)	366
Walter, Thomas	23 (1786-93)	398
Walter, William	11 (1767-71)	138
Ward, Alicia	3 (1731-33)	53
Ward, Ann	43 (1839-45)	616
Ward, Elizabeth	37 (1826-34)	74
Ward, James McCall	36 (1818-26)	887
Ward, John	1 (1720-21)	23
Ward, John	8 (1757-60)	172
Ward, John	20 (1783-86)	131
Ward, John	24 (1786-93)	795
Ward, John	33 (1807-18)	1140

Name	Volume	Page
Ward, Jonathan	3 (1732-37)	212
Ward, Joseph	13 (1767-71)	902
Ward, Joshua	28 (1800-07)	252
Ward, Love	26 (1793-1800)	578
Ward, Mary Grimke	35 (1818-26)	685
Ward, Peter	31 (1807-18)	395
Ward, Sarah	39 (1826-34)	990
Ward, Sarah Elizabeth	42 (1839-45)	355
Wardlow, James H.	38 (1826-34)	567
Waren, John	24 (1786-93)	1049
Warham, Charles	27 (1793-1800)	779
Waring, Ann	43 (1839-45)	555
Waring, Archar	15 (1771-74)	557
Waring, Benjamin	9 (1760-67)	350
Waring, Harriet	36 (1818-26)	845
Waring, Jane Ladson	48 (1856-62)	258
Waring, Joseph	7 (1752-56)	137
Waring, Joseph [Warring]	9 (1760-67)	182
Waring, Josiah	5 (1740-47)	370
Waring, Lydia Jane	42 (1839-45)	273
Waring, Mary	9 (1760-67)	293
Waring, Mary John	34 (1818-26)	21
Waring, Morton (A.)	50 (1862-68)	73
Waring, Richard	7 (1752-56)	71
Waring, Richard	7 (1752-56)	548
Waring, Richard	19 (1780-83)	204
Waring, Richard	20 (1783-86)	58
* Waring, Sarah	7 (1752-56)	388
Waring, Sarah	8 (1757-60)	110
Waring, Sarah	22 (1786-93)	321
Waring, Sarah F.	39 (1826-34)	842
Waring, Thomas	7 (1752-56)	135
Waring, Thomas	13 (1767-71)	882
Warley, Ann	41 (1834-39)	488

Name	Volume	Page
Warley, Ann Eliza	49 (1856-62)	971
Warley, Elizabeth	40 (1834-39)	109
Warley, Felix	32 (1807-18)	891
Warley, Martha	33 (1807-18)	1191
Warley, Mary	41 (1834-39)	486
Warley, Melchion ⌊Werley⌋	19 (1780-83)	143
Warley, Melchior	20 (1783-86)	43
Warley, Paul	30 (1800-07)	1121
Warley, William	35 (1818-26)	622
Warmington, George	42 (1839-45)	320
Warner, Benjamin	37 (1826-34)	118
Warner, Jane	48 (1856-62)	277
Warner, Penelope	40 (1834-39)	246
Warnock, Abraham (Sen$^{r.}$)	2 (1724-25)	35
Warnock, Andrew	2 (G1729-31)	17
Warnock, Andrew	6 (1747-52)	323
Warnock, Feriby	47 (1851-56)	655
Warnock, Samuel	7 (1752-56)	413
Warnock, Samuel	19 (1780-83)	12
Warren, Henry	39 (1826-34)	902
Warren, John	38 (1826-34)	519
Warren, Joseph	33 (1807-18)	989
Warren, Jubah	45 (1845-51)	501
Warren, Lydia	32 (1807-18)	567
Warren, Mary A.	51 (1862-68)	625
Warren, William	27 (1793-1800)	798
Warring see Waring		
Warshing, Abraham	11 (1767-71)	246
Wartenberg, Peter	33 (1807-18)	1273
Washington, Thomas	24 (1786-93)	910
Waters, Frances	10 (1760-67)	697
Waters, John	1 (1671-1727)	6
Watfon see Watson		
Waties, Ann Elizabeth	49 (1856-62)	937

Name	Volume	Page
Waties, John	8 (1757-60)	551
Waties, Thomas	9 (1760-67)	332
* Waties, William	6 (1747-52)	461
Watkins, Charles	4 (1736-40)	1
Watkins, William	5 (1740-47)	671
Watson, Alexander	42 (1839-45)	178
Watson, Caroline	48 (1856-62)	434
Watson, David	3 (1731-33)	46
Watson, James	14 (1771-74)	46
Watson, John (Jun$^{r.}$)	6 (1747-52)	73
Watson, John	7 (1752-56)	184
Watson, John	10 (1760-67)	860
Watson, John	23 (1786-93)	457
Watson, John	31 (1807-18)	316
Watson, John	42 (1839-45)	49
Watson, Lydia	38 (1826-34)	769
Watson, Mary	26 (1793-1800)	508
Watson, Thomas ₍Watfon₎	5 (1740-47)	677
Watson, William	3 (1732-37)	305
Watson, William	8 (1757-60)	109
Watson, William	8 (1757-60)	402
Watson, William	19 (1780-83)	399
Watt, James	39 (1826-34)	1162
Watt, Janet Craig	38 (1826-34)	598
Watt, John	18 (1776-84)	163
Watts, Bridget	36 (1818-26)	895
Watts, Charles	32 (1807-18)	510
Watts, David	18 (1776-84)	246
Watts, Francis	7 (1752-56)	231
Way, Aaron (Senr)	3 (1731-33)	21
Way, Aaron (Senr)	3 (1732-37)	231
Way, David	43 (1839-45)	709
Way, Ebenezer	4 (1736-40)	312

Name	Volume	Page
Way, Jacob G.	43 (1839-45)	810
Way, Jacob H.	50 (1862-68)	370
Way, Moses	4 (1736-40)	294
Way, Parmenas	24 (1786-93)	1089
Way, Samuel	5 (1740-47)	392
Way, William (Senr)	2 (1724-25)	71
Way, Wm., Sr.	2 (1729-31)	28
Weatherick, Robert	1 (1671-1727)	5
Weatherley, Richard	13 (1767-71)	701
Weatherley, Thomas	6 (1747-52)	148
Weatherly, Isaac	10 (1760-67)	735
Weatherspoon, James (Witherspoon)	12 (1767-71)	461
Weaver, Thomas	7 (1752-56)	250
Weavor, Aaron	33 (1807-18)	1328
Webb, Benjamin	3 (1732-37)	126 } Dupli
Webb, Benjamin	3 (1732-37)	271
Webb, Benjamin	17 (1774-79)	483
Webb, Benjamin	23 (1786-93)	491
Webb, Daniel Cannon	45 (1845-51)	791
Webb, David	16 (1774-79)	59
Webb, Deborah	16 (1774-79)	324
Webb, Elizabeth	31 (1807-18)	92
Webb, George	5 (1740-47)	459
Webb, Job see Webb, (Thomas) Job		
Webb, (Thomas) Job	40 (1834-39)	63
Webb, John	31 (1807-18)	96
Webb, John	51 (1862-68)	652
Webb, Magdalene	20 (1783-86)	332
Webb, Margaret	13 (1767-71)	824
Webb, Mathew	27 (1793-1800)	745
Webb, Michael	49 (1856-62)	872
Webb, Richard	5 (1740-47)	81
Webb, Samuell	1 (1711-18)	86

Name	Volume	Page
Webb, William	6 (1747-52)	611
Webb, William	15 (1771-74)	530
Webb, William M.	46 (1851-56)	243
Webber, Ann	26 (1793-1800)	374
Webber, John	20 (1783-86)	375
Webber, Samuel W.	40 (1834-39)	433
Webber, William	34 (1818-26)	235
Weber, Charlotte	49 (1856-62)	848
Weber, George	48 (1856-62)	59
Webley, John	38 (1826-34)	553
✻ ✻ Wedderburn, James		
Wedemeyer, Frederick	49 (1856-62)	599
Weeb, William	3 (1732-37)	19
Weed, Jane	51 (1862-68)	721
Weekley, Richard	1 (1720-21)	3
Weekly, Edward	3 (1732-37)	206
Weeks, Joseph C.	51 (1862-68)	811
Weeks, Joseph H.	42 (1839-45)	158
Wehlert, Jacob C.	46 (1851-56)	230
Weights, John	17 (1774-79)	458
Weinand, Joseph	39 (1826-34)	1052
Weinholtz, John P.	47 (1851-56)	480
Weldin, John	5 (1740-47)	572
Welkanson see Wilkinson		
Wells, Arnold	30 (1800-07)	896
Wells, Dianna	44 (1845-51)	17
Wells, Edgar	7 (1752-56)	553
Wells, Edgar	26 (1793-1800)	534
Wells, Elizabeth	35 (1818-26)	650
Wells, James	39 (1826-34)	982
Wells, James Laroche	30 (1800-07)	1077
Wells, John	20 (1783-86)	270
Wells, John	32 (1807-18)	559

Name	Volume	Page
Wells, Joseph	6 (1747-52)	380
Wells, Mary	6 (1747-52)	506
Wells, Moses	34 (1818-26)	139
Wells, Rachel	45 (1845-51)	553
Wells, Samuel	10 (1760-67)	460
Wells, Samuel	20 (1783-86)	36
Wells, Susanah	39 (1826-34)	1067
Wells, William	20 (1783-86)	66
Welsby, William	8 (1757-60)	182
Welsh, Thomas	2 (1729-31)	120
Welsh, Thomas	26 (1793-1800)	487
Welsh, Walter	3 (1732-37)	296
Werley see Warley		
Werner, Jacob	19 (1780-83)	383
Wernicke, Lewis	20 (1783-86)	297
Wershing, Casper	25 (1796-1800)	59
Wershing, John	30 (1800-07)	989
Wesberry, Jonathan [Wesbury]	26 (1793-1800)	575
Wesbery see Westberry		
Wesbury see Wesberry		
Wescoat, Thomas [Westcoat]	19 (1780-83)	381
Wescott, Samuel	23 (1786-93)	764
Wesner, Barbara	27 (1793-1800)	755
Wesner, Elizabeth A.	48 (1856-62)	209
Wesner, Henry Philip	25 (1793-1800)	27,2
West, Ann	40 (1834-39)	454
West, Ann	40 (1834-39)	459 }Dupl
West, John	32 (1807-18)	876
West, Samuel	44 (1845-51)	293
West, Thomas S.	49 (1856-62)	1052
Westberry, Elizabeth	22 (1786-93)	199
Westberry, Joshua [Westbery, Wesbery]	7 (1752-56)	488
✳ Westberry, William	6 (1747-52)	436

Name	Volume	Page
Westbery see Westberry		
Westcoat see Wescoat		
Weston, Jacob	12 (1767-71)	422
Weston, Jacob	50 (1862-68)	221
Weston, John	38 (1826-34)	758
Weston, Paul, Dr.	41 (1834-39)	601
Weston, Plowden	37 (1826-34)	165
Weston, Plowden	38 (1826-34)	570
Weston, William	27 (1793-1800)	822
Weyman, Cath.	39 (1826-34)	1174
* Weyman, Edward	25 (1793-1800)	7
Weyman, Edward	32 (1807-18)	694
Weyman, Francis	41 (1834-39)	586
Weyman, Rebecca ⌈Rebekah⌉	25 (1793-1800)	278
Whaley, Edward	49 (1856-62)	601
Whaley, John B. see Whaley Mary M.		
Whaley, Mary	32 (1807-18)	671
Whaley, Mary M. ⌈John B.⌉	48 (1856-62)	131
Whaley, Mary O.	51 (1862-68)	796
Whaley, Thomas	30 (1800-07)	932
Whaley, Thomas	30 (1800-07)	934
Wheeler, Ann L.	42 (1839-45)	22
Wheeler, Benjamin	20 (1783-86)	387
Wheeler, Henry	37 (1826-34)	141
Wheeler, John	32 (1807-18)	886
Wheeler, William	35 (1818-26)	620
Whelden, Jonathan ⌈Whilden; Jonathin⌉	4 (1736-40)	7
Whilden, Dorcas	25 (1793-1800)	173
Whilden, Elias, Senr·	40 (1834-39)	256
Whilden, Elisha, Senr.	23 (1786-93)	624
Whilden, Elisha, Sen.	36 (1818-26)	916
Whilden, John	2 (1724-25)	68
Whilden, Joseph	25 (1793-1800)	91

310

Name	Volume	Page
Whilden, Louis A	50 (1862-68)	294
Whilden see also Whelden		
Whipple, Samuel	27 (1793-1800)	844
Whitaker, Mary H.	44 (1845-51)	256
White, Ann	32 (1807-18)	536
White, Anna E.	49 (1856-62)	1036
White, Charlotte Constantia	48 (1856-62)	524
White, Elipha	45 (1845-51)	608
White, Eliza B.	50 (1862-68)	86
White, Eve	20 (1783-86)	172
White, Hannah	4 (1736-40)	171
White, Hannah	16 (1774-79)	109
White, Jacob	19 (1780-83)	256
White, James	36 (1818-26)	1102
White, James Hudson	49 (1856-62)	1017
White, Jane	45 (1845-51)	722
White, Jane M.	49 (1856-62)	950
White, John	2 (1724-25)	103
White, John	9 (1760-67)	46
White, John	14 (1771-74)	76
White, John	28 (1800-07)	330
White, John	32 (1807-18)	897
White, John	43 (1839-45)	930
White, John Blake	48 (1856-62)	511
White, Joseph	8 (1757-60)	242
White, Joseph	11 (1767-71)	306
White, Joseph	14 (1771-74)	212
White, Leonard	6 (1747-52)	353
White, Nathan	3 (1732-37)	334
White, Patty	39 (1826-34)	1062
White, Samuel	20 (1783-86)	42
White, Thomas	9 (1760-67)	313
White, Thomas	21 (1783-86)	448
White, William, Junr.	7 (1752-56)	563

Name	Volume	Page
White, William	18 (1776-84)	37
White, William	25 (1793-1800)	53
White, William	51 (1862-68)	702
White, William Hawes	44 (1845-51)	411
White, William J.	49 (1856-62)	593
Whitefield, William [Whitfield]	31 (1807-18)	57
Whitehart, Peter	38 (1826-34)	641
Whitehouse, Catharine	31 (1807-18)	321
Whiteside, Thomas	9 (1760-67)	305
Whiteside see also Whitesides		
Whitesides, John	40 (1834-39)	148
Whitesides, Mary	46 (1851-56)	37
Whitesides, Moses	31 (1807-18)	334
Whitesides, Moses [Whiteside]	46 (1851-56)	240
Whitesides, Thomas	23 (1786-93)	646
Whitesides, Thomas	29 (1800-07)	515
Whitesides, Thomas I.	44 (1845-51)	190
Whitfield, John	3 (1732-37)	336
Whitfield, Luke, Senr.	11 (1767-71)	223
Whitfield see also Whitefield		
Whiting, George	30 (1800-07)	769
Whitley, Rodger	2 (1726-27)	29
Whitmarsh, John	1 (1720-21)	12
Whitmarsh, John	1 (1722-24)	40
Whitney, Archibald	44 (1845-51)	202
Whitridge, Joshua B.	51 (1862-68)	503
Whittelock, John [Witlock]	8 (1757-60)	317
Whittlesey, Richard	30 (1800-07)	1118
Whitty, Edward	44 (1845-51)	227
Wiare, Eliza	32 (1807-18)	645
Wiare, James Gray [Wiares]	28 (1800-07)	250
Wiares see Wiare		
Wickham, Nathaniel	5 (1740-47)	485
Wiedau, Jacob	51 (1862-68)	819

312

Name	Volume	Page
Wienges, Conrad	47 (1851-56)	625
Wienges, Jacob	51 (1862-68)	700
Wienges, Jacob (executors' bond)	51 (1862-68)	820
Wienges, Jacob (executors' bond)	51 (1862-68)	823
Wienges, Jacob (executors' bond)	51 (1862-68)	826
Wigfall, Benjamin	17 (1774-79)	619
Wigfall, Catharine [Catherine]	19 (1780-83)	387
Wigfall, Constantia	34 (1818-26)	340
Wigfall, Eliza Moore	50 (1862-68)	290
Wigfall, John	25 (1793-1800)	61
Wigfall, Joseph	28 (1800-07)	4
Wigfall, Samuel	30 (1800-07)	826
Wigfall, Samuell	2 (1724-25)	92
Wigfall, Thomas, Jr.	42 (1839-45)	99
Wigfall, Thomas	43 (1839-45)	669
Wigg, Richard	2 (1726-27)	58
Wigg, Thomas	8 (1757-60)	323
Wiggins, Mary L.	46 (1851-56)	310
Wiggins, Thomas	41 (1834-39)	610
Wightman, Jane	46 (1851-56)	258
Wightman, William	40 (1834-39)	262
Wilbraham see Willbraham		
Wilbur, William W.	49 (1856-62)	920
Wilds, Samuel	13 (1767-71)	841
Wilhelmi, John Philip	33 (1807-18)	1354
Wilkening, John H. [Wilkenning]	49 (1856-62)	620
Wilkenning, Gesina	50 (1862-68)	127
Wilkenning, Gesina	50 (1862-68)	131
Wilkenning see also Wilkening		
Wilkerson, Francis [Wilkinson]	24 (1786-93)	874
Wilkes, Clelia	50 (1862-68)	187
Wilkey, John [Wilkie]	7 (1752-56)	159
Wilkie, John	13 (1767-71)	1051
Wilkie, William	40 (1834-39)	356

Name	Volume	Page
Wilkie, William B.	41 (1834-39)	660
Wilkie see also Wilkey		
Wilkins, Eliza Berkley	50 (1862-68)	347
Wilkins, John	2 (1729-31)	112
Wilkins, John	7 (1752-56)	574
Wilkins, Martha C.	41 (1834-39)	749
Wilkins, Martin L.	43 (1839-45)	693
Wilkins, Mary S.	36 (1818-26)	1199
Wilkins, Paul	11 (1767-71)	248
Wilkins, William	5 (1740-47)	267
Wilkins, William	10 (1760-67)	547
Wilkinson, Christopher	3 (1732-37)	16
Wilkinson, Christopher	18 (1776-84)	28
Wilkinson, Edward (Junr)	14 (1771-74)	63
Wilkinson, Eleonora	50 (1862-68)	157
Wilkinson, Joseph	5 (1740-47)	403
Wilkinson, Mary ₍Welkanson₎	16 (1774-79)	302
Wilkinson, Richard	25 (1793-1800)	182
Wilkinson, Susanna	34 (1818-26)	125
Wilkinson, Thomas	1 (1721-22)	10
Wilkinson, Thomas	2 (1727-29)	73
Wilkinson, William	19 (1780-83)	385
Wilkinson, Willis	45 (1845-51)	635
Wilkinson see also Wilkerson		
Will, Margaret	51 (1862-68)	663
Will, Robert W.	43 (1839-45)	508
Willbraham, Edward ₍Wilbraham₎	5 (1740-47)	215
Willdy, Benjamin	1 (1692-93)	66
Wille, Charles	45 (1845-51)	587
Williamfon, Nathaniel	1 (1711-18)	14
Williamfon, Nathainel ₍Williamson₎	1 (1711-18)	72
Williamfon see also Williamson		
Williams, Abimeleck	35 (1818-26)	719
Williams, Benjamin Paul	31 (1807-18)	327

Name	Volume	Page
Williams, Daniel	10 (1760-67)	710
Williams, Daniel	12 (1767-71)	463
Williams, David	10 (1760-67)	765
Williams, David	17 (1774-79)	451
Williams, David	18 (1776-84)	280
Williams, Elizabeth	26 (1793-1800)	478
Williams, George P.	39 (1826-34)	1226
Williams, Hardy	20 (1783-86)	285
Williams, Henrietta	31 (1807-18)	174
Williams, Isham	44 (1845-51)	75
Williams, John	3 (1732-37)	160
Williams, John	6 (1747-52)	193
Williams, John	10 (1760-67)	693
* Williams, John	18 (1776-84)	168
Williams, John	23 (1786-93)	579
Williams, Joseph	12 (1767-71)	533
williams, Mark Lewis	44 (1845-51)	176
Williams, Mary	47 (1851-56)	603
Williams, Michael	14 (1771-74)	79
Williams, Nathaniel	2(G1729-31)	34
Williams, Paul	7 (1752-56)	232
Williams, Philip	19 (1780-83)	397
Williams, Pouncey	31 (1807-18)	405
Williams, Robert	12 (1767-71)	397
Williams, Robert	17 (1774-79)	419
Williams, Samuel	8 (1757-60)	469
Williams, Sarah	28 (1800-07)	73
Williams, Stephen	48 (1856-62)	242
Williams, Susan	45 (1845-51)	817
Williams, Thomas	12 (1767-71)	601
* williams, Thomas	18 (1776-84)	248
Williams, Thomas	33 (1807-18)	1390
Williams, West Capers	49 (1856-62)	945

Name	Volume	Page
Williams, William	1 (1711-18)	24
Williams, William	3 (1731-33)	9
Williams, William	13 (1767-71)	784
*Williamson, Andrew	21 (1783-86)	820
Williamson, Benjamin	6 (1747-52)	22
Williamson, Captain	47 (1851-56)	457
Williamson, Champernoun ⌜Champernown⌝	11 (1767-71)	314
Williamson, David	21 (1783-86)	675
Williamson, Dove ⌜Williamfon⌝	1 (1711-18)	12
Williamson, Elizabeth ⌜williamfon⌝	9 (1760-67)	97
Williamson, Elizabeth	46 (1851-56)	308
Williamson, Emelia	31 (1807-18)	90
Williamson, Henry	5 (1740-47)	506
Williamson, John	3 (1732-37)	82
Williamson, John	38 (1826-34)	743
Williamson, John	43 (1839-45)	762
Williamson, Manley ⌜Williamfon⌝	3 (1732-37)	132
Williamson, Mary	26 (1793-1800)	574
Williamson, Richard	4 (1736-40)	251
Williamson, William	11 (1767-71)	225
Williamson, William	13 (1767-71)	1044
Williamson, William	15 (1771-74)	662
Williamson, William	21 (1783-86)	776
Williamson see also Williamfon		
Williman, Christopher	32 (1807-18)	744
Williman, Christopher (Substitution of Trustee)	41 (1834-39)	868
Williman, Elizabeth	47 (1851-56)	681
Williman, George	32 (1807-18)	755
Williman, Jacob	34 (1818-26)	337
Willingham, Joseph	23 (1786-93)	409
Willingham, Thomas Henry	27 (1793-1800)	853
Willington, Aaron Smith	49 (1856-62)	941
Willis, David	33 (1807-18)	1061

Name	Volume	Page
Willis, Henry	29 (1800-07)	484
Willis, Henry	50 (1862-68)	317
Willis, James	42 (1839-45)	307
willis, John G.	49 (1856-62)	922
Willisford, William	4 (1736-40)	265
Willkes, John	34 (1818-26)	33
Willpen, Friederick	49 (1856-62)	1041
Willson, Charles	41 (1834-39)	490
Willson, David	13 (1767-71)	913
Willson, John	47 (1851-56)	855
Wilson, Alexander	27 (1793-1800)	674
Wilson, Alexander B.	42 (1839-45)	212
Wilson, Algernoon	16 (1774-79)	311
Wilson, Daniel	25 (1793-1800)	212
Wilson, Elizabeth	30 (1800-07)	789
Wilson, Elizabeth	50 (1862-68)	261
wilson, Francis	32 (1807-18)	693
Wilson, George	25 (1793-1800)	202
Wilson, Henrietta S.	47 (1851-56)	540
Wilson, Henry	22 (1786-93)	78
Wilson, Hugh	16 (1774-79)	304
Wilson, Hugh	34 (1818-26)	377
Wilson, Hugh	50 (1862-68)	254
wilson, James	40 (1834-39)	140
Wilson, Jehu	37 (1826-34)	153
Wilson, Joanna	40 (1834-39)	153
Wilson, John	3 (1732-37)	178
Wilson, John	5 (1740-47)	10
Wilson, John	17 (1774-79)	418
wilson, John	22 (1786-93)	88
Wilson, John	27 (1793-1800)	749
Wilson, John	50 (1862-68)	228
Wilson, Jonathan	5 (1740-47)	115
Wilson, Joseph Nicholes	24 (1786-93)	921

Name	Volume	Page
Wilson, Mary	7 (1752-56)	541
Wilson, Mary B.	46 (1851-56)	38
Wilson, Mary E.	50 (1862-68)	344
Wilson, Mary Elizabeth	36 (1818-26)	863
Wilson, Moses ⌐Mofes⌐	4 (1736-40)	119
Wilson, Robert	32 (1807-18)	663
Wilson, Robert	35 (1818-26)	488
Wilson, Robert	44 (1845-51)	107
Wilson, Samuel	37 (1826-34)	211
Wilson, Samuel	49 (1856-62)	865
Wilson, Sarah	28 (1800-07)	176
Wilson, Susan S.	44 (1845-51)	135
Wilson, Susanna	32 (1807-18)	737
Wilson, Thomas	13 (1767-71)	984
Wilson, Thos., Capt.	19 (1780-83)	296
Wilson, William	9 (1760-67)	158
Wilson, William	19 (1780-83)	51
Wiltberger, John B.	51 (1862-68)	809
Wilton, Joseph Dacre	11 (1767-71)	182
Winborn, Samuel	9 (1760-67)	266
Winborn, Susannah	19 (1780-83)	64
Winborn, Thomas	7 (1752-56)	422
Winborne, Willm	32 (1807-18)	715
Winchester, Martha A.	45 (1845-51)	899
Winderas, William	2 (1727-29)	46
Windsor, Thomas, Captain	35 (1818-26)	441
Wing, Sarah C.	39 (1826-34)	1246
Wing, Sarah C. (Petition)	39 (1826-34)	1253
Wingate, Ann	15 (1771-74)	654
Wingate, Edward	9 (1760-67)	106
Wingate, Edward	27 (1793-1800)	679
Wingood, Charvil	5 (1740-47)	60
Wingood, Charvil	22 (1786-93)	279
Wingood, John	37 (1826-34)	384

Name	Volume	Page
Wingood, John Sauseau	10 (1760-67)	656
✳ Winman, Leonard ₍Leanord₎	9 (1760-67)	407
Winn, Robert	4 (1736-40)	133
Winstanley, Sarah	38 (1826-34)	535
Winstanley, Thomas	39 (1826-34)	1072
Winthrop, Ann S.	48 (1856-62)	34
Winthrop, Augustus	43 (1839-45)	758
Winthrop, Frederick	45 (1845-51)	885
Winthrop, Jane	49 (1856-62)	946
Winthrop, Joseph A.	50 (1862-68)	210
Winthrop, Mary	44 (1845-51)	84
Wise, Henry	15 (1771-74)	491
Wish, John	21 (1783-86)	460
Wish, William	31 (1807-18)	392
Witherfpoon see Witherspoon		
Withers, Frances	39 (1826-34)	892
Withers, Francis	44 (1845-51)	268
Withers, James	7 (1752-56)	537
Withers, Richard, Junr.	22 (1786-93)	10
Withers, Richard	23 (1786-93)	572
Withers, Thomas	25 (1793-1800)	129
Witherspoon, David ₍Witherfpoon₎	8 (1757-60)	394
Witherspoon, Elizabeth	18 (1776-84)	268
Witherspoon, Gavin	16 (1774-79)	250
Witherspoon, James (Junior)	15 (1771-74)	670
Witherspoon, John	26 (1793-1800)	404
Witherspoon, Robert	8 (1757-60)	283
Witherspoon, Robert ₍Wotherspoon₎	47 (1851-56)	732
Witherspoon, Ruth ₍Witherspoons₎	10 (1760-67)	517
Witherspoon see also Weatherspoon		
Witherspoons see Witherspoon		
Witlock see Whittelock		
Witten, Peter	22 (1786-93)	248
Witten, Peter Robert	34 (1818-26)	132

Name	Volume	Page
Witten, Robert	16 (1774-79)	143
Witten, Thomas	4 (1736-40)	292
Witter, Benjamin	6 (1747-52)	222
Witter, James	2 (1729-31)	85
Witter, James	22 (1786-93)	334
Witter, Jane	29 (1800-07)	416
Witter, Joanah	23 (1786-93)	533
Witter, John	8 (1757-60)	184
* Witter, John	20 (1783-86)	245
Witter, Matthew	26 (1793-1800)	592
Witter, Samuel	7 (1752-56)	383
Witter, Susanna	43 (1839-45)	840
Witter, Susannah [Susanna]	42 (1839-45)	240
Witter, Susannah (Substitution of Trustee)	42 (1839-45)	262
Witter, Susannah (Substitution of Trustee)	42 (1839-45)	263
Witter, Thomas, Senr.	24 (1786-93)	841
Wittpenn, Joanna E. S. D.	51 (1862-68)	581
Wittschen, Henry	50 (1862-68)	366
Wittschen, John Frederic	49 (1856-62)	870
Woddrop, Ann	39 (1826-34)	932
Woddrop see also Woodrop		
Wolf, John Frederic	28 (1800-07)	115
Wolfe, John	29 (1800-07)	436
Wolfe, John Lewes	13 (1767-71)	850
Wolff, Mathias	30 (1800-07)	811
Wolter, Eibe Horeisz	41 (1834-39)	763
Womack, John B.	49 (1856-62)	862
Wood, Ann	22 (1786-93)	45
* Wood, Benjamin	6 (1747-52)	654
Wood, Edward	42 (1839-45)	313
Wood, George	18 (1776-84)	287
Wood, George	51 (1862-68)	735
Wood, James	43 (1839-45)	814

Name	Volume	Page
Wood, James P.	39 (1826-34)	917
Wood, John	14 (1771-74)	93
Wood, John	19 (1780-83)	39
Wood, Jonathan	17 (1774-79)	613
Wood, Joseph	16 (1774-79)	343
Wood, Rachel	23 (1786-93)	623
Wood, Robert	5 (1740-47)	597
Wood, Robert	37 (1826-34)	334
Wood, Thomas	4 (1736-40)	126
Wood, William	5 (1740-47)	505
Wood, William	8 (1757-60)	580
Wood, William	21 (1783-86)	808
Wood, William E.	34 (1818-26)	144
Wood, Willoughby	6 (1747-52)	304
Woodbridge see Woodridge		
Woodcraft, Martha	12 (1767-71)	399
Woodcraft, Richard	23 (1786-93)	784
Woodil, John Anthony [Woodill]	30 (1800-07)	790
Woodill see Woodil		
Woodin, Thomas	16 (1774-79)	183
Woodman, Edward	28 (1800-07)	264
Woodmancy, Ann	32 (1807-18)	899
Woodridge, Robert [Woodbridge]	28 (1800-07)	38
Woodrop, John [Woddrop]	38 (1826-34)	438
Woodrop, John	50 (1862-68)	422
Woodrouffe, Elizabeth A. [Eliza]	34 (1818-26)	364
Woodruff, Jane Campbell	40 (1834-39)	119
Woodsides, Alexander	17 (1774-79)	781
Woodward, Elizabeth [Elisabeth]	5 (1740-47)	101
Woodward, Henry	1 (1671-1727)	3
Woodward, John	2 (1727-29)	67
Woodward, Margaret	27 (1793-1800)	653
Woodward, Richard (Capt.)	2 (1724-25)	100
Woodward, Richard	5 (1740-47)	340

Name	Volume	Page
Woodward, Sarah	6 (1747-52)	335
Woodward, William	26 (1793-1800)	639
Woolf, Margaret	31 (1807-18)	120
Woolf, Rachel	40 (1834-39)	317
Woolford, Elizabeth	12 (1767-71)	475
Word, Henry	32 (1807-18)	884
Worrel see Worrell		
✷Worrell, William ₎Worrel₎	18 (1776-84)	217
Wotherspoon see Witherspoon		
Wragg, Dick	28 (1800-07)	21
Wragg, Elizabeth	45 (1845-51)	529
Wragg, George	30 (1800-07)	1064
Wragg, John	19 (1780-83)	1
✷ Wragg, Joseph	6 (1747-52)	527
Wragg, Joseph, Jr.	6 (1747-52)	541
Wragg, Judith	12 (1767-71)	667
Wragg, Judith	20 (1783-86)	89
Wragg, Thomas L.	48 (1856-62)	396
Wragg, William	19 (1780-83)	3
Wrainch, Richard	30 (1800-07)	982
Wright, Anthony	9 (1760-67)	240
Wright, Daniel	7 (1752-56)	343
Wright, George	16 (1774-79)	265
Wright, Mrs. Harriett	47 (1851-56)	478
Wright, James	20 (1783-86)	133
Wright, James	23 (1786-93)	658
Wright, James	26 (1793-1800)	548
Wright, John	19 (1780-83)	333
Wright, Peel	38 (1826-34)	811
Wright, Rebecca	39 (1826-34)	939
Wright, Richard	5 (1740-47)	351
Wright, Robert	42 (1839-45)	367
Wright, Thomas	11 (1767-71)	203
Wright, Thomas	17 (1774-79)	583

Name	Volume	Page
Wright, Thomas	23 (1786-93)	578
Wright, Thomas B.	46 (1851-56)	326
Wright see also McGill		
Wrixham, James	1 (1722-24)	1
Wulff, Jacob	40 (1834-39)	367
Wulff, Jacob	41 (1834-39)	600
Wurdemann, Christina Dorothea	46 (1851-56)	41
Wurdemann, J.G.F.	45 (1845-51)	532
Wurthmann, Henry	48 (1856-62)	475
Wurtzer, Henry	8 (1757-60)	422
Wyatt, Delia	32 (1807-18)	648
Wyatt, Elizabeth	39 (1826-34)	1192
Wyatt, John	26 (1793-1800)	645
Wyatt, John Richardson	40 (1834-39)	307
Wyatt, Mary	2 (1724-25)	8
Wyatt, Peter	34 (1818-26)	329
Wyatt, Peter (Substitution of Trustee)	34 (1818-26)	393
Wyatt, Robert	1 (1722-24)	48
Wyatt, Stephen	1 (1721-22)	3
Wyatt, Violetta	39 (1826-34)	851
Wyly, Samuel	12 (1767-71)	357

Y

* Yarborough, Moses	15 (1771-74)	357
Yates, Deborah	45 (1845-51)	783
Yates, Elisha	18 (1776-84)	7
Yates, Francis S. ⌐J. S.⌐	48 (1856-62)	142
Yates, Joseph	35 (1818-26)	642
Yates, Joseph. Senr.	49 (1856-62)	714
Yates, J. S. see Yates, Francis S.		
Yates, Mary Ann	44 (1845-51)	206
Yates, Samuel	34 (1818-26)	367
Yates, Seth	31 (1807-18)	400
Yeadon, Samuel V.	47 (1851-56)	624

Name	Volume	Page
Yeadon, William	45 (1845-51)	598
Yeates, James	13 (1767-71)	812
Yeates, Robert	14 (1771-74)	112
Yeoman see Yeomans		
Yeomans, Mary ⌐Yeoman⌐	18 (1776-84)	177
Yeomans, William	7 (1752-56)	49
Yoer, Jacob	31 (1807-18)	469
Yonge, Francis	19 (1780-83)	40
Yonge, Francis	22 (1786-93)	269
Yonge, Francis, Senr.	23 (1786-93)	480
Yonge, Robert	6 (1747-52)	578
Yonge see also Young		
York, Lewis	5 (1740-47)	673
York, William	3 (1732-37)	288
You, Dandridge C. ⌐Dandredge⌐ ⌐Mary L. L.⌐	48 (1856-62)	166
You, Eliz^th	38 (1826-34)	828
You, Mary L. L. see You, Dandridge		
You, Thomas	22 (1786-93)	31
Young, Archibald ⌐Younge, Yonge⌐	6 (1747-52)	177
Young, Dinah	43 (1839-45)	805
Young, Eliza Maria	48 (1856-62)	28
Young, George	27 (1793-1800)	897
Young, John	11 (1767-71)	312
Young, John	19 (1780-83)	266
Young, Joseph	41 (1834-39)	804
Young, Robert	3 (1732-37)	188
Young, Thomas	25 (1793-1800)	27
Young, William	14 (1771-74)	163
Young, William	14 (1771-74)	200
Young, William	24 (1786-93)	868
Young, William Price	35 (1818-26)	423
Youngblood, David	24 (1786-93)	1105
Youngblood, Peter	25 (1793-1800)	248

Name	Volume	Page

Younge   see Young

Name	Volume	Page
Younghusband, John	26 (1793-1800)	347
Yrola, Anastacio	44 (1845-51)	373
Yulzy, Vallentine	14 (1771-74)	149

Z

Name	Volume	Page
Zelle, W (C) H.	47 (1851-56)	461
Zerbst, G. H.	50 (1862-68)	339
Zubly, David	8 (1757-60)	35
Zubly, John Jaachim	19 (1780-83)	306
Zylstra, Anna Jacoba	36 (1818-26)	1056
Zylstra, Peter	31 (1807-18)	385

www.ingramcontent.com/pod-product-compliance
Lightning Source LLC
Chambersburg PA
CBHW030236030426
42336CB00009B/131